Apache Polaris:
The Definitive Guide

Enriching Apache Iceberg Data Lakehouses with an Open Source Catalog

Alex Merced, Andrew Madson, and Tomer Shiran

O'REILLY®

Apache Polaris: The Definitive Guide

by Alex Merced, Andrew Madson, and Tomer Shiran

Published by O'Reilly Media, Inc., 141 Stony Circle, Suite 195, Santa Rosa, CA 95401.

O'Reilly books may be purchased for educational, business, or sales promotional use. Online editions are also available for most titles (*http://oreilly.com*). For more information, contact our corporate/institutional sales department: 800-998-9938 or *corporate@oreilly.com*.

Acquisition Editor: Aaron Black	**Indexer:** Krsta Technology Solutions
Development Editor: Gary O'Brien	**Cover Designer:** Susan Brown
Production Editor: Aleeya Rahman	**Cover Illustrator:** José Marzan Jr.
Copyeditor: Piper Content Partners	**Interior Designer:** David Futato
Proofreader: Helena Stirling	**Interior Illustrator:** Kate Dullea

September 2025:   First Edition

Revision History for the First Edition

2025-09-16:   First Release

See *http://oreilly.com/catalog/errata.csp?isbn=9798341608146* for release details.

979-8-341-60814-6

[LSI]

Table of Contents

Part III.   Hands-on with Apache Polaris

Foreword

The lakehouse ecosystem has matured significantly over the last few years. Apache Iceberg emerged as the main table format, especially for analytics.

Apache Iceberg brings the reliability and simplicity of SQL queries on top of data files. To achieve this, Apache Iceberg materialized the data files as tables. This opens many new possibilities: ACID transaction, schema evolution, partitioning, and time travel. A table is essentially a set of data files and metadata. This means that we need a way to access the metadata describing a table. That's the primary role of a catalog: to act as a reference and to provide a pointer to the metadata for a table, thus providing atomicity.

The Iceberg Catalog is now a key component, telling where the tables are located and how to access them safely. The catalog is the keystone of data governance, managing table accesses, auditing and tracking, and atomic operations on metadata.

The Apache Iceberg REST Catalog specification has dramatically changed the catalog ecosystem by providing an interoperable approach for Iceberg, where any language or tool can use the same API. But Iceberg doesn't provide an implementation of this specification.

That's the purpose of Apache Polaris (incubating): an Iceberg Catalog REST implementation first but with additional features like multi-catalog support and fine-grained access control at the catalog level.

Apache Polaris: The Definitive Guide is a timely, well-written book that perfectly presents Iceberg REST Catalog concepts and the Apache Polaris (incubating) catalog. The book provides everything you need to know to master Apache Polaris, from its core values (interoperability, run anywhere, and security) to specific features in detail (generic tables, federated catalogs, and more). It covers every aspect of Polaris, from how to run Polaris in a minute through advanced security and access configuration.

This book is a must have for anyone interested in using the Iceberg Catalog ecosystem and understanding Apache Polaris (incubating) in detail.

— JB Onofré
Director of The Apache Software Foundation

Preface

Welcome to *Apache Polaris: The Definitive Guide*. This book is designed to guide you through the journey of building and managing scalable, secure, and flexible data lakehouses with *Apache Polaris™*, an innovative, community-driven catalog project. As data lakehouses continue to evolve, Polaris represents the next generation of catalog solutions, offering unified data management, role-based access control, and multi-catalog support, all while promoting open standards and interoperability across cloud and on-premise environments.

The story of Apache Polaris begins with the *data lakehouse architecture* and the critical role that *Apache Iceberg™* plays in making data lakehouses performant, reliable, and accessible. In the first part of this book, we'll dive deep into the origins and architecture of data lakehouses, explore the challenges they were designed to solve, and walk through the capabilities that Apache Iceberg brings to modern data lakes. As data becomes increasingly central to all aspects of business operations, Iceberg's robust table format has emerged as an essential tool for managing data at scale, providing essential features like ACID transactions, schema evolution, and efficient querying. We'll also look at how Iceberg catalogs originally developed to bring this table format to life, allowing data lakehouses to become more accessible and consistent.

Apache Polaris is an effort undergoing incubation at The Apache Software Foundation (ASF), sponsored by the Apache Incubator. Incubation is required of all newly accepted projects until a further review indicates that the infrastructure, communications, and decision making process have stabilized in a manner consistent with other successful ASF projects. While incubation status is not necessarily a reflection of the completeness or stability of the code, it does indicate that the project has yet to be fully endorsed by the ASF.

But even with the power of Iceberg, the need for a new generation of catalogs has grown clearer. Chapter 2 introduces the diverse world of Iceberg catalogs, highlighting their unique advantages and the challenges that come with having multiple catalog options. From file-based catalogs to service-driven solutions, you'll see how each catalog provides unique features but also introduces complexity, especially when deployed across diverse environments and data tools. This leads us to the *Apache Iceberg REST Catalog Specification*, which was developed to streamline client interactions across catalog implementations, making cross-language support and integration with managed services simpler and more consistent.

The foundation of Polaris builds on this REST specification, taking it further by tackling some of the most pressing challenges in data management today. In Part II, we'll explore Apache Polaris as a new kind of Iceberg catalog. Polaris brings a multi-catalog architecture, enabling organizations to maintain multiple catalogs with distinct roles and access controls, ensuring that each catalog serves its specific purpose while being centrally governed. Additionally, Polaris allows users to connect external catalogs that support the REST Spec, creating a unified environment where Iceberg tables are discoverable across catalog systems. In this part, you'll gain a deeper understanding of Polaris's security model, including *role-based access control (RBAC)*, and learn best practices for managing permissions at scale. We'll also delve into *Git-for-Data*, a unique ecosystem feature that allows for versioned data operations, branching, and tagging—powerful capabilities that make data versioning as straightforward as software versioning.

In Part III, we take a hands-on approach to working with Polaris, starting with deployment and configuration in Chapter 6. Here, you'll learn how to set up Polaris locally, manage multiple catalogs, configure access roles, and integrate security controls. The following chapters provide practical guides on using Polaris with popular data tools, including Apache Spark™, Snowflake, and Dremio. These chapters will walk you through setting up connections, executing queries, managing data, and utilizing each tool's unique capabilities, demonstrating how Polaris can serve as the backbone of a robust, tool-agnostic data lakehouse environment.

Keep in mind that Apache Polaris, like any technology, will evolve. As things change, we will aim to reflect those updates in the book's companion GitHub repository:

https://github.com/developer-advocacy-dremio/apache-polaris-the-definitive-guide

If you have Polaris content you'd like to submit to the repo, such as tutorials or new integrations, please submit a pull request.

By the end of this book, you'll be well-equipped to leverage the full power of Apache Polaris in your data lakehouse architecture. You'll understand the theory and architecture behind catalogs and the practical steps needed to deploy Polaris as a central, scalable, and secure solution for data management. Whether you're a data engineer, architect, or analyst, *Apache Polaris: The Definitive Guide* will provide the insights and tools you need to take your data lakehouse to the next level.

If you'd like to take your learning further, here are some additional resources to consider:

- Apache Polaris Documentation (*https://polaris.apache.org*)
- Apache Iceberg Documentation (*https://iceberg.apache.org*)
- Directory of Apache Iceberg Resources (*https://oreil.ly/TPOP6*)

Conventions Used in This Book

The following typographical conventions are used in this book:

Italic
> Indicates new terms, URLs, email addresses, filenames, and file extensions.

`Constant width`
> Used for program listings, as well as within paragraphs to refer to program elements such as variable or function names, databases, data types, environment variables, statements, and keywords.

`Constant width bold`
> Shows commands or other text that should be typed literally by the user.

`Constant width italic`
> Shows text that should be replaced with user-supplied values or by values determined by context.

This element signifies a tip or suggestion.

This element signifies a general note.

This element indicates a warning or caution.

Using Code Examples

Supplemental material (code examples, exercises, etc.) is available for download at *https://github.com/developer-advocacy-dremio/apache-polaris-the-definitive-guide*.

If you have a technical question or a problem using the code examples, please send email to *support@oreilly.com*.

This book is here to help you get your job done. In general, if example code is offered with this book, you may use it in your programs and documentation. You do not need to contact us for permission unless you're reproducing a significant portion of the code. For example, writing a program that uses several chunks of code from this book does not require permission. Selling or distributing examples from O'Reilly books does require permission. Answering a question by citing this book and quoting example code does not require permission. Incorporating a significant amount of example code from this book into your product's documentation does require permission.

We appreciate, but generally do not require, attribution. An attribution usually includes the title, author, publisher, and ISBN. For example: "*Apache Polaris: The Definitive Guide* by Alex Merced, Andrew Madson, and Tomer Shiran (O'Reilly). Copyright 2025 O'Reilly Media, Inc., 979-8-341-60814-6."

If you feel your use of code examples falls outside fair use or the permission given above, feel free to contact us at *permissions@oreilly.com*.

O'Reilly Online Learning

O'REILLY® For more than 40 years, *O'Reilly Media* has provided technology and business training, knowledge, and insight to help companies succeed.

Our unique network of experts and innovators share their knowledge and expertise through books, articles, and our online learning platform. O'Reilly's online learning platform gives you on-demand access to live training courses, in-depth learning paths, interactive coding environments, and a vast collection of text and video from O'Reilly and 200+ other publishers. For more information, visit *https://oreilly.com*.

How to Contact Us

Please address comments and questions concerning this book to the publisher:

O'Reilly Media, Inc.
141 Stony Circle, Suite 195
Santa Rosa, CA 95401
800-889-8969 (in the United States or Canada)
707-827-7019 (international or local)
707-829-0104 (fax)
support@oreilly.com
https://oreilly.com/about/contact.html

We have a web page for this book, where we list errata and any additional information. You can access this page at *https://oreil.ly/apache-polaris-definitive-guide*.

For news and information about our books and courses, visit *https://oreilly.com*.

Find us on LinkedIn: *https://linkedin.com/company/oreilly-media*.

Watch us on YouTube: *https://youtube.com/oreillymedia*.

Acknowledgments

Alex Merced, Andrew Madson, and Tomer Shiran would like to extend their heartfelt gratitude to their families for their unwavering support and encouragement throughout the process of writing this book. Their patience and understanding have been invaluable as we dedicated countless hours to bring *Apache Polaris: The Definitive Guide* to life.

We would also like to thank the exceptional team at O'Reilly, who consistently make the publishing process both smooth and enjoyable. Their professionalism and dedication are truly appreciated. Special thanks go out to our technical reviewers: Robert Stupp, Bhargavi Reddy, Michal Gancarski, Saurav Varma, Dmitiri Bourlatchkov, and Alex Dutra and the forward writer, JB Onofré, whose insights and feedback have helped make this book the best it can be. Thank you all for your contributions to this journey.

## PART I

Data Lakehouses and Apache Iceberg Fundamentals

Before diving into the specifics of Apache Polaris, it's essential to understand the broader context in which it operates: the world of data lakehouses and Apache Iceberg. The lakehouse architecture that turns data lakes into flexible data warehouses combines the scalability and cost-effectiveness of data lakes with the performance and reliability of data warehouses. Apache Iceberg is at the core of this architecture, a table format designed to bring structure, consistency, and efficiency to massive datasets stored in data lakes. This section lays the foundation for understanding how Polaris fits into this ecosystem by exploring the challenges that led to the rise of lakehouses, the pivotal role of Iceberg in enabling them, and the critical need for robust cataloging solutions to manage and govern data effectively.

## CHAPTER 1

Data Lakehouse and Apache Iceberg

Organizations are generating massive amounts of information, making it crucial to store, manage, and analyze that data efficiently. The sheer volume and variety of data pose unique challenges, from ensuring accessibility to maintaining performance at scale. This is where modern data architectures come into play. To fully grasp the value of Apache Polaris, an open source data lakehouse catalog, it's essential first to understand the origins of the Data Lakehouse concept and the role that Apache Iceberg plays in enabling scalable, high-performance data management.

This chapter aims to lay the foundation for those concepts, beginning with an exploration of the modern data challenges that led to the evolution of the lakehouse architecture. We will then dive into the role of table formats in simplifying data management and ensuring consistency across systems, focusing on Apache Iceberg, a table format designed for the cloud data era. By the end of this chapter, you'll have a solid understanding of the data lakehouse and Iceberg's pivotal role in creating scalable, manageable, and cost-effective data solutions, setting the stage for a deeper dive into the unique contributions of Apache Polaris.

Modern Data Challenges

The explosion of data in the digital age brought about the need for systems optimized to handle large-scale analytics. Traditional databases designed for transactional processing were simply not equipped to meet the demands of modern analytical workloads. This led to the rise of data warehouses—systems purpose-built to deliver high performance for querying structured data. Over time, as organizations needed to store and analyze more diverse forms of data, data lakes emerged as a solution, allowing the storage of vast amounts of structured, semistructured, and unstructured data at a lower cost.

However, as data volumes surged into the petabyte range, both data warehouses and data lakes began to show their limitations. Data warehouses, while powerful, came with high storage costs and lacked the flexibility needed to handle unstructured data. On the other hand, data lakes, while flexible and scalable, suffered from performance issues when it came to delivering the speed and reliability needed for real-time analytics.

Further innovation came with cloud-based deployment, allowing organizations to scale their infrastructure more flexibly and cost effectively. In addition, the rise of analytics-optimized file formats such as Apache Parquet and ORC (Optimized Row Columnar) improved data processing efficiency by making storage formats better suited for large-scale query workloads.

Yet, even with these advances, the challenge remained: how to bring the best of both worlds together—combining the flexibility and scalability of data lakes with the performance and structure of data warehouses. This challenge led to the creation of the data lakehouse, a unified architecture designed to address the evolving needs of modern data management.

We will explore how these systems evolved and how their limitations eventually paved the way for the data lakehouse, setting the stage for the innovations that followed—including Apache Iceberg and, ultimately, Apache Polaris.

The World of Data Warehouses

Traditional relational databases, designed for transactional workloads, struggled to deliver the speed and efficiency needed for analytical queries significantly as data volumes grew. *Data warehouses* were built to solve this problem by optimizing data storage and query execution for *online analytical processing (OLAP)*. This allowed organizations to generate reports, run *business intelligence (BI)* tools, and make data-driven decisions faster and more effectively.

Data warehouses were architecturally distinct from *online transaction processing (OLTP)* systems, which were designed to handle high volumes of short, transactional queries, like inserting, updating, or deleting a few records at a time. OLTP databases optimized for these fast, row-based operations focused on consistency and the ability to support many users making frequent, small changes to the data. In contrast, data warehouses were built specifically for OLAP, where the goal is to analyze large volumes of historical data to extract trends, patterns, and insights. Architecturally, this meant that data warehouses were optimized for batch processing and complex read-heavy queries that spanned large datasets, rather than handling individual transactions.

Key differences under the hood included the use of columnar storage, where data is stored in columns rather than rows (illustrated in Figure 1-1). This made data warehouses much more efficient at querying specific fields across large datasets because only the relevant columns needed to be loaded into memory. Data warehouses often employ techniques like denormalization and materialized views, which involve pre-computing and storing aggregates or summary tables to speed up analytical queries. Unlike OLTP systems, which are designed for frequent updates, data warehouses emphasize read performance by reducing the complexity of joins and grouping operations, enabling them to handle complex analytical workloads far more effectively.

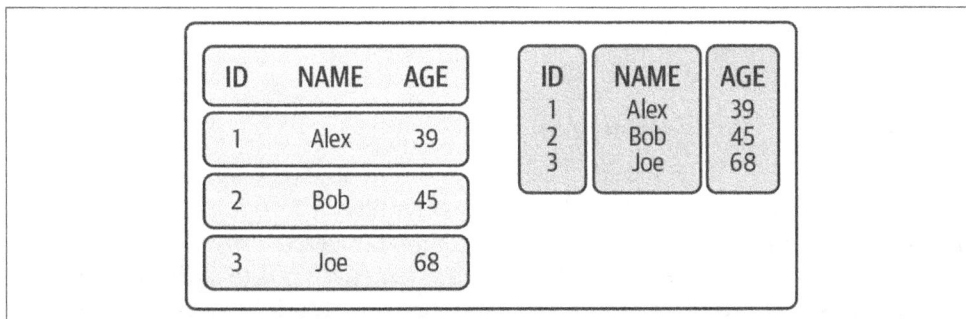

Figure 1-1. The differences between row-based and columnar data

However, as the volume and variety of data increased over time, some significant limitations of data warehouses began to surface:

Cost
Storing large amounts of data in a data warehouse was expensive, particularly as data storage costs were tied to premium, high-performance hardware. This made it impractical to store all business data within a data warehouse, especially as the data grew into the terabyte and petabyte ranges.

Lack of flexibility
Data warehouses were designed primarily for structured data, meaning data that fits neatly into tables with defined rows and columns. This made it difficult to handle semistructured or unstructured data, such as logs, multimedia, and sensor data, which became increasingly important for modern business analytics.

Scaling issues
Scaling a data warehouse was no easy task. As more data needed to be ingested and queried, performance could degrade without significant hardware investment and optimization efforts. This rigidity made it hard to accommodate rapidly changing business needs.

ETL bottlenecks
> Moving data into a data warehouse required extract, transform, load (ETL) processes that were often time consuming and error prone. The need to clean, structure, and format data before loading it into a warehouse meant there were delays between when data was generated and when it became usable for analytics.

While data warehouses were revolutionary for their time and solved many early data management challenges, these limitations began to hinder their effectiveness in a world that was producing increasingly large and diverse datasets. As organizations sought more scalable, flexible solutions, the era of data lakes began, offering a way to manage growing volumes of varied data more affordably—but with their own set of trade-offs, as we will explore in the next section.

Moving Forward with Data Lakes

As the limitations of data warehouses became more apparent—particularly around cost, scalability, and the rigidity of their schema requirements—organizations needed a more flexible and cost-effective way to handle the increasing diversity and volume of data. This need gave rise to the *data lake*, a system designed to store vast amounts of data in its raw form, whether structured, semistructured, or unstructured. The introduction of Hadoop in the mid-2000s was a key innovation that made data lakes practical and accessible for organizations looking to manage growing datasets without the constraints of traditional data warehouses.

Hadoop, an open source framework, revolutionized data storage and processing by introducing a *distributed storage system* and a *distributed computing engine*. This allowed organizations to store data across a cluster of inexpensive, commodity hardware, drastically reducing the cost of storing large amounts of data compared to data warehouses, which relied on high-performance, expensive hardware.

Hadoop's architecture

At its core, Hadoop is composed of two primary components: the *Hadoop Distributed File System (HDFS)* and the *MapReduce* processing framework.

Hadoop Distributed File System (HDFS)
> HDFS is a highly scalable file system designed to store data across multiple machines in a distributed manner. Data is broken into blocks, typically 128MB or 256MB in size, and stored across the cluster, with redundancy to ensure fault tolerance. This architecture allowed organizations to scale their storage needs by adding more inexpensive servers to the cluster, addressing the storage cost issue that data warehouses struggled with.

MapReduce

MapReduce is a programming model that enables large-scale data processing by distributing computational tasks across multiple nodes in the Hadoop cluster. The *Map* function processes data by breaking it into key-value pairs, and the *Reduce* function aggregates those results to produce a final output. This distributed computing approach allowed Hadoop to process massive datasets in parallel, making it possible to analyze petabytes of data efficiently.

The evolution of the Hadoop ecosystem saw the introduction of several key technologies that addressed some of Hadoop's initial shortcomings and contributed to the growth of the data lake. Apache Hive was one of the first major developments, introducing a SQL-like interface for Hadoop. Hive allowed users to query large datasets stored in HDFS without needing to write complex MapReduce jobs, which was a significant step forward in making Hadoop more accessible to a broader range of users, particularly data analysts accustomed to SQL. The *Hive Metastore* played a crucial role in managing metadata within Hive, serving as a centralized catalog to track information about data stored in HDFS, such as table structures, partitions, and data types. This helped to bring more structure and organization to the otherwise schemaless world of data lakes, making it easier to manage and query large datasets.

As the need for faster, more flexible data processing grew, *Apache Spark* emerged as a key player in the Hadoop ecosystem, offering an in-memory processing engine that was much faster than MapReduce for many types of analytical workloads. Spark not only supported batch processing but also enabled real-time stream processing, machine learning, and iterative computations, all of which were limitations of Map-Reduce. Spark's integration with the Hadoop ecosystem allowed it to work seamlessly with HDFS and Hive Metastore, while providing a more powerful and flexible toolset for data processing and analytics.

Together, these technologies—Hive, Hive Metastore, and Spark—helped shape the modern data lake by improving accessibility, metadata management, and processing performance, making it easier for organizations to harness the power of big data. However, even with these innovations, the complexity of managing and optimizing large data lakes remained a challenge.

Challenges with data lakes

While data lakes solved many of the challenges posed by data warehouses, they introduced their own set of problems. One of the primary issues was that, unlike the carefully structured environments of data warehouses, data lakes could easily turn into "*data swamps*"—vast pools of raw data that were difficult to manage, curate, or query effectively. This lack of structure led to several challenges:

Lack of data governance
Because data lakes stored raw data without strict schema enforcement, maintaining data quality, consistency, and governance became difficult. Organizations struggled to ensure that data in the lake was trustworthy and usable, particularly as the lake grew in size.

Performance issues
While Hadoop's distributed architecture made it cost effective to store large amounts of data, the performance of analytical queries on these datasets often lagged behind that of traditional data warehouses. Hadoop's MapReduce framework, while powerful for batch processing, was not optimized for real-time analytics, which limited its use in scenarios requiring fast insights.

Complexity of access
Accessing and using data stored in a data lake often required specialized skills in distributed computing and programming. This meant that business users or data analysts couldn't easily interact with the data in a self-service manner. In many cases, the data stored in lakes remained underutilized due to the complexity involved in querying and processing it.

While Hadoop and the data lake addressed key limitations of traditional data warehouses—namely cost, flexibility, and scalability—these challenges revealed the need for further innovation. As organizations continued to evolve, they began exploring cloud-based solutions that offered the best of both worlds: the flexibility and low-cost storage of data lakes combined with the performance and structure of data warehouses. This evolution led to the next phase of data management, which we'll cover in the following section.

The Cloud Revolution

As organizations grappled with data management's growing scale and complexity, the next significant shift came with the move to the cloud. Both data warehouses and data lakes found new life in the cloud, where they could use scalable, elastic infrastructure. This shift addressed many limitations of on-premise systems, offering unprecedented flexibility, reduced operational overhead, and cost efficiency. With cloud-based solutions, organizations no longer needed to invest in and maintain expensive hardware. Instead, they could store and process data on demand, paying only for their used resources.

For data warehouses, cloud providers introduced fully managed services like Amazon Redshift, Google BigQuery, and Snowflake, which delivered the performance of traditional data warehouses with the added benefits of cloud elasticity and scalability. This meant that organizations could scale their computing and storage resources independently, ensuring they had the power to handle large analytical queries without overprovisioning their infrastructure. Furthermore, the cloud allowed for near-limitless storage, alleviating one of the key cost concerns of on-premise data warehouses.

Similarly, data lakes in the cloud allow organizations to store vast amounts of structured, semistructured, and unstructured data at a meager cost. Services like Amazon S3, Azure Data Lake Storage, and Google Cloud Storage provide highly durable, scalable storage with pay-per-use pricing models. This shift to the cloud also made it easier to manage data lakes, as cloud providers handled many operational challenges that previously burdened on-premise Hadoop clusters. Cloud data lakes offered the flexibility of storing raw data and the ability to layer various processing frameworks on top, from Spark to Dremio, further expanding their use cases.

Despite the massive benefits of moving data warehouses and data lakes to the cloud, several issues persisted. One of the primary challenges was data performance. While cloud data lakes offered low-cost storage, retrieving and processing large volumes of data was still slow, particularly for real-time analytics. Additionally, the absence of a standardized format for organizing and querying data in data lakes led to fragmentation and inefficiencies. As organizations stored data in various formats, querying across these disparate sources became cumbersome, especially when performance and optimization were key considerations.

The cloud revolution needed a data format optimized for both storage efficiency and query performance, something that could work natively within the cloud data lake and bridge the gap between the raw flexibility of data lakes and the high-performance querying capabilities of data warehouses.

File-Based Analytics with Apache Parquet

The introduction of Apache Parquet was a turning point for data lakes, transforming them into much more viable environments for large-scale analytics. Parquet, a *columnar storage format*, was explicitly designed to address many performance challenges when querying large datasets in data lakes in less analytics-optimized formats like CSV and JSON. Its efficient design allowed for faster analytics by minimizing the amount of data that needed to be read from storage, optimizing query performance and storage efficiency.

How Apache Parquet works

Parquet stores data in columns rather than rows, unlike traditional row-based storage formats (such as CSV or JSON). This columnar design means that when a query only needs to access a few specific fields or columns from a dataset, Parquet can read just the relevant columns without loading the entire row into memory. This is particularly advantageous in analytical queries, which often aggregate or filter data across several columns over large datasets. By reading only what is necessary, Parquet dramatically reduces the *I/O* overhead and the amount of data transferred from disk, leading to faster query execution and lower storage costs.

Parquet also employs several techniques to improve performance further and reduce storage costs:

Compression
Parquet natively supports a variety of compression algorithms—like Snappy and Gzip—allowing it to store data in a much smaller footprint than uncompressed formats. This reduces storage costs and speeds up queries by reducing the amount of data that needs to be read from disk.

Encoding
Parquet uses advanced encoding techniques like *run-length encoding (RLE)* and *dictionary encoding*, which further compress the data and improve query performance by reducing the amount of data scanned during a query.

Metadata and statistics
Parquet files store metadata and *min/max statistics* for each column, which allows query engines to skip over irrelevant portions of the dataset. This optimization, called *predicate pushdown*, helps further reduce the I/O required to answer queries, particularly when filtering large datasets.

These design choices made Parquet a game changer for data lakes, significantly improving the efficiency of reading, writing, and querying data at scale (Figure 1-2 illustrates the Parquet format). For organizations storing petabytes of data in cloud-based data lakes, Parquet enabled much faster and more cost-effective analytics, bridging some of the gap between the performance of data lakes and traditional data warehouses.

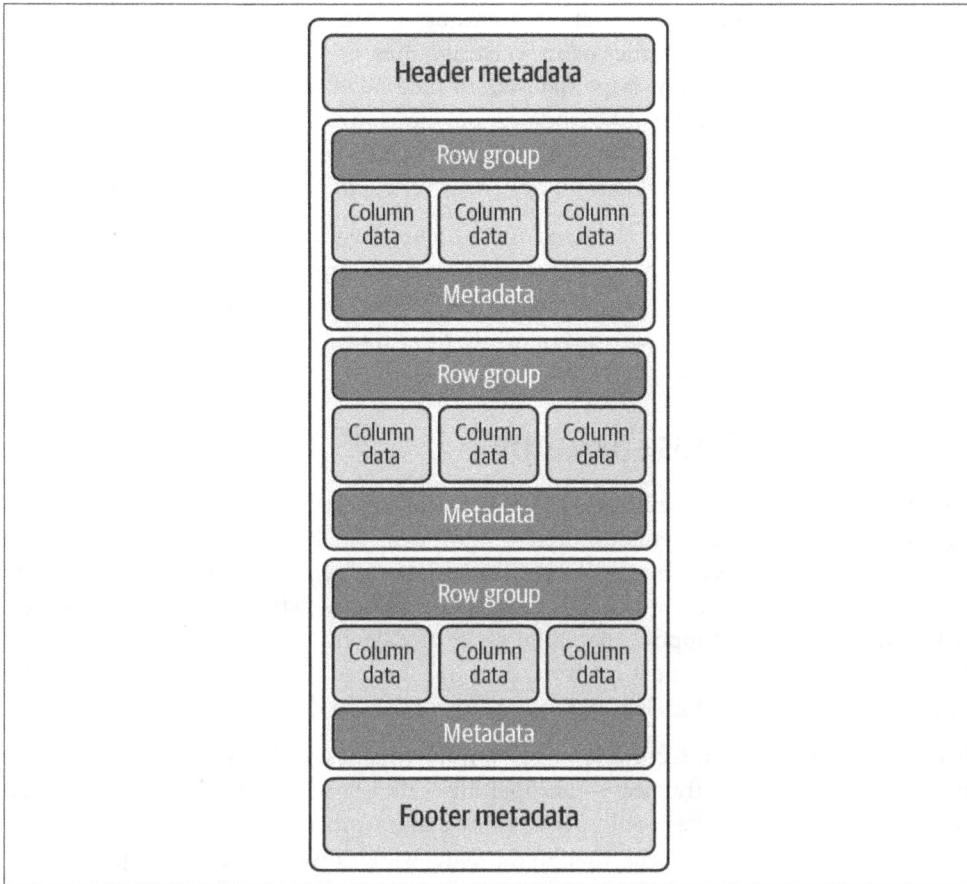

Figure 1-2. The design of an Apache Parquet file

Challenges with multi-file datasets

While Apache Parquet brought significant performance gains, it didn't solve all the challenges of managing large datasets in a data lake. One of the major issues with data lakes, even when using Parquet, was the complexity of managing *multi-file datasets*. As datasets grew, they were often broken into thousands or even millions of individual Parquet files. This fragmentation made it difficult to manage and query datasets efficiently.

For example, when adding new data to a Parquet-based dataset, there was no built-in mechanism to merge new files with existing ones or to optimize the dataset for future queries. Additionally, large datasets in data lakes lacked a *transactional layer*, which meant that operations like updates, deletions, or concurrent writes could lead to inconsistencies. Managing multi-file datasets became error prone and complicated without a way to handle *schema evolution*, *data versioning*, and *atomic transactions*.

These challenges highlighted the need for a higher level of abstraction that could sit on top of Parquet files, managing datasets as cohesive units rather than collections of independent files. This abstraction must address issues like file management, schema enforcement, and query optimization while providing the transactional guarantees necessary for reliable data operations.

The Data Lakehouse Solution

As organizations began to embrace the benefits of data lakes for storing vast amounts of raw data, they quickly encountered a significant challenge: data lakes lacked the *transactional guarantees* central to traditional data warehouses. Without the ability to manage data updates, enforce schemas, or reliably handle concurrent writes, data lakes could not support the same level of data integrity and consistency that organizations had come to expect from data warehouses. This gap presented a crucial opportunity for innovation, leading to the concept of the data lakehouse.

The data lakehouse architecture aims to combine the best of both data lakes and data warehouses by layering transactional capabilities on top of the flexible storage offered by a data lake. If data lakes could provide the same Atomicity, Consistency, Isolation, Durability (ACID) guarantees that make data warehouses so reliable for complex analytics, it would allow organizations to use their data lake for raw storage and fast, reliable analytics. By creating a transactional layer on top of file formats like Apache Parquet, data lakehouses enable data to be treated like a table in a data warehouse, with a structured, schema-driven interface that analysts, engineers, and data scientists can work with confidently.

The Key Benefits of a Data Lakehouse

Let's examine some of the most crucial benefits of leveraging data lake storage using a data lakehouse strategy, making your data lake behave more like a data warehouse.

Unified data storage
   One of the primary values of the data lakehouse is its ability to serve as a single source of truth for all data. Organizations no longer need to maintain separate systems for raw data (in a data lake) and structured, query-ready data (in a data warehouse). With a lakehouse, data can be stored once and used for both opera-

tional and analytical purposes without needing to create costly, time-consuming copies of the data.

ACID transactions

By introducing a transactional layer, the data lakehouse ensures that data operations—such as writes, updates, and deletes—are executed in a transactionally safe manner. This means that even if multiple users or processes are interacting with the data concurrently, the lakehouse can maintain data consistency and prevent issues such as partial writes or corrupted datasets, which were common problems in early data lakes.

Schema enforcement and evolution

Another essential feature of a data lakehouse is the ability to enforce schemas at the table level. Lakehouses take what is possible via metadata tracking at the file level with formats like Parquet and applies it over multiple files using table formats like Apache Iceberg. Unlike traditional data lakes, where data could be dumped into storage without structure, a data lakehouse ensures that the data adheres to a defined schema. At the same time, it supports schema evolution, allowing changes to the data structure (such as adding new columns) without breaking existing pipelines or queries.

Performance optimization

With the transactional layer, a lakehouse can optimize data storage and retrieval in ways that traditional data lakes could not. For example, compaction processes can combine small files into larger ones to improve query performance. At the same time, data pruning techniques can automatically exclude irrelevant data during query execution, significantly speeding up analytics. This makes it possible to perform real-time analytics on data stored in a lakehouse, which was often a challenge in raw data lakes. Lakehouse tables also maintain a list of data files, enabling users to pinpoint the specific files needed for a query without expensive file listing.

Cost efficiency

Since a data lakehouse builds on top of distributed storage like object storage or HDFS, it retains the cost benefits of data lakes while reducing the need to maintain separate, expensive data warehouses. This unified approach minimizes data sprawl and eliminates the need to replicate data across multiple systems. In essence, the lakehouse provides the performance benefits of a warehouse without the associated storage costs.

Support for streaming and batch processing

Lakehouses are designed to handle both real-time streaming data and batch processing seamlessly. This makes them a versatile solution for handling a wide range of use cases, from real-time business intelligence dashboards to historical data analysis.

Open standards and flexibility
By building on open file formats like Parquet and using open source frameworks, the data lakehouse can avoid the vendor lock-in often associated with proprietary data warehouse solutions. This open architecture allows organizations to use a variety of tools and processing engines—such as Spark, Presto, or Dremio— without being tied to a single platform.

The Path Forward: Data Lakehouse Table Formats

The concept of the data lakehouse rests on the ability to treat data in the lake with the same structure and reliability as a traditional warehouse. Achieving this requires more than just file formats like Parquet—it needs table formats that can provide the necessary abstraction and transactional guarantees on top of the raw data. These table formats bring the structure and control needed to make data lakehouses practical and performant at scale.

The Role of Table Formats

As organizations adopted data lakehouse architecture, the need for better management, performance, and reliability of large-scale datasets became increasingly clear. While efficient, simply storing files in a format like Apache Parquet was not enough to meet the transactional, performance, and schema requirements of modern analytics workloads. This gap led to the rise of *table formats*, which add a layer of abstraction on top of raw files, transforming them into manageable, queryable tables with transactional guarantees.

The Benefits of Table Formats

Table formats are the key to unlocking the full potential of data lakehouses. They provide several critical benefits:

ACID transactions
Table formats ensure ACID compliance, meaning that complex data operations (such as concurrent reads and writes) are handled safely without risking data corruption or partial updates. This was a major challenge in traditional data lakes, which lacked these guarantees.

Schema enforcement and evolution
Users can enforce and evolve schemas over time with table formats. This means that data can be validated against a defined structure before being written,

ensuring consistency while also allowing changes to the schema (e.g., adding, dropping, or modifying columns) without the need to rewrite the table.

Data versioning
Table formats allow for *time travel* or the ability to query historical versions of a dataset. This makes debugging, auditing, and rolling back data changes within a single table easier.

Efficient query performance
Table formats optimize query performance by managing metadata, handling file compaction, and providing advanced partitioning strategies, significantly speeding up analytical workloads.

Partition management
They offer powerful partitioning mechanisms that help query engines skip irrelevant data, reduce the data scanned, and improve query performance. Some formats also introduce innovations like *partition evolution*, which allows partitions to change over time without restructuring the dataset.

Existing Table Formats

Several table formats have emerged to solve these challenges, each with its own strengths and features:

Apache Iceberg
Originally developed at Netflix, Iceberg is a powerful table format designed for handling petabyte-scale data in data lakes with high-performance analytics. It provides strong ACID guarantees, schema evolution, and unique features such as partition evolution and hidden partitioning, making it one of the most flexible and scalable options for building data lakehouses.

Apache Hudi
Hudi, created at Uber, is another open source table format focused on transactional updates and streaming data. It offers ACID guarantees and real-time ingestion of data, which makes it useful for streaming use cases. Hudi is particularly strong in incremental data processing and ensuring up-to-date data for real-time analytics.

Delta Lake
Delta Lake, developed at Databricks, focuses on improving the reliability and performance of data lakes by offering ACID transactions and schema enforcement. While initially focused on Spark-based workloads, Delta Lake has grown in popularity and usage due to its tight integration with the Databricks platform.

Apache Paimon

Formerly known as Flink Table Store, Paimon is a table format designed to integrate deeply with stream processing frameworks like Apache Flink. It supports both streaming and batch data, making it a powerful option for real-time and low-latency workloads.

Apache Iceberg

Apache Iceberg has become a staple for data lakehouse architectures. Its flexibility, performance, and open governance have led to widespread adoption across the data ecosystem. Several factors have contributed to Iceberg's adoption:

Broad ecosystem support

Apache Iceberg was built to be tool-agnostic and boasts a vast ecosystem of tools and platforms that have built first-class support for Iceberg tables. These include Dremio, Snowflake, AWS, Google Cloud, Upsolver, and many more. This broad adoption represents Iceberg's versatility and reliability across various environments, making it a go-to solution for data lakehouses.

Databricks acquisition of Tabular

In a significant industry move, Databricks, the creators of Delta Lake, acquired Tabular, a company founded by Ryan Blue, Daniel Weeks, and Jason Reid, who created and led the development of Iceberg while at Netflix. This acquisition highlights the growing importance of Iceberg.

Transparent, community-driven project

Apache Iceberg operates as a community-driven, open source project, unlike other formats that single vendors tightly control. It has a public mailing list, regular development meetings, and multiple channels for transparent feedback. This open governance model encourages collaboration from across the industry, allowing players from various organizations to contribute to and influence the project's direction.

Unique features

Iceberg's advanced features set it apart from other table formats. Partition evolution allows partitions to change without having to rewrite entire datasets, solving a common challenge in large data lakes. Iceberg's hidden partitioning abstracts away the complexities of managing partitions, allowing for more flexible and efficient data organization. These innovations make Iceberg highly adaptable and easy to use for teams managing large-scale, complex datasets.

With strong transactional guarantees, flexibility in handling complex data layouts, and a vast ecosystem of support, Apache Iceberg has become a fixture in modern data lakehouses.

What Is Apache Iceberg?

Apache Iceberg is a modern, open table format designed to manage large-scale datasets within data lakes, providing the functionality and performance of traditional data warehouses. Iceberg introduces powerful capabilities such as ACID transactions, schema evolution, time travel, and partition evolution, allowing organizations to efficiently query, manage, and evolve their data over time.

At its core, Apache Iceberg leverages a metadata-driven architecture that enables fast, reliable data management (see Figure 1-3). This architecture revolves around several key metadata files that track the state of the dataset, ensuring seamless handling of operations like queries, updates, and deletions.

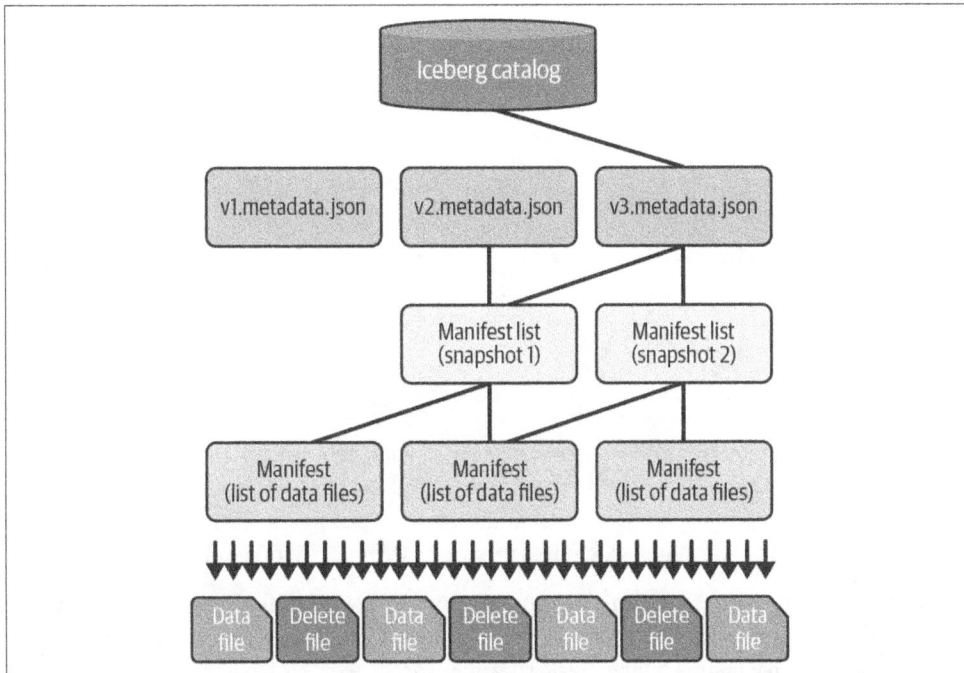

Figure 1-3. The Structure of an Apache Iceberg Table

In the following sections we'll break down the main types of Iceberg metadata files and explain their roles in the format.

Metadata File (metadata.json)

The *metadata file*, also known as *metadata.json*, is the central file that manages the overall state of the table. Think of it as the brain of the Iceberg table, tying together the structure and history of the dataset. Each Iceberg table has one primary metadata file that tracks critical information, including:

Table schema
> The table's structure, including column names, data types, and any schema changes that have occurred over time.

Snapshots
> The metadata file tracks all the table's historical versions (snapshots), enabling time travel so users can query the table as it existed at previous points in time.

Current snapshot
> A reference to the latest snapshot, representing the current state of the table.

Partitioning
> Details about how the table is partitioned and partition evolution—any changes to partitioning over time.

Table properties
> Configuration details such as file formats used, compression settings, and other optimization-related settings.

The metadata file is updated with each table modification (such as adding or deleting data), ensuring that Iceberg maintains an accurate, up-to-date view of the entire dataset.

Manifest List

The *manifest list* is a higher-level metadata file that references all the *manifest files* associated with a table. It is a table of contents that Iceberg consults when determining which manifest files to scan for a query or operation. This structure allows Iceberg to efficiently manage large datasets by scanning only relevant data sections.

Using the manifest list, Iceberg can quickly locate the manifest files containing the data needed for a particular query. This helps reduce the amount of data read from storage, leading to faster query performance and lower I/O costs, especially when dealing with petabyte-scale datasets.

Manifest Files

Each manifest file contains detailed metadata about a group of data files in the dataset. It records information such as:

File paths
> The locations of the actual data files in the storage system (e.g., Object Storage or HDFS)

Partition values

The partitioning information for each file, which allows Iceberg to perform partition pruning—filtering out unnecessary partitions to reduce query scope

File statistics

Min/max values for each column, enabling predicate pushdown (filtering rows before reading them) for more efficient querying

The manifest files are the key to Iceberg's ability to scale across large datasets, as they allow the system to manage groups of data files in an organized and optimized way. By storing metadata about the data files separately, Iceberg also supports partition evolution—the ability to adjust partitioning schemes over time without rewriting the entire dataset.

Data Files

The data files are where the actual records in the dataset are stored. These files are typically in columnar formats like Apache Parquet or ORC, optimized for analytical queries. Data files contain the raw data that is processed during reads and writes, and the manifest files reference them.

Iceberg abstracts the complexity of managing these files, allowing users to interact with their datasets through high-level table interfaces. When new data is added, Iceberg writes it into new data files and updates the associated metadata, ensuring that the latest state of the table is always accessible. Data files are the core storage units that Iceberg manages through its metadata layers, enabling efficient data operations.

Delete Files

Delete files are a particular type of file in Apache Iceberg that track row-level deletions within a dataset. Iceberg stores deletion markers in separate delete files rather than physically removing rows from a data file. These markers reference rows in existing data files, marking them as "deleted" without needing to rewrite the data file itself. This approach significantly reduces the cost and complexity of managing large datasets, especially when deletions are frequent.

There are two types of delete files in Iceberg:

Position deletes

These files store each deleted row's path and row position within the data files.

Equality deletes

These files store row-level conditions (e.g., "delete rows where customer_id = 123") that indicate which rows should be considered deleted.

Delete files allow Iceberg to maintain fast query performance by applying deletions dynamically at query time, without needing to rewrite entire data files. This also supports Iceberg's ability to perform time travel queries, as previous versions of the data remain intact and deletions can be applied selectively.

Conclusion

The modern data landscape is characterized by the exponential growth of data volumes, the diversification of data types, and the increasing demand for real-time analytics. Traditional architectures, such as data lakes and data warehouses, often struggle to meet these evolving requirements due to scalability limitations or high operational costs. Adopting a lakehouse architecture—in particular, using Apache Iceberg—has emerged in response to these challenges.

Apache Iceberg's architecture brings a new level of control and optimization to data lakes, transforming them into true data lakehouses that can handle the scale, complexity, and performance demands of modern analytics. By introducing a series of metadata files—such as the metadata.json, manifest list, manifest files, and specialized delete files—Iceberg provides powerful capabilities such as ACID transactions, schema evolution, and time travel. This architecture allows data engineers and analysts to work with massive datasets efficiently without being overwhelmed by the complexities of managing thousands of underlying data files and to easily revert to previous states if needed.

However, as organizations scale their data lakehouses, it becomes critical to have a centralized way of tracking and organizing the growing number of Iceberg tables. Managing each table's metadata, snapshots, and schema versions across a distributed environment requires a robust system that can act as a central catalog for all tables, providing visibility and governance across the organization's entire data infrastructure.

In the next chapter, we will explore how Iceberg catalogs provide this crucial functionality, enabling organizations to manage their Iceberg tables easily. Whether operating in the cloud or on-premise, catalogs ensure that every table is discoverable, version-controlled, and accessible, while also supporting integrations with a wide range of query engines and data tools. With a catalog in place, Iceberg truly becomes the backbone of a modern, scalable, and efficient data lakehouse architecture.

## CHAPTER 2

The Role of Apache Iceberg Catalogs

As we've seen in the previous chapter, Apache Iceberg brings powerful table management capabilities to data lakehouses, enabling reliable, scalable data operations with features like ACID transactions, schema evolution, and time travel. But to fully unlock the potential of Iceberg tables, we need a way to manage and organize them across the vast and diverse ecosystem of lakehouse tools. This is where Apache Iceberg catalogs come in, providing the final piece of the lakehouse puzzle.

Iceberg catalogs act as a centralized layer that tracks, organizes, and governs the growing number of tables in a lakehouse environment. They make tables discoverable by different tools and frameworks, ensuring that data engineers, analysts, and other users can easily access the latest state of any table, regardless of where the data resides. Without catalogs, managing large-scale datasets across different query engines and environments would become chaotic and error prone, resulting in a lack of a unified view of table metadata, versions, and schema changes.

More than just a tracking system, Iceberg catalogs provide a governance layer that enforces access controls and auditability across your lakehouse. Iceberg catalogs can ensure that the right users have the appropriate access to the correct data, all while providing the transparency needed for regulatory compliance and operational security. In this chapter, we will explore how Iceberg catalogs enable these capabilities and examine the different types of catalogs available, along with the challenges that come with diverse catalog options. Finally, we will delve into the Apache Iceberg REST Catalog specification, which provides a flexible, scalable approach to managing Iceberg tables across any environment.

What Is and Isn't an Apache Iceberg Catalog

The term *catalog* has long been used in data architecture, but it can refer to many different things depending on the context. Before the rise of technologies like Apache Iceberg, the word "catalog" primarily referred to enterprise metadata catalogs. Tools such as Collibra, Alation, and others served as platforms for data consumers—business users, data analysts, and data scientists—to discover datasets across an organization. These catalogs were designed to document data, providing descriptions, lineage, and access policies to ensure that users could locate the data they needed, understand its context, and request access from data stewards or owners. In this sense, enterprise metadata catalogs act as gateways for human discoverability and management of data.

In contrast, *Apache Iceberg catalogs*, which we'll refer to as *lakehouse catalogs*, serve a different but equally important purpose. Instead of being a tool for end users to find datasets, lakehouse catalogs act as a backbone for the tools that those users rely on. They provide *machine-driven discoverability* of data, enabling various engines, like Spark, Dremio, Snowflake, or Flink, to know which datasets exist in your lakehouse. Without a lakehouse catalog, these tools would only see files in storage—a raw, unstructured data view. By leveraging a lakehouse catalog, tools can treat the data as tables, allowing for easy access, querying, and management as though the data were housed in a traditional data warehouse. Figure 2-1 summarizes the differences.

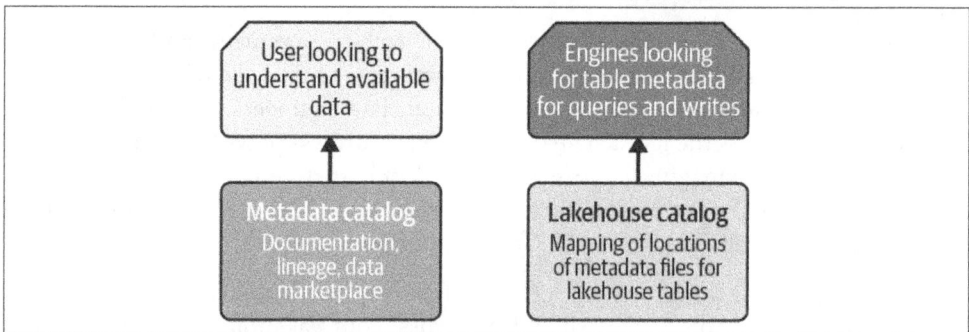

Figure 2-1. The difference between enterprise data catalogs and lakehouse catalogs

The Mechanics of Apache Iceberg Catalogs

The need for a lakehouse catalog stems from how Apache Iceberg manages data. Each Iceberg table generates a new *metadata.json* file every time the table is updated. This file contains essential information about the table's schema, partitions, snapshots, and more, making it the central source of truth for the current state of the table. However, without a catalog to manage these files, there would be no mechanism for tools to determine which version of the *metadata.json* is the correct one to use. Every query engine, processing tool, or user would potentially see different versions of the table, leading to inconsistencies.

This is where the lakehouse catalog comes into play. The catalog serves as the source of truth, providing a consistent way for tools to discover and access the correct *metadata.json* file for any given table, as illustrated in Figure 2-2. By having all tables and views registered in the lakehouse catalog, all tools querying the table are working with the current and correct version of the data. This prevents issues like tools accessing outdated metadata files or reading stale data.

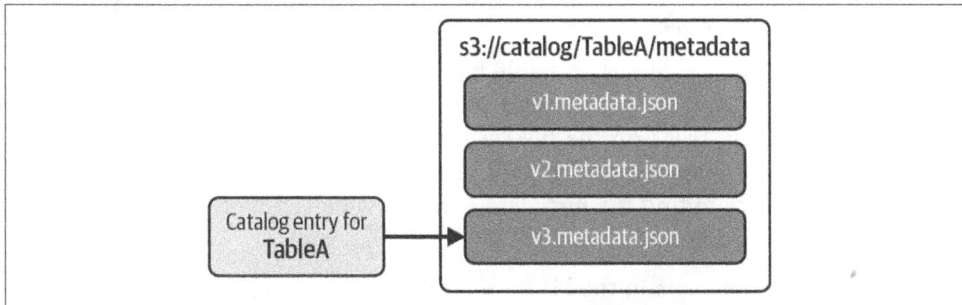

Figure 2-2. The catalog as the source of truth for the table metadata

Moreover, the catalog plays the central role in enabling safe concurrent transactions. When a write operation begins, the tool checks the current state of the table, as recorded in the catalog. After the operation is complete, the catalog verifies that no conflicting changes have occurred in the meantime before committing the new data. If another write operation has modified the table during this time, the transaction will fail and likely be retried, ensuring data consistency and preventing conflicts.

By acting as a global registry for Iceberg tables, lakehouse catalogs ensure that all users and tools in the data ecosystem have access to the same, up-to-date view of each table, paving the way for consistent and reliable operations.

In the next section, we will explore the various types of Apache Iceberg catalogs available and their implementation across different environments, ranging from cloud-native solutions to on-premise systems.

Types of Apache Iceberg Catalogs

When Apache Iceberg was initially developed, it offered several methods for managing and tracking datasets through various types of catalogs. These Iceberg catalogs can be broadly categorized into two main types: file-system catalogs and service catalogs. Each type has its strengths and weaknesses, particularly in terms of scalability, consistency, and ease of integration with various environments. In this section, we'll explore both types of catalogs and discuss how they operate under the hood, as well as the challenges they may encounter in production environments.

File-System Catalogs

File-system catalogs manage Iceberg tables by storing metadata references directly in the underlying file system. The file-system catalog, also known as the Hadoop catalog, maintains metadata for each Iceberg table within a directory structure on a distributed file system, such as HDFS, Amazon S3, or Google Cloud Storage.

How the Hadoop Catalog works

In the Hadoop catalog, each Iceberg table has its directory, and the metadata for the table (such as the *metadata.json* file and the table's *snapshots*) is stored within that directory. The catalog relies on the file system's structure to organize and reference tables. When a query engine or other tool needs to interact with an Iceberg table, it consults the directory to find the *metadata.json* file, which contains the latest schema and partitioning information.

One of the key components in the Hadoop catalog is the *VERSION-HINT.TEXT* file. This file serves as a pointer to the most recent version of the *metadata.json* file. Each time a table is updated, a new metadata file is created, and the *VERSION-HINT.TEXT* file is updated to reflect the latest version. When a tool queries a table, it reads the *VERSION-HINT.TEXT* file to know which version of the metadata to use, as illustrated in Figure 2-3.

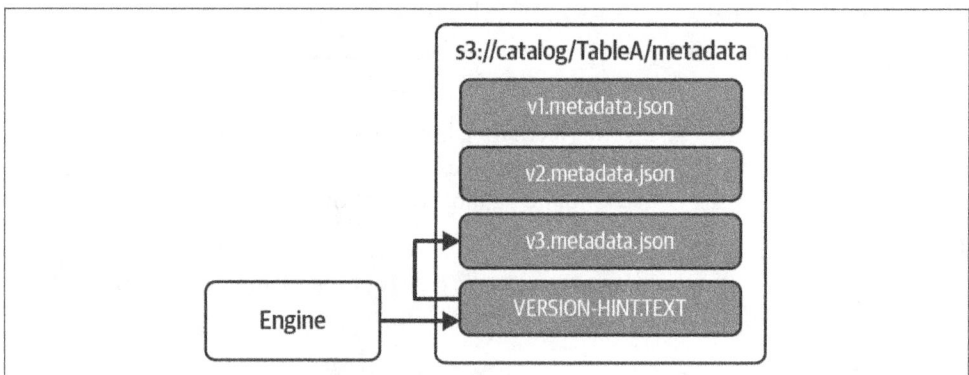

Figure 2-3. How the Hadoop (File-System) catalog works

The challenges with file-system catalogs

While the Hadoop catalog works well for smaller-scale or test environments, it introduces some significant challenges when used in production settings. One of the key issues is consistency. Not all file systems provide the same guarantees when it comes to updating and reading files, and in particular, the update of the *VERSION-HINT.TEXT* file may not always be atomic. For instance, in some cloud storage systems, there may be a delay between when a file is updated and when that change is visible to other clients (eventual consistency). This can lead to situations where the query engine reads the old version of the *VERSION-HINT.TEXT* file, causing it to reference an outdated metadata file and leading to inconsistencies in the data that is accessed.

Additionally, file-system catalogs often lack the built-in locking mechanisms necessary for managing concurrent writes and reads. As a result, production environments that require high levels of consistency, reliability, and scalability may find that file-system catalogs are not robust enough to meet their needs.

Service Catalogs

To address the challenges faced by file-system catalogs, *service catalogs* exist. Unlike file-system catalogs, service catalogs rely on an external service—typically a database or specialized catalog service—to store metadata and manage transactions. These services can leverage locking mechanisms and other features to ensure data consistency and handle concurrent operations safely, making them much more reliable for large-scale production environments. Figure 2-4 shows how service catalogs work.

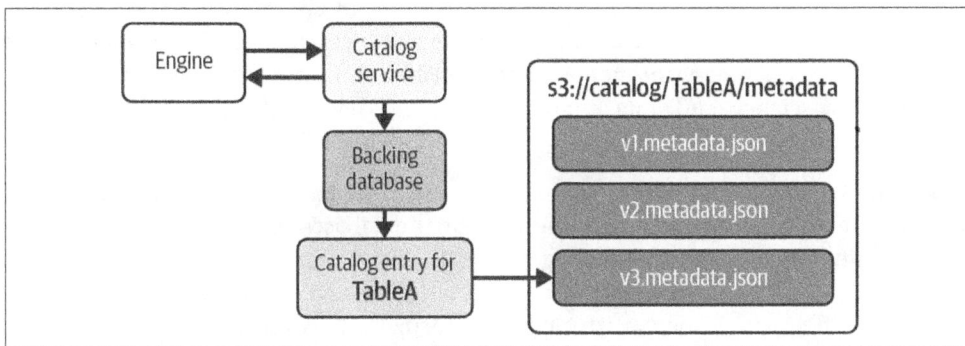

Figure 2-4. How service catalogs deliver the location of metadata to engines

Hive catalog

The Hive catalog is one of the earliest service catalogs for Apache Iceberg. Built on top of the Apache Hive Metastore, this catalog stores Iceberg metadata in a relational database (such as MySQL or PostgreSQL) through Hive's table management system. The Hive catalog integrates well with query engines that already rely on Hive for metadata management, such as Apache Spark and Apache Flink.

Hive provides a more consistent and transactionally safe environment compared to file-system catalogs. Its relational database backend allows it to lock tables during updates, ensuring that changes are correctly handled and reducing the risk of inconsistencies. However, Hive's metastore was not initially designed for the scale of modern data lakes, and this can become a limiting factor as the number of tables and datasets grows. Hive can also be challenging to deploy and manage.

JDBC catalog

The *JDBC catalog* works similarly to the Hive catalog, but instead of relying on Hive, it uses a direct connection to a relational database via the JDBC interface. This provides organizations with more flexibility in selecting their database system to serve as the Iceberg catalog. For example, organizations can use MySQL, PostgreSQL, or even cloud-based managed databases to store metadata for Iceberg tables.

The JDBC catalog provides the same benefits as the Hive catalog in terms of consistency and transactional safety. By leveraging the locking capabilities of relational databases, it ensures that concurrent writes and reads are handled properly, avoiding issues like partial updates or stale data being read by query engines. It's an ideal choice for organizations that prefer a lightweight, relational database-driven approach to catalog management.

Nessie catalog

The *Nessie catalog* is a service catalog designed for catalog-level version control and multi-branch data management. It operates similarly to Git, allowing data engineers to create branches, tags, and commits for their Iceberg tables. This makes Nessie particularly useful in environments where collaboration and versioning are critical, such as data science and data engineering teams that need to work on multiple versions of a dataset simultaneously.

Nessie stores its metadata in a versioned key-value store, which can be backed by a variety of storage systems, including relational databases or cloud-native solutions like DynamoDB. The Nessie catalog provides ACID transactions and concurrent write safety, while also allowing teams to roll back to previous versions of their tables or branch off to experiment with new transformations without affecting the main production dataset.

AWS Glue catalog

The *AWS Glue catalog* is a fully managed service for tracking metadata for data stored in Amazon S3. Originally designed to manage metadata for a variety of AWS analytics services (like Athena, Redshift Spectrum, and EMR), Glue now supports Apache Iceberg tables as well. The Glue catalog integrates tightly with the AWS ecosystem, making it an ideal choice for organizations that run their data infrastructure on AWS.

Glue provides serverless metadata management, meaning that AWS handles the scaling, availability, and operational aspects of the catalog. It supports schema versioning, concurrent operations, and partition discovery—all of which are critical for managing large datasets in production environments. As a managed service, AWS Glue is particularly appealing for organizations that don't want to manage the operational complexity of running their own catalog service.

Challenges of Diverse Catalog Options

As Apache Iceberg adoption grew, so did the number of catalog implementations designed to manage Iceberg tables. While having multiple catalog options—ranging from file-system-based solutions to service-driven catalogs like Hive, JDBC, Nessie, and AWS Glue—provided flexibility, it also introduced a new set of challenges. Each catalog had its own way of managing metadata and transactions, and integrating these catalogs with different data processing engines became increasingly complex and error prone.

One of the most significant challenges was that each catalog required a dedicated *client class* to be implemented in every language that used the Iceberg API. Whether you were working in Java, Python, Rust, or Go, you needed a specialized client that could interact with the chosen catalog, as illustrated in Figure 2-5.

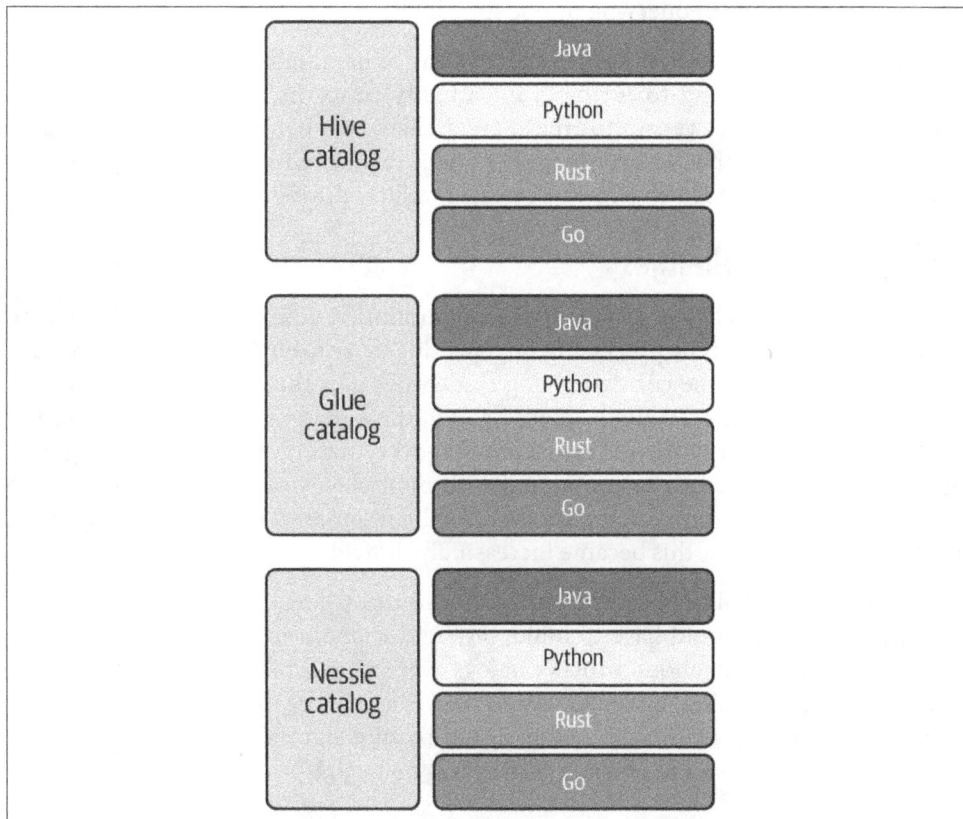

Figure 2-5. The challenges of maintaining all the client libraries for a single catalog

This requirement created significant overhead for catalog maintainers and developers, as each catalog had to ensure compatibility across multiple programming languages and environments. The lack of standardization across these implementations also meant that bugs, inconsistencies, or mismatches between catalog versions and client libraries could easily arise.

Client-Side Complexity

Much of the catalog logic was handled on the client side, meaning that the responsibility for correctly managing metadata, interacting with table snapshots, and ensuring consistent reads and writes were placed on the application or processing engine using the catalog. This client-side approach led to issues with version mismatches. For example, if an organization upgraded their catalog server but failed to update the corresponding catalog client library in their data processing tools, inconsistencies or errors could occur when querying or updating tables.

In addition, each catalog had its own specific way of handling metadata and interacting with storage, leading to further compatibility concerns. It became essential to ensure that the correct version of the catalog client was being used for the version of the catalog server that was running. If a client was out of sync with the catalog, it could lead to unexpected behaviors or outright failures during data operations.

Configuration Challenges

Another significant challenge was the configuration required when working with Iceberg catalogs. Different processing engines (like Spark, Flink, or Dremio) needed to be configured with the correct catalog credentials plus the object storage configuration and the storage credentials to access both the metadata and the data stored in the underlying storage system. This meant that every tool or engine interacting with an Iceberg table needed to be configured with multiple layers of credentials, leading to a tedious and error-prone setup process. As the number of tools and catalogs used in an organization grew, this became increasingly difficult to manage.

For organizations using managed services, the situation was even more complicated. Managed platforms would have to build, test, and support each catalog individually. This led to confusion about which catalogs were supported on which platforms, and differences in catalog implementations between services meant that transitioning from one managed platform to another could require significant reconfiguration or even a complete overhaul of how the catalog was managed.

Authorization Challenges

Governing access privileges to data, as well as metadata, is critical for many organizations. While some Iceberg catalog implementations provided some access control to the tables, views and namespaces, access to the actual data had to be separately managed via the object storage configuration and storage credentials, forcing users to manage two different authorization systems for the same thing, the tables' data.

The Need for a Unified Approach

These challenges—the proliferation of client libraries, the complexity of client-side logic, version mismatches, tedious configuration, access privilege concerns, and fragmented managed service support—highlighted the need for a different server-client paradigm. Organizations required a standardized way of interacting with Iceberg catalogs that would simplify integration, ensure compatibility across different environments, and reduce the operational burden of managing metadata and governing data access.

The Apache Iceberg REST Catalog Specification

The *Apache Iceberg REST Catalog Specification* was created to address the growing complexities and challenges associated with managing Apache Iceberg catalogs. This specification is designed to simplify the interaction between Iceberg tables and the diverse range of catalogs by establishing a uniform client interface that would work seamlessly across multiple programming languages. At the core of this effort is an OpenAPI Spec, which provides a blueprint for building a RESTful catalog service. By adhering to this specification, any catalog can implement the necessary endpoints, ensuring compatibility with Iceberg while solving many of the issues faced by earlier catalog implementations, as illustrated in Figure 2-6.

This approach moves the complexity and specialties of each catalog from all the different client libraries to the service. Access privileges to metadata and data are governed by the catalog service, allowing integration with organization IdPs running, for example, Keycloak, Authelia or Okta and leveraging IAM policies for table level data access control.

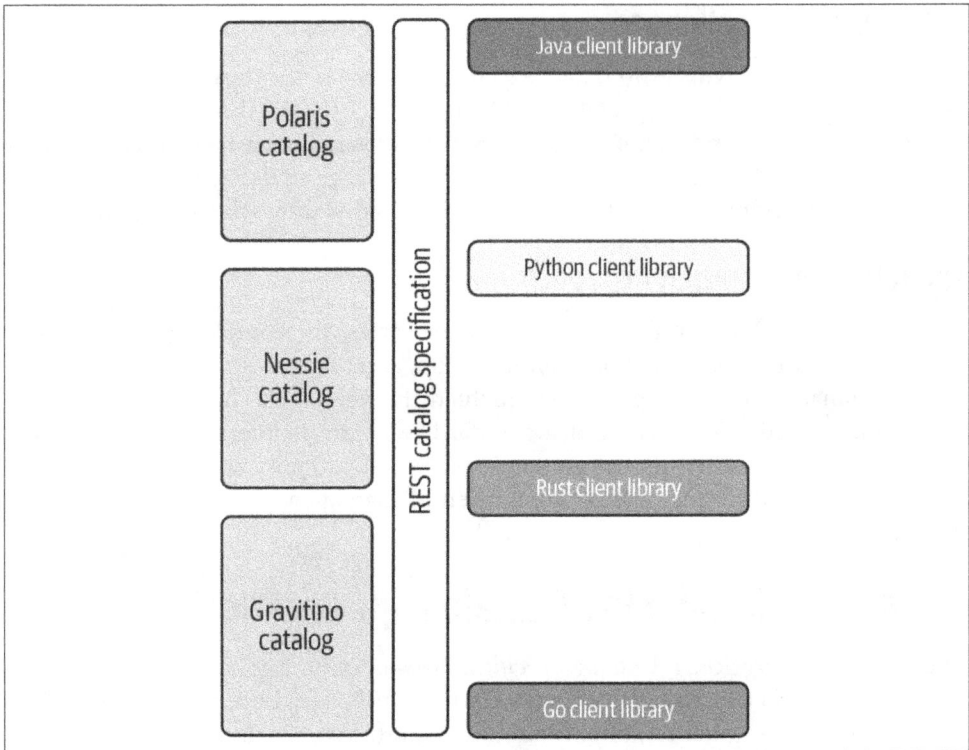

Figure 2-6. The simplification enabled by the REST catalog specification

Key Benefits of the REST Catalog Specification

By providing a uniform way to talk to catalogs for read/write operations on Apache Iceberg tables, the REST catalog interface provides the following key benefits:

Server-side logic handling
> One of the most significant improvements the REST catalog specification brings is that it shifts much of the catalog-specific logic from the client to the server. Instead of the client managing intricate details such as metadata, snapshots, and transactions, these operations are now handled directly by the catalog service itself. This move reduces the versioning issues that previously arose when catalog clients and servers were out of sync. Since the catalog service takes responsibility for most operations, the client-side implementation becomes much lighter and simpler.

Unified client across catalogs
> The REST catalog specification standardizes how clients interact with catalogs. Once a catalog supports the REST specification, it can be accessed using the same REST catalog client. Data processing engines, query tools, or any service inter-

acting with the catalog no longer need custom, catalog-specific clients. Instead, they can use a single, standardized client, making it much easier to connect to multiple catalogs without needing to adapt to different APIs or implementations.

Cross-language simplicity

By introducing a common interface, the REST catalog specification eliminates the need for separate client classes for each catalog in different programming languages. Now, a single REST client can be implemented for each language (Java, Python, Rust, Go, etc.), and that client will work with any catalog that implements the REST specification. This significantly reduces the complexity of maintaining cross-language compatibility and ensures that future updates or improvements can be rolled out consistently across all supported environments.

Simplified support for managed services

For managed services, the REST catalog specification offers substantial benefits. Previously, managed platforms needed to build and test support for each individual catalog, leading to confusion and fragmented catalog support across different services. With the REST catalog, managed services only need to implement the REST catalog client. Once this client is in place, the platform can automatically support any catalog that complies with the REST specification. This opens the door to a much wider range of catalogs being available for users on managed platforms, all while reducing the operational overhead for service providers.

The Evolution of REST Catalog Implementations

When the REST catalog specification was first introduced, the only option available was a commercial catalog service from Tabular. Founded by the original creators of Apache Iceberg, Tabular was the first to implement the REST specification, offering enterprises a fully managed Iceberg catalog with all the benefits of the specification. This provided early adopters with a robust solution. Still, it remained a commercial offering that closed off its availability after Tabular was purchased by Databricks, which closed registration and sunsetted the product after the acquisition.

As the value of the REST catalog specification became clear, the open source community began to implement the specification, leading to the creation of several open source catalog services that supported REST-based interactions, catalogs that can be self-managed into perpetuity without the need to worry about corporate actions leading to a need to migrate. Today, several open source catalogs have adopted the REST specification, including:

Nessie

The original open source catalog was explicitly made for modern post-Hive lake-houses, which was initially created at Dremio. Nessie provides a Git-like catalog that allows for catalog-level data versioning, branching, and tagging, enabling these kinds of semantics across multiple tables.

Apache Gravitino

Gravitino is an open source project working to provide a robust REST-based catalog service that meets the needs of modern data lakehouses. Gravitino aims to be a metadata catalog not just for tables, but also a schema and ML model registry that can be geo-distributed, initially created and donated to the Apache Software Foundation by Datastrato.

Apache Polaris

Polaris is an Iceberg REST catalog implementation designed to become the center of your lakehouse, providing robust role-based access controls (RBAC), integration with organizations' IdPs, and the ability to connect external catalogs, thereby unifying the catalog ecosystem. Polaris, with contributors from Dremio, Snowflake, AWS, Google, Microsoft, Confluent, LanceDB, and many more, was initially created and donated to the Apache Software Foundation by Snowflake.

These open source implementations of the REST catalog specification have made it easier for organizations to adopt Iceberg and leverage its advanced features in a standardized way. The REST catalog specification ensures a consistent, scalable, and manageable approach to organizing and interacting with Iceberg tables in modern data lakehouses.

Apache Polaris

With the rise of the data lakehouse, many of the significant challenges in data management—such as maintaining data consistency across fragmented teams and tools—have been addressed, especially with the introduction of open source catalogs like Nessie, Gravitino, and others. These catalogs, each with unique features such as Nessie's versioning and Gravitino's geo-distributed availability, have provided flexibility and engine interoperability. However, a few key issues remained that the current ecosystem of catalogs hadn't quite solved.

One major limitation was that while different catalogs had their own strengths, organizations often found themselves forced to center their entire lakehouse architecture around a single catalog. Choosing one catalog meant forgoing the benefits of others. For instance, if a team wanted to use Nessie's versioning capabilities, they'd be locked into Nessie's catalog, unable to leverage Gravitino's geo-distribution. This created a siloed effect, where the choice of catalog dictated the entire structure of the lakehouse, thus reducing flexibility.

Another critical challenge was governance. In many cases, access controls and security were implemented at the engine level, meaning each tool interacting with Apache Iceberg tables had to implement its own access rules. This approach led to inconsistency and operational overhead, as teams had to manage multiple layers of access control across different tools, and these access rules weren't portable from one tool to another.

The Birth of Apache Polaris

Recognizing these limitations, Snowflake announced the development of a new catalog called Polaris. With collaboration from major players such as Dremio, AWS, Google, and Microsoft, Polaris quickly gained momentum. The project was accepted into the Apache Software Foundation Incubator, officially becoming a community-driven project guided by developers from various companies and organizations. The creation of Polaris was a major step forward in addressing the remaining challenges of data lakehouse catalogs, pushing the boundaries of what catalogs could do in a multi-tool, multi-cloud environment.

Polaris: A New Era of Lakehouse Catalogs

Polaris introduced several innovative features that helped position it at the center of the Iceberg catalog ecosystem. Figure 2-7 illustrates how some of these features fit in.

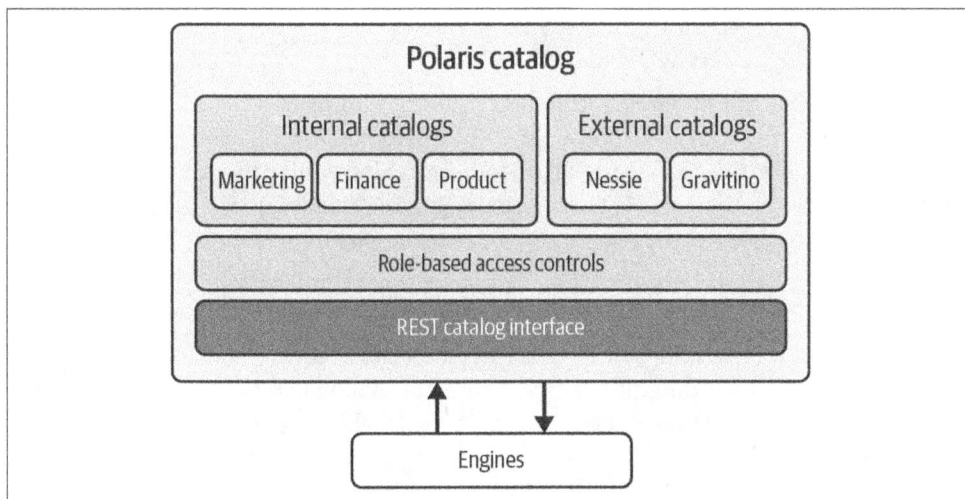

Figure 2-7. Unifying the Iceberg lakehouse catalog ecosystem with Apache Polaris

Multi-catalog support

One of the most innovative features of Polaris is its ability to create and manage multiple catalogs within a single system. Each catalog in Polaris can have its own set of *catalog roles*, allowing fine-grained control over access to tables, namespaces, and views. This means that organizations no longer have to choose a single catalog to manage their entire lakehouse. Instead, Polaris allows for *flexible cataloging*, where different catalogs can serve different purposes, each with its own security and governance structure.

External connectivity

Perhaps the most powerful feature of Polaris is its ability to connect to external catalogs that support the Apache Iceberg REST Specification. This allows Polaris to serve as a central point of discoverability for all Iceberg tables, even if they are managed by other catalogs like Nessie or Gravitino. By integrating external catalogs, Polaris enables users to leverage the unique features of other catalog implementations while still viewing and managing all their tables from a single, unified interface.

RBAC (role-based access control)

Polaris also provides robust role-based access control (RBAC), ensuring that data access is handled at the catalog level. Users, referred to as *principals*, can be assigned *roles*, which consist of collections of catalog-specific permissions. These roles determine the level of access each user has across the various catalogs within Polaris, ensuring consistent, centralized security across the entire data environment. With RBAC built into Polaris, access control no longer depends on individual tools or engines but is instead portable and consistent across the lakehouse.

Conclusion

With features like multi-catalog support, external connectivity, and RBAC, Polaris has quickly become a central player in the Iceberg catalog ecosystem. Its ability to unify and simplify the management of Iceberg tables while providing flexibility in choosing which catalog features to leverage makes it a powerful tool for organizations building modern data lakehouses. Backed by the largest names in the cloud and data space, Polaris is poised to redefine how catalogs operate in distributed, multi-cloud environments.

As we explore the capabilities of Polaris in greater detail throughout this book, you'll gain a deeper understanding of how this powerful catalog can help solve some of the most complex data management challenges in the lakehouse paradigm.

## PART II

Apache Polaris

With the foundational concepts of data lakehouses, Apache Iceberg, and catalogs established, it's time to explore the next frontier in catalog innovation: Apache Polaris. As a new-generation catalog in the Apache ecosystem, Polaris addresses key challenges in the lakehouse architecture, offering groundbreaking solutions for governance, security, and multi-catalog integration.

In this section, we'll look closer at Polaris's unique features and role in advancing the lakehouse paradigm. Chapter 3 begins with an in-depth exploration of Polaris's security model, a cornerstone of its architecture. Here, you'll learn how Polaris implements catalog-level access controls through roles, principals, and permissions, ensuring robust and scalable governance for even the most complex data ecosystems. You'll also gain insights into best practices for managing access and security in Polaris-powered lakehouses, enabling you to maintain compliance while empowering data consumers.

Chapter 4 focuses on one of Polaris's most innovative capabilities: external catalog integration. Polaris is designed to connect with other catalogs, allowing you to unify datasets across systems while still leveraging the unique features of each catalog. We'll explore integrations with prominent catalogs like Nessie, Gravitino, Lakekeeper, and Unity, highlighting how Polaris simplifies data discoverability and governance across diverse environments.

By the end of this section, you'll have a comprehensive understanding of Polaris's role in solving critical challenges in lakehouse management and enabling seamless integration across the data ecosystem.

## CHAPTER 3

The Apache Polaris Security Model

This chapter explores the security model of Apache Polaris, focusing on how it enables fine-grained access control, ensures compliance, and facilitates seamless collaboration across teams. Through a combination of principals, principal roles and catalog roles, Polaris empowers organizations to enforce access control policies that are both flexible and scalable. You'll also discover best practices for implementing Polaris's security model, ensuring that your lakehouse remains secure across different tooling.

What Is Polaris?

Apache Polaris is a catalog designed to address the challenges of managing and governing data in modern lakehouse environments. As data becomes more distributed across systems, tools, and platforms, Polaris provides a unified cataloging solution that simplifies data discoverability, enhances governance, and ensures security across the entire data ecosystem.

At its core, Polaris is built around a multi-catalog architecture, allowing organizations to create and manage multiple catalogs under a single system. Each catalog operates independently, with its own catalog roles, permissions, and namespaces, providing unparalleled flexibility for managing diverse datasets. This architecture is particularly valuable in complex environments where different teams, regions, or use cases require distinct data governance policies.

Polaris's security model is one of its defining features, centralizing access controls to ensure that governance policies are applied consistently across all connected tools and engines. By implementing role-based access control (RBAC) at the catalog level, Polaris allows administrators to define precise permissions for users and groups, ensuring that sensitive data remains protected while enabling authorized users to access the datasets they need.

Another feature of Polaris is its external catalog integration. Organizations can connect Polaris to other catalogs supporting the Apache Iceberg REST specification, enabling centralized management and governance while leveraging the unique capabilities of external catalogs like Nessie and Gravitino.

As we move through this chapter, we'll explore how Polaris catalogs, principals, principal roles, and catalog roles interact to create a secure and governable environment for your lakehouse and provide practical guidance on deploying these features effectively. These elements make Polaris a powerful tool for balancing security, collaboration, and accessibility in modern data systems.

Catalogs

At the heart of the Apache Polaris security model lies the concept of catalogs. A catalog in Polaris serves as a logical grouping of tables, namespaces, and views and is the foundation upon which access control and governance policies are built. Unlike traditional data catalog systems that are often tied to a single data engine or service, Polaris introduces a multi-catalog architecture that allows organizations to create and manage multiple catalogs within the same system, as seen in Figure 3-1. This architecture provides unparalleled flexibility in managing diverse data needs while maintaining centralized governance.

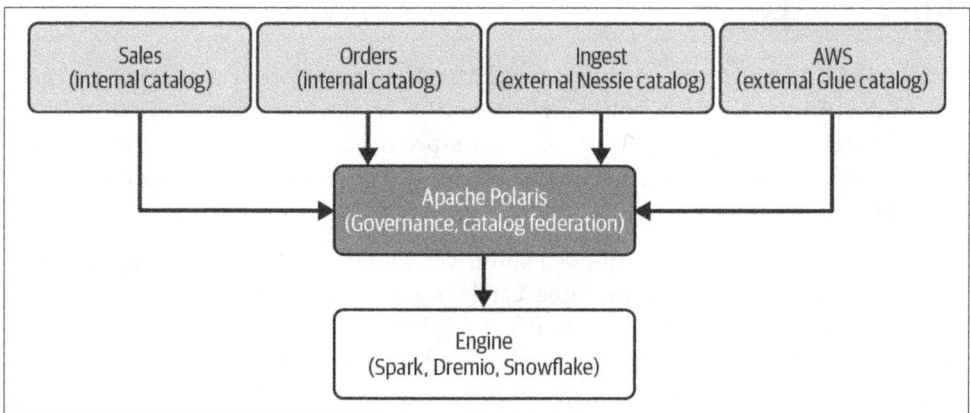

Figure 3-1. Apache Polaris's multi-catalog architecture

Each catalog in Polaris is an independent entity with its metadata, roles, and access policies. This independence enables the design of catalogs tailored to specific use cases, teams, business units, or geographic regions. For example, an organization might create separate catalogs for marketing, sales, and compliance-critical data, each with its access controls tailored to the needs and sensitivities of the data it contains.

Polaris catalogs are more than just containers for tables—they are governance units that enforce RBAC at the catalog level. This ensures that only authorized users can access or modify the data within a given catalog/namespace/table/view, making it easier to meet compliance requirements and maintain data security across the lakehouse.

Key Features of Polaris Catalogs

Apache Polaris provides various features to make it easier to organize, manage, and govern your data lakehouse datasets:

Namespace management
Within a catalog, Polaris organizes tables and views into namespaces, which act as subdirectories for structuring data (think of it as a folder on your laptop's filesystem). This hierarchical organization makes it easy to manage large datasets, enforce granular access controls, and align the data structure with business domains.

Catalog roles
Each catalog has its own set of catalog roles, which define the permissions for accessing and managing the tables, namespaces, and views within a catalog. Roles can be as granular or broad as needed, allowing administrators to fine-tune access for different user groups.

Isolation and independence
Catalogs in Polaris are isolated from one another, meaning that changes or permissions applied in one catalog do not affect other catalogs. This isolation provides a level of security and control that is essential for managing diverse datasets in multi-tenant or multi-use environments.

Multi-catalog integration
Polaris allows for the creation of multiple catalogs under a single system. This multi-catalog approach simplifies the management of large-scale, distributed data environments by providing a unified governance framework while allowing each catalog to serve its specific purpose.

Integration with external catalogs
Polaris catalogs are not limited to internal datasets. With support for the Apache Iceberg REST specification, Polaris can integrate with external catalogs such as Nessie or Gravitino, making it a central hub for managing all your Iceberg tables across various platforms.

Benefits of Multi-Catalog Architecture

The multi-catalog design of Polaris offers several benefits for modern data lakehouses:

Flexibility
Organizations can design catalogs to align with their unique business, operational, or regulatory requirements.

Scalability
As datasets grow in complexity, multiple catalogs allow for better organization and performance by isolating metadata and access controls.

Security
Isolated catalogs reduce the risk of accidental or unauthorized access to sensitive data by limiting the scope of permissions to specific catalogs.

Collaboration
Teams working on different projects or datasets can operate independently within their catalogs, while administrators maintain centralized oversight and governance.

Polaris catalogs are the cornerstone of its governance model, providing a robust, scalable framework for organizing and securing data in the lakehouse.

Principals

In Apache Polaris, principals are unique identities representing users or services interacting with the system. These principals are the foundational entities assigned to access permissions, enabling secure and governed access to Polaris catalogs, namespaces, tables, and views. Whether a data engineer is running jobs through Apache Spark, a data analyst is serving a dashboard from Dremio, or a data scientist is training models using Polaris-managed data, each user or service is mapped to a distinct principal.

What Are Principals?

A principal in Polaris can represent either a user or a service:

User
An individual accessing Polaris directly or through an application.

Service
An automated process or tool that requires access to Polaris for operations like querying, transforming, or cataloging data.

Each principal operates within Polaris's security and governance framework, which ensures that every interaction adheres to the organization's access policies.

Managing Principals

Principals in Polaris are assigned specific principal roles to determine their access rights within the system. These principal roles serve as groups of catalog roles, enabling administrators to manage access efficiently without having to handle individual privileges for each principal. This role-based approach simplifies security management and aligns with industry standards for governance, for example:

- A *data_engineer* principal role might grant permissions to create, update, and query tables in different catalogs.
- A *data_scientist* principal role might allow querying and reading data only from specific catalogs to different catalogs.

Principal Lifecycle

Principals represent those who will access your data lakehouse datasets, and each principal goes through a three-stage lifecycle:

Creation
> Principals are created to represent users or services requiring access to Polaris.

Assignment
> Each principal is assigned one or more principal roles, granting them specific access permissions.

Revocation
> When a user leaves the organization or a service is decommissioned, their principal and associated roles can be revoked, ensuring security and compliance.

This lifecycle helps you think through things that you will want to verify when doing regular audits of your access roles:

- Are all the principals I need created?
- Are they assigned the roles they require?
- Did retired or updated principals have their access revoked?

Catalog Roles

Catalog roles in Apache Polaris are another building block of its RBAC model, enabling fine-grained control over who can access or manage data within a catalog. These roles define a set of permissions that determine what actions a principal role assigned the catalog role can perform on the resources—such as tables, namespaces, and views—contained within a specific catalog. By assigning catalog roles to principal roles (which are then assigned to principals/users), administrators can ensure that access is secure and aligned with organizational policies. An illustration of Apache Polaris's RBAC framework is in Figure 3-2.

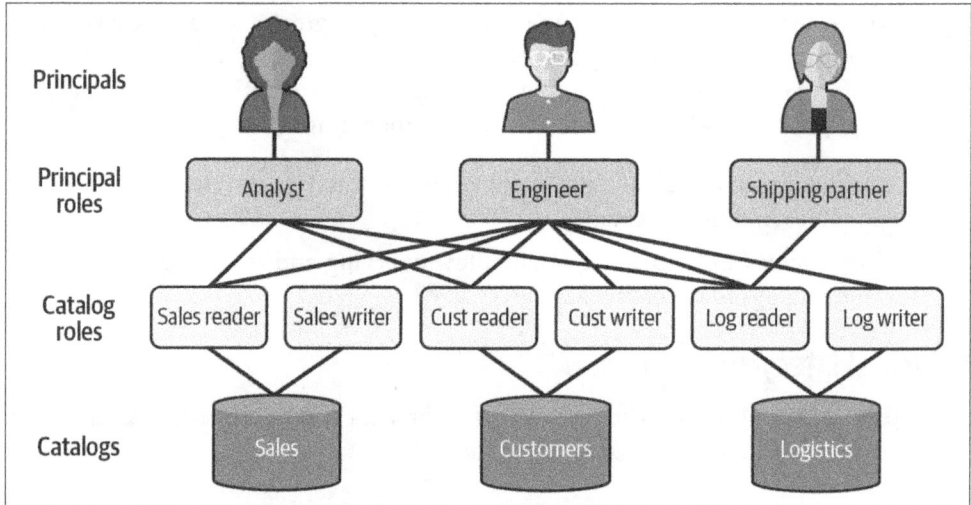

Figure 3-2. Overview of Apache Polaris's RBAC architecture

A *catalog role* is a collection of permissions that grant specific operations within a catalog. Permissions can range from basic read access to more advanced privileges, such as creating new tables, modifying schemas, or managing namespaces. Catalog roles are highly flexible, allowing administrators to tailor access policies to the unique needs of their organization, business units, or teams, for example:

- A data analyst role might include permissions for querying tables and reading metadata but restrict the ability to modify schemas or delete data.

- A data engineer role might include permissions for creating and managing tables, updating schemas, and organizing namespaces.

- A catalog admin role might have full control over all catalog resources, including assigning roles and managing access policies.

These roles would then be assigned to principal roles that would inherit these privileges, and then those principal roles would be assigned to individual principals.

Defining Permissions in Catalog Roles

Catalog roles in Apache Polaris are constructed using a comprehensive set of permissions that define specific actions a user or service can perform within a catalog. These permissions allow for fine-grained control over tables, views, namespaces, and the catalog itself. Next, we delve into the key types of permissions and their associated privileges.

Table Privileges

Table permissions manage interactions with the data tables within a catalog. These privileges include:

TABLE_CREATE
> Allows registering a new table within the catalog

TABLE_DROP
> Permits deleting a table from the catalog

TABLE_LIST
> Enables listing all tables in the catalog

TABLE_READ_PROPERTIES
> Grants access to read the properties and metadata of a table, such as schema details and partition information

TABLE_WRITE_PROPERTIES
> Allows modifying the properties of a table, including updating configurations.

TABLE_READ_DATA
> Provides read-only access to the table data by issuing short-lived read-only storage credentials.

TABLE_WRITE_DATA
> Grants permission to write data to a table by issuing short-lived read+write storage credentials

TABLE_FULL_METADATA
> Includes all table-related privileges except TABLE_READ_DATA and TABLE_WRITE_DATA, which must be granted individually.

These privileges ensure precise control over how data tables are created, modified, accessed, or removed within a catalog.

View Privileges

Views allow users to create and manage virtual representations of data. The privileges associated with views include:

VIEW_CREATE
Allows registering a new view within the catalog

VIEW_DROP
Enables dropping an existing view from the catalog

VIEW_LIST
Grants the ability to list all views in the catalog

VIEW_READ_PROPERTIES
Provides access to read the properties and metadata of a view

VIEW_WRITE_PROPERTIES
Allows updating the properties and configurations of a view

VIEW_FULL_METADATA
Grants all privileges related to views, including creation, deletion, and property management

These permissions enable users to create and manage virtual datasets effectively while maintaining governance controls.

Namespace Privileges

Namespaces serve as logical groupings of tables and views, often corresponding to schemas or databases in other systems (the hierarchy being catalog → namespaces → tables/views). Namespace privileges include:

NAMESPACE_CREATE
Grants the ability to create new namespaces within a catalog

NAMESPACE_DROP
Permits deleting namespaces from a catalog

NAMESPACE_LIST
Enables listing objects (e.g., tables, views) within a namespace, including nested namespaces

NAMESPACE_READ_PROPERTIES
Provides access to read properties and metadata associated with namespaces

NAMESPACE_WRITE_PROPERTIES
Allows configuring properties for namespaces, such as defining organizational structures

NAMESPACE_FULL_METADATA
Grants all privileges for managing namespaces, including creation, deletion, and property updates

These privileges allow for structured organization and management of datasets, ensuring a clear hierarchy within catalogs.

Catalog Privileges

Catalog-level privileges control overarching actions and governance across the catalog. These include:

CATALOG_MANAGE_ACCESS
Allows granting or revoking permissions on objects within a catalog and assigning catalog roles to principal roles

CATALOG_MANAGE_CONTENT
Provides full control over catalog content, including managing metadata, tables, namespaces, and views. This privilege encompasses:

- CATALOG_MANAGE_METADATA
- TABLE_FULL_METADATA
- NAMESPACE_FULL_METADATA
- VIEW_FULL_METADATA
- TABLE_WRITE_DATA
- TABLE_READ_DATA
- CATALOG_READ_PROPERTIES
- CATALOG_WRITE_PROPERTIES

CATALOG_MANAGE_METADATA
Grants full control over metadata and roles within the catalog, including tables, namespaces, and views

CATALOG_READ_PROPERTIES
Enables listing catalogs and reading catalog properties

CATALOG_WRITE_PROPERTIES
Allows modifying catalog-wide settings and configurations

These privileges ensure secure and centralized management of the catalog and its associated resources, enabling administrators to enforce governance policies effectively.

By defining permissions at multiple levels—tables, views, namespaces, and catalogs—Apache Polaris offers a highly flexible, granular security model. This structure enables organizations to govern their data lakehouses with precision, ensuring that users and services have the exact level of access required to perform their roles while safeguarding sensitive resources.

Assigning Catalog Roles to Principals

In Polaris, catalog roles are assigned to principal roles, which grant privileges to individual users or groups. This assignment process ensures that each principal's access to the resources within a catalog is governed by the permissions defined in their assigned roles. A single principal can have multiple principal roles with multiple catalog roles, allowing for complex and nuanced access policies.

For example, a compliance officer and a user working as a data engineer might be assigned roles that grant them write access to tables for engineering tasks and read-only access to compliance-critical datasets.

Benefits of catalog roles in Polaris

Catalog roles provide several benefits in the Polaris architecture such as:

Granular control
> By defining roles at the catalog level, Polaris allows for particular access policies tailored to an organization's needs.

Centralized governance
> Roles ensure consistent access controls across all resources within a catalog, reducing the risk of misconfiguration or accidental data exposure.

Relationship between principal roles and catalog roles

Principal roles and catalog roles are tightly integrated in Polaris's RBAC model:

Catalog roles
> Define the permissions for a specific catalog (e.g., Catalog Reader, Catalog Contributor)

Principal roles
> Aggregate catalog roles, assigning them to principals based on their responsibilities

This relationship enables fine-grained control over access to Polaris resources.

Best Practices for Catalog Roles

Here are some principles to apply to maximize the manageability and security provided by your catalog roles:

Proper planning
> Collect the requirements and needs before creating the first role. Play around with multiple ideas, consider how things may evolve, and plan for the future.

Least privilege principle
> Assign roles that grant the minimum access required for a user's responsibilities. Avoid overly broad permissions to reduce security risks.

Role-naming conventions
> Use clear, consistent naming conventions for roles to simplify administration and reduce confusion.

Regular reviews
> Regularly review roles and their assigned permissions to ensure they align with current business needs and compliance requirements.

Testing and validation
> Test roles in a nonproduction environment to validate that permissions are applied correctly and do not inadvertently grant excess privileges.

Catalog roles are central to the governance framework of Apache Polaris, providing the structure and flexibility needed to secure data lakehouses at scale.

Principal Roles

While principals define who interacts with Polaris, principal roles define what they can do. Principal roles act as a grouping of catalog roles, abstracting away the complexities of managing permissions for individual users or services for each catalog. This abstraction allows administrators to enforce access policies consistently across multiple principals.

What Are Principal Roles?

A principal role in Polaris is a collection of permissions granted through catalog roles. By assigning a principal role to a principal, Polaris ensures that the user or service inherits the permissions associated with that role across the specified catalogs, namespaces, tables, or views, for example:

- The data engineer role might be granted catalog roles like Catalog Contributor, which includes permissions to write data, create namespaces, and update tables.

- The data scientist role might be granted a Catalog Reader role, allowing read-only access to data.

Benefits of Principal Roles

Principal roles allow you to group the different access roles across catalogs for multiple principles and provide these benefits:

Logical grouping
Principal roles enable administrators to group permissions based on job functions, making assigning access rights to new users or services easier.

Scalability
A single principal role can be assigned to multiple principals, reducing the administrative overhead of managing access for large teams or services.

Consistency
Roles ensure consistent access policies across the organization, minimizing the risk of accidental overpermission.

Best Practices for Principal Roles

Best practices to apply when designing your principal roles for best results include:

Proper planning
Collect the requirements and needs before creating the first role. Play around with multiple ideas, consider how things may evolve, and plan for the future.

Define clear roles
Create principal roles that align with organizational roles and responsibilities (e.g., data_engineer, data_scientist, compliance_officer).

Least privilege principle
Follow the principle of least privilege, granting only the access necessary for a principal to perform their job.

Review regularly
Periodically audit principal roles to ensure they align with current business needs and compliance requirements.

Use naming conventions
Adopt clear, consistent naming conventions for roles to reduce confusion and improve maintainability.

Polaris provides a scalable, secure framework for managing access in complex lakehouse environments by integrating principals and principal roles. These entities work seamlessly with catalog roles to ensure every user and service interacts with data according to defined governance policies. In the next section, we'll explore best practices for combining these elements to optimize security and operational efficiency in Polaris.

Polaris Security Best Practices

Apache Polaris provides a flexible security model tailored to fit various organizational use cases. The key to effective governance and access control lies in structuring catalogs, catalog roles, and principal roles to align with your organization's operational and security needs. This section will explore everyday use cases and recommend best practices for setting up catalogs and principal roles for each scenario.

When implementing these different use cases, follow these best practices:

Align roles with business functions
> Define catalog and principal roles that closely mirror your organizational structure and workflows. This simplifies administration and ensures that access policies align with business needs.

Apply the principle of least privilege
> Assign roles that grant only the permissions required for a principal's responsibilities. Avoid overly broad privileges to minimize security risks.

Use hierarchical namespace structures
> Organize datasets into namespaces to group related data and simplify access control within catalogs.

Assign privileges via roles on namespaces
> Prefer assigning catalog roles to namespaces, leveraging inheritance instead of individual tables and views. This drastically reduces the number of role assignments and thus the overall complexity of your security model.

Regularly audit roles and permissions
> Review roles and assignments regularly to ensure they remain aligned with organizational needs and compliance requirements.

Leverage multi-catalog architecture
> Use Polaris's multi-catalog capabilities to segment data based on sensitivity, use case, or organizational unit, to simplify management and improve security.

Now let's explore some of these Polaris use cases.

Multi-Tenant Environments

In multi-tenant environments, where multiple teams or business units share the same data lakehouse infrastructure, isolating data access while maintaining centralized governance is critical.

Setup recommendations for multi-tenant environments include:

Catalogs
> Create separate catalogs for each team or business unit (e.g., marketing, finance, engineering). Each catalog serves as an isolated workspace for the respective team's data.

Catalog roles
> Define catalog roles specific to each team, such as:
>
> - `Marketing_Admin`: Full access to manage tables and views within the marketing catalog.
> - `Marketing_Analyst`: Read-only access to marketing datasets.

Principal roles
> Assign principal roles to users or services based on their team and job function, for example:
>
> - `Marketing_Data_Engineer`: Map to `Marketing_Admin`.
> - `Marketing_Analyst`: Map to `Marketing_Analyst`.

This structure ensures that teams have access only to their data while enabling centralized management of roles and permissions. You can also leverage the "realms" feature in Polaris that allows you to create isolated environments with their catalogs and principles. This feature will be discussed in a later chapter.

Cross-Team Collaboration

When multiple teams need to collaborate on shared datasets, you can configure shared access to specific catalogs or namespaces while limiting access to other resources.

Setup recommendations for cross-team collaboration include:

Catalogs
> Create a shared catalog for collaborative datasets (e.g., *cross_team_data*) while maintaining separate catalogs for each team's private data.

Catalog roles
> Define roles for shared access, for example:

- Shared_Contributor: Grants read and write access to collaborative datasets.
- Shared_Viewer: Grants read-only access.

Principal roles
> Assign shared access roles to specific users or teams:
>
> - A data engineer from one team might have both Shared_Contributor and a team-specific admin role.
> - Analysts from multiple teams might have Shared_Viewer roles.

This approach promotes collaboration while maintaining clear boundaries around private data.

Compliance and Sensitive Data Governance

Organizations handling sensitive data—such as personally identifiable information (PII) or financial records—need governance to comply with regulations like GDPR or HIPAA.

Setup recommendations for handling sensitive data include:

Catalogs
> Create separate catalogs for sensitive and nonsensitive data (e.g., *sensitive_data*, *public_data*).

Catalog roles
> Sensitive_Data_Admin grants full access to manage sensitive data, limited to trusted personnel
>
> Sensitive_Data_Viewer grants restricted read-only access for auditors or compliance teams

Principal roles
> Assign compliance teams Sensitive_Data_Viewer roles.
>
> Ensure sensitive data roles are assigned only to trusted users with proper credentials and monitoring.

By segregating sensitive data and using role-based access controls, you can meet compliance requirements while minimizing the risk of unauthorized access.

Cloud-Native Deployments

In cloud-native deployments, where data is distributed across multiple storage providers, access control must account for resource distribution and external catalog integration.

Setup recommendations for cloud-native deployments include:

Catalogs
> Create catalogs for each cloud provider or storage type (e.g., *AWS_S3*, *Azure_Blob*).

Catalog roles
> `Cloud_Storage_Admin` grants full access to manage resources in a specific storage catalog.
>
> `Cloud_Storage_Viewer` grants read-only access for monitoring or cost analysis.

Principal roles
> Assign roles to cloud operations teams based on their provider focus, e.g., `AWS_Admin`, `Azure_Viewer`.

External catalog integration
> Use Polaris's ability to integrate external catalogs to centralize visibility while delegating catalog-specific permissions to the external systems.

This setup provides clear boundaries and governance while leveraging Polaris as a unifying interface across multi-cloud deployments.

Organizations can create a secure, scalable, and collaborative environment with Apache Polaris while maintaining robust governance and flexibility by tailoring catalog and principal role configurations to specific use cases.

Conclusion

Apache Polaris's robust security model provides a scalable, flexible framework for managing access control in modern data lakehouses. By leveraging catalog roles, principal roles, and RBAC, Polaris enables governance across catalogs, namespaces, tables, and views. This architecture allows organizations to meet diverse use cases, from multi-tenant environments to compliance-driven data governance, while simplifying role management and ensuring consistent enforcement of access policies.

However, the true power of Polaris extends beyond its internal capabilities. Organizations often rely on multiple catalog implementations in today's complex data ecosystems, each with unique features and benefits. Polaris addresses this challenge by acting as a unifying layer that integrates with external catalogs through the Apache Iceberg REST Specification. This capability enables centralized discoverability of all Iceberg tables, regardless of their underlying catalog, making Polaris a pivotal tool for unifying the catalog ecosystem. In the next chapter, we'll explore how Polaris connects with external catalogs like Nessie, Gravitino, and others to bring cohesion to distributed data environments and maximize the flexibility of your lakehouse architecture.

## CHAPTER 4

External Catalogs

Organizations sometimes manage multiple Iceberg catalogs, each tailored to specific workloads, teams, regulatory requirements, or operational needs. While this diverse array of catalogs allows organizations to optimize their data strategies, it also introduces challenges in unifying access and ensuring seamless integration. Apache Polaris addresses this problem by enabling connections to external Iceberg catalogs by integrating those using the Apache Iceberg REST Catalog Specification. This innovative feature enables Polaris to serve as a central access point for all Iceberg tables, regardless of the underlying catalog, thereby simplifying multi-catalog use cases and enhancing operational flexibility.

With Polaris, users can query and manage Iceberg tables from external catalogs as if they were part of Polaris. By connecting their Polaris catalog to their favorite engines, end users gain unified access to datasets across multiple catalogs without managing separate credentials or interfaces (Figure 4-1). This capability makes it significantly easier to leverage the best features of different catalogs while maintaining a cohesive and user-friendly experience.

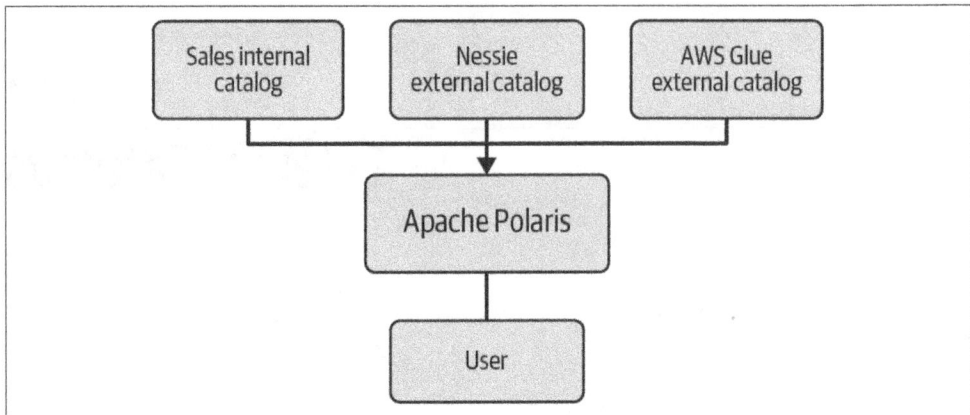

Figure 4-1. Access to Polaris can be access to all catalogs on the lakehouse

Organizations across industries often find themselves managing multiple Iceberg catalogs, sometimes due to regional compliance, sometimes because of tooling preferences, and often simply as a result of organic growth. Polaris simplifies this complexity by enabling cross-catalog access through a unified interface. Here are several common scenarios where external catalog integration with Polaris proves especially valuable for data engineers and architects:

Gradual migration
> If you've been using other catalogs and are transitioning to Polaris, you can maintain access to all your Iceberg tables during the migration process. This ensures minimal disruption to users and workflows while centralizing management under Polaris over time.

Partner data integration
> For organizations accessing data from external partners, connecting an external catalog enables seamless use of partner datasets alongside internal data. This unified access, playing hand-in-hand with a good role/privilege model, streamlines collaboration and enhances data-driven decision-making.

Workload optimization
> Some catalogs offer specialized features for specific workloads. For example, Nessie's versioning capabilities are ideal for isolating data changes during ingestion. Polaris allows you to use these features without sacrificing a centralized user experience.

Regulatory compliance
> In scenarios where regulatory requirements mandate separate catalog deployments in different regions, Polaris's external catalog connections ensure users

can work with all data while maintaining proper security boundaries without juggling multiple catalog credentials or interfaces.

In this chapter, we'll explore several key external catalogs that implement the Apache Iceberg REST Catalog Specification. We'll highlight their unique features and capabilities, providing insight into how they can be integrated into a multi-catalog strategy with Polaris as the unifying layer. By leveraging Polaris's external catalog connections, organizations can achieve a balance of flexibility, scalability, and centralized governance, making it easier than ever to manage diverse and distributed data ecosystems.

Nessie

Nessie is often described as "Git-for-data" as it brings the familiar concepts of version control to the world of data. By implementing branches, tags, and commits to changes at the catalog level, Nessie enables organizations to isolate changes, track history, and manage data lifecycles with a level of granularity previously only seen in source code repositories.

What Makes Nessie Unique?

Nessie introduces a "data-as-code" approach to data lake management, solving several challenges inherent to traditional data lake operations:

Branching and merging
  Nessie allows users to create *branches* for specific workloads, such as staging, development, or analytics experiments. These branches isolate changes from the main data branch until they are ready to be merged. For example:

  - A data engineer can perform transformations on a staging branch without affecting production data.

  - Analytics jobs can create temporary branches to aggregate data and merge only the finalized results.

Commit history and tags
  Nessie tracks every change through *commits*, which can be tagged for easier reference. This provides a complete audit trail of modifications, enabling reproducibility and regulatory compliance.

Multi-table transactions
  Nessie supports transactional updates across multiple tables, allowing related changes to be committed simultaneously. This capability is invaluable for complex data workflows.

Why Use Nessie with Polaris?

Integrating Nessie with Apache Polaris allows organizations to unify their data lakehouse ecosystems while leveraging Nessie's unique versioning capabilities. Here's why you might want to use Nessie alongside Polaris:

Seamless migration
> The external catalog integration feature ensures you can continue accessing Nessie-managed tables through Polaris if you're migrating from Nessie to Polaris. This reduces disruption and provides a central access point for all your data during the transition.

Data change isolation
> Nessie's branching and versioning capabilities make it worthwhile for data ingestion work while using Polaris to enable end-user access for use cases where data changes need to be isolated, such as:
>
> - Data ingestion: Use branches to safely test and validate data ingestion processes before merging changes into production.
> - Analytics workloads: Run experiments on data branches without affecting live datasets.

Example: Nessie and Polaris in Action

Consider a scenario where an organization ingests daily sales data into a data lake. With Nessie, a data engineer creates a branch specifically for the ingestion job, allowing raw data to be processed and validated without affecting production data.. Once the job is complete, the branch is merged into the main branch, ensuring a consistent and accurate update to production datasets.

At the same time, Polaris's external catalog integration enables analysts to query the sales data using their preferred tools without needing to understand the complexities of branching and merging. This unified approach improves productivity, minimizes errors, and retains consistency across all tables and views.

Nessie's features, such as branching, versioning, and multi-table transactions, make it a unique tool for managing data lakes. With Polaris, you can unify data that leverage Nessie's features with all your other data for your data consumers.

Gravitino

Apache Gravitino is a federated metadata management system designed to manage metadata in a geo-distributed, multi-regional environment. By providing a Single Source of Truth (SSOT) for metadata across diverse sources and regions, Gravitino offers unified metadata access for both data and AI assets.

What Makes Gravitino Unique?

Gravitino is built to manage metadata across various systems, regions, and data types. Here are some of its features:

Geo-distributed metadata management
> Gravitino's architecture supports deployments across multiple regions or clouds, enabling seamless metadata synchronization and access. Users gain a global view of metadata across disparate environments, which is useful for organizations operating in multiple geographic locations with distinct regulatory or operational requirements.

Unified metadata models
> Gravitino abstracts metadata from various sources—such as relational databases (Hive, MySQL, PostgreSQL) and file systems (HDFS, S3)—into a unified metadata model. This abstraction allows users and tools to interact with metadata consistently, regardless of its origin.

Direct metadata management
> Unlike traditional systems that collect metadata through periodic synchronization, Gravitino interacts with underlying systems directly. Changes made in Gravitino are immediately reflected in the source systems, and vice versa, ensuring up-to-date metadata without manual intervention.

Centralized security
> Gravitino centralizes metadata governance, including access control, discovery, and auditing. This centralized security model simplifies compliance and ensures consistent governance across regions and sources.

Why Use Gravitino with Polaris?

Integrating Gravitino with Apache Polaris creates a powerful combination for managing metadata across distributed environments. Gravitino's geo-distributed architecture ensures that metadata stays synchronized and accessible across regions, which is essential for global organizations dealing with regulatory boundaries or operational silos. By connecting Gravitino as an external catalog in Polaris, data teams gain a centralized interface for discovering and managing metadata regardless of where it originates, reducing friction and improving visibility across the entire ecosystem.

Example: Distributed Metadata Governance

Consider an enterprise with operations in North America, Europe, and Asia. Each region has its own data governance requirements, necessitating separate deployments of metadata systems. By deploying Gravitino in each region and connecting these deployments to Polaris, the organization can achieve:

- Localized metadata control to meet regulatory requirements.
- A unified global view of all metadata for simplified discovery and auditing.
- Centralized access for end users through Polaris, eliminating the need to manage multiple credentials or interfaces.

Apache Gravitino is a solution for geo-distributed metadata management, providing unified access and governance across regions, sources, and data types. Gravitino's capabilities are enhanced when integrated with Polaris, offering organizations a centralized, flexible, and secure metadata ecosystem.

Lakekeeper

Written in Rust, Lakekeeper is a solution for managing Iceberg metadata, offering features such as fine-grained access control, soft deletion of tables, and built-in support for authentication protocols. Its focus on secure and fast metadata management makes it an option for organizations operating in distributed and multi-tenant environments.

What Makes Lakekeeper Unique?

Lakekeeper's architecture and feature set address many challenges organizations face when managing metadata in large-scale data lakehouses. Key features include:

Rust-based design
> As a Rust-based implementation, Lakekeeper provides a single, lightweight binary that eliminates the need for external runtimes and the performance overhead of code interpretation.

Multi-tenancy and role-based access control
> A single Lakekeeper instance can serve multiple projects, each with distinct configurations and access controls. Projects can contain multiple warehouses, namespaces, and roles, efficiently supporting complex multi-tenant setups. Polaris can achieve this natively through multiple internal catalogs.

Soft deletion
> Lakekeeper supports soft deletion for tables and views, allowing accidental deletions to be reversed within a configurable time frame. This feature enhances operational safety in production environments.

Why Use Lakekeeper with Polaris?

While Lakekeeper is a robust standalone solution, integrating it with Apache Polaris unlocks even greater potential by centralizing access and governance for Iceberg tables. Here's why you might want to use Lakekeeper alongside Polaris:

Real-time metadata visibility
> Lakekeeper's built-in change events and approval workflows allow organizations to monitor and manage metadata updates in real time.
> These capabilities complement Polaris's role as a central catalog, enabling real-time updates to be reflected across the broader ecosystem. There is currently a proposal to bring this functionality to Apache Iceberg more broadly in the future.

Disaster recovery and table management
> Lakekeeper's soft deletion feature adds a safety net for metadata operations, ensuring recoverability in case of accidental changes.

Example: Multi-Tenant Metadata Governance

Imagine an organization with multiple data teams working on isolated projects, each with its metadata and storage requirements. Using Lakekeeper, the organization can:

- Create separate projects for each team, each containing dedicated warehouses and namespaces.
- Manage permissions using Lakekeeper's fine-grained access control and roles.

By integrating Lakekeeper with Polaris, the organization gains:

- A unified view of all metadata across projects.
- Centralized access for querying and governance, ensuring consistency across tools and teams.
- The ability to monitor changes and enforce data contracts through Lakekeeper's change event system.

When integrated with Polaris, Lakekeeper's capabilities are amplified, offering organizations centralized governance, real-time metadata updates, and enhanced security for multi-tenant and distributed deployments.

AWS Glue

The AWS Glue Catalog, a central metadata repository in the AWS ecosystem, has recently added support for the Apache Iceberg REST Catalog interface. This enhancement allows the Glue Catalog to function as an Iceberg-compatible catalog, enabling connecting and managing your Iceberg tables directly from Apache Polaris. For teams deeply embedded in the AWS ecosystem, this integration bridges the gap between AWS-native tools and a unified, cross-environment Iceberg catalog.

Why Use the AWS Glue Catalog?

AWS Glue Catalog has long been a cornerstone for data management in the AWS ecosystem, offering seamless integration with services such as Amazon S3, Athena, Redshift Spectrum, and AWS Glue ETL. With its Iceberg REST Catalog support, Glue now extends its capabilities to include transactional metadata for Iceberg tables, enabling ACID compliance, schema evolution, and time travel.

Key benefits of using the Glue Catalog include:

Deep AWS integration
> Glue is tightly integrated with AWS services, making it easy to manage and analyze metadata alongside your AWS workloads. Tools like Athena and Redshift Spectrum can natively query Iceberg tables managed in the Glue Catalog.

Managed infrastructure
> As a fully managed service, Glue reduces the operational overhead associated with maintaining metadata systems. Glue automates tasks like schema inference, metadata updates, and data crawling, simplifying Iceberg table management.

Security and compliance
> Glue leverages AWS Identity and Access Management (IAM) for robust, fine-grained access control. AWS-native encryption and compliance features ensure that sensitive metadata is protected.

Serverless flexibility
> Glue's serverless model allows you to scale metadata management dynamically without worrying about infrastructure limits.

Why Use Glue with Polaris?

While the AWS Glue Catalog excels in AWS-centric environments, its utility can be enhanced by integrating it with Polaris. This combination enables organizations to unify metadata access across AWS and non-AWS environments, ensuring consistent governance and discoverability. Here's why you might leverage both:

Centralized metadata across environments
> AWS-heavy teams can continue to use Glue for their Iceberg metadata while using Polaris as a central interface for managing and accessing these tables across other tools and platforms.

Cross-team collaboration
> Polaris allows teams outside the AWS ecosystem to access Glue-managed Iceberg tables without additional configuration or AWS-specific knowledge. This facilitates cross-team workflows, enabling seamless collaboration between teams using AWS and those in other environments.

Hybrid and multi-cloud strategies

In hybrid or multi-cloud architectures, Glue's metadata can be unified with other catalogs through Polaris, enabling organizations to work with all their Iceberg tables in one place without duplicating metadata or creating silos.

Leverage AWS tools without lock-in

Teams can continue to use Glue for AWS-native tools like Athena and Redshift Spectrum while ensuring metadata remains accessible and governable across the broader data ecosystem through Polaris.

Example: Hybrid Team Collaboration

Consider an enterprise where one team works primarily in AWS, using S3 for storage and Glue for metadata management, while another team operates on a non-AWS environment. By integrating Glue with Polaris:

- The AWS team can continue leveraging Glue's deep integration with AWS services for their workflows.
- The non-AWS team can query and manage the same Iceberg tables via Polaris, using their preferred tools and environments.
- Governance policies defined in Polaris ensure consistent security and access control across both teams.

Adding Apache Iceberg REST Catalog support to the AWS Glue Catalog marks a significant milestone for Iceberg adoption in the AWS ecosystem. Organizations can unify their metadata management by connecting Glue to Polaris, enabling seamless collaboration across AWS and non-AWS environments. This integration ensures teams can benefit from Glue's tight AWS integrations while maintaining centralized governance, discoverability, and flexibility across their entire data landscape. Whether you're running workloads entirely on AWS or adopting a hybrid approach, Glue and Polaris together create a powerful solution for managing Iceberg metadata in modern data lakehouses.

Conclusion

The rise of interoperable catalogs using the Iceberg REST Catalog interface—like Nessie, Gravitino, Lakekeeper, and AWS Glue—highlights the growing need for flexible and unified metadata management in modern data lakehouses. By integrating these catalogs with Apache Polaris, organizations can consolidate their metadata ecosystem into a single, centralized interface while leveraging the unique strengths of each catalog. Whether it's Nessie's version control, Gravitino's geo-distributed architecture, Lakekeeper's security-focused design, or Glue's deep integration with AWS, Polaris provides the tools to unify these diverse capabilities seamlessly.

This ability to manage and access data across multiple catalogs isn't just a win for organizational governance; it directly impacts how data engineers, architects, and analysts work every day. Instead of wrangling credentials for separate environments, writing brittle integrations, or waiting on metadata sync jobs to complete, teams can use Polaris as a single point of discovery and access across all Iceberg tables, regardless of where they live. For example, an engineer building ingestion pipelines in AWS can continue using Glue to manage metadata, while Polaris exposes those same tables to downstream users in other environments, without duplicating logic or compromising access control. This streamlines collaboration across teams, reduces redundant engineering work, and makes debugging and auditing far more manageable. In a landscape where data platforms are increasingly hybrid and distributed, Polaris doesn't just unify metadata—it unblocks workflows, accelerates delivery, and gives practitioners confidence that they're building on consistent, governed ground.

In the next chapter, we'll dive into Polaris's Catalog Management REST API, which is the foundation for configuring and managing catalogs, roles, principals, and namespaces in a Polaris deployment. Understanding these APIs will empower you to design and implement robust metadata strategies that scale with your organization's needs. Let's explore leveraging Polaris's API to efficiently set up and manage your lakehouse environment.

## CHAPTER 5

Polaris REST API

In this chapter, we will delve into the REST API provided by Apache Polaris for managing catalogs, roles, namespaces, tables, and views. The Polaris REST API enables seamless and programmatic interaction with the catalog layer of your data lakehouse, making it easier to orchestrate complex operations across distributed environments.

Whether adding a new catalog, defining access control through roles and principals, or performing granular namespace and table operations, the Polaris REST API provides the flexibility to handle these tasks efficiently. By leveraging this API, teams can automate catalog management tasks, ensuring scalability, consistency, and improved governance within their data platform.

We will break down each endpoint, exploring its purpose and showcasing its usage with cURL and Python's requests library. By the end of this chapter, you will have a solid understanding of how to programmatically manage your Polaris deployment and integrate it into your workflows.

The following sections examine the Polaris Management REST API endpoints specifically, grouped by functionality (this differs from the Apache Icicle REST catalog spec and endpoints). There is also a Python CLI built into the Polaris Repo that can be used to execute most of the tasks without having to write custom scripts or use an HTTP client like cURL, Postman, or Insomnia.

You can always find the latest version of this REST Spec here:

https://github.com/apache/polaris/blob/main/spec/polaris-management-service.yml

All endpoints in sections 5.1-5.3 are prefixed with `/api/management/v1`. For example, the `/catalogs` endpoint becomes `/api/management/v1/catalogs`.

Catalog Operations

The Polaris REST API provides endpoints for performing Create, Read, Update, and Delete (CRUD) operations on catalogs. These operations form the foundation of catalog management, enabling you to define, query, update, and remove catalogs programmatically.

List Catalogs

Retrieve a list of all catalogs in the Polaris deployment.

Endpoint:

```
GET /catalogs
```

Sample cURL request:

```
curl -X GET https://polaris.example.com/api/management/v1/catalogs \
    -H "Authorization: Bearer <ACCESS_TOKEN>" \
    -H "Content-Type: application/json"
```

Sample Python request:

```
import requests
url = "https://polaris.example.com/api/management/v1/catalogs"
headers = {
    "Authorization": "Bearer <ACCESS_TOKEN>",
    "Content-Type": "application/json"
}
response = requests.get(url, headers=headers)
print(response.json())
```

Sample response:

```
{
  "catalogs": [
    {
      "type": "INTERNAL",
      "name": "example_catalog",
      "properties": {
        "default-base-location": "s3://bucket/path"
      },
      "createTimestamp": 1622547800000,
      "lastUpdateTimestamp": 1622547900000,
      "entityVersion": 1,
      "storageConfigInfo": {
        "storageType": "S3",
        "allowedLocations": "For AWS [s3://bucketname/prefix/],
        for AZURE [abfss://container@storageaccount.blob.core.windows.net
        /prefix/],
        for GCP [gs://bucketname/prefix/]"
      }
    }
```

```
        ]
    }
```

Create a Catalog

Add a new catalog to the Polaris deployment. Catalogs can be internal or external.

Endpoint:

```
POST /catalogs
```

Sample cURL request:

```
curl -X POST https://polaris.example.com/api/management/v1/catalogs \
    -H "Authorization: Bearer <ACCESS_TOKEN>" \
    -H "Content-Type: application/json" \
    -d '{
            "catalog": {
                "type": "INTERNAL",
                "name": "example_catalog",
                "properties": {
                    "default-base-location": "s3://bucket/path"
                }
            }
        }'
```

Sample Python request:

```
import requests
url = "https://polaris.example.com/api/management/v1/catalogs"
headers = {
    "Authorization": "Bearer <ACCESS_TOKEN>",
    "Content-Type": "application/json"
}
payload = {
    "catalog": {
        "type": "INTERNAL",
        "name": "example_catalog",
        "properties": {
            "default-base-location": "s3://bucket/path"
        }
    }
}
response = requests.post(url, headers=headers, json=payload)
print(response.status_code, response.json())
```

Sample response:

```
{
  "catalog": {
    "type": "INTERNAL",
    "name": "example_catalog",
    "properties": {
```

```
      "default-base-location": "s3://bucket/path"
    },
    "createTimestamp": 1533547800000,
    "lastUpdateTimestamp": 1627647800000,
    "entityVersion": 1
  }
}
```

Get Catalog Details

Retrieve detailed information about a specific catalog by name.

Endpoint:

```
GET /catalogs/{catalogName}
```

Sample cURL request:

```
curl -X GET https://polaris.example.com/api/management/v1
/catalogs/example_catalog \
    -H "Authorization: Bearer <ACCESS_TOKEN>" \
    -H "Content-Type: application/json"
```

Sample Python request:

```
import requests
url = "https://polaris.example.com/api/management/v1/catalogs/example_catalog"
headers = {
    "Authorization": "Bearer <ACCESS_TOKEN>",
    "Content-Type": "application/json"
}
response = requests.get(url, headers=headers)
print(response.json())
```

Sample response:

```
{
  "type": "INTERNAL",
  "name": "example_catalog",
  "properties": {
    "default-base-location": "s3://bucket/path",
    "property1": "value1",
    "property2": "value2"
  },
  "createTimestamp": 143547800000,
  "lastUpdateTimestamp": 1538547900000,
  "entityVersion": 1
}
```

Update a Catalog

Update the details of an existing catalog. The request must include the current
entityVersion of the catalog.

Endpoint:

```
PUT /catalogs/{catalogName}
```

Sample cURL request:

```
curl -X PUT https://polaris.example.com/api/management/v1
/catalogs/example_catalog \
    -H "Authorization: Bearer <ACCESS_TOKEN>" \
    -H "Content-Type: application/json" \
    -d '{
        "currentEntityVersion": 1,
        "properties": {
            "default-base-location": "s3://new_bucket/path"
        }
    }'
```

Sample Python request:

```
import requests
url = "https://polaris.example.com/api/management/v1/catalogs/example_catalog"
headers = {
    "Authorization": "Bearer <ACCESS_TOKEN>",
    "Content-Type": "application/json"
}
payload = {
    "currentEntityVersion": 1,
    "properties": {
        "default-base-location": "s3://new_bucket/path"
    }
}
response = requests.put(url, headers=headers, json=payload)
print(response.status_code, response.json())
```

Sample response:

```
{
  "type": "INTERNAL",
  "name": "example_catalog",
  "properties": {
    "default-base-location": "s3://new_bucket/path",
    "property1": "value1",
    "property2": "value2"
  },
  "createTimestamp": 1622547800000,
  "lastUpdateTimestamp": 1622548000000,
  "entityVersion": 2
}
```

Delete a Catalog

Remove an existing catalog. The catalog must be empty before deletion.

Endpoint:

```
DELETE /catalogs/{catalogName}
```

Sample cURL request:

```
curl -X DELETE https://polaris.example.com/api/management/v1/catalogs
/example_catalog \
    -H "Authorization: Bearer <ACCESS_TOKEN>" \
    -H "Content-Type: application/json"
```

Sample Python request:

```
import requests

url = "https://polaris.example.com/api/management/v1/catalogs/example_catalog"
headers = {
    "Authorization": "Bearer <ACCESS_TOKEN>",
    "Content-Type": "application/json"
}
response = requests.delete(url, headers=headers)
print(response.status_code)
```

Sample response:

Empty response if successful.

Principal Operations

Principals in Apache Polaris represent entities (such as users or services) that interact with the system. The REST API provides CRUD (Create, Read, Update, Delete) operations for managing principals and the ability to rotate credentials. This section covers each of these endpoints with sample requests and responses.

List Principals

Retrieve all the principals currently available in the Polaris catalog.

Endpoint:

```
GET /principals
```

Sample cURL request:

```
curl -X GET \
  https://polaris.example.com/api/management/v1/principals \
  -H "Authorization: Bearer <ACCESS_TOKEN>"
```

Sample Python request:

```
import requests
url = "https://polaris.example.com/api/management/v1/principals"
headers = {"Authorization": "Bearer <ACCESS_TOKEN>"}
```

```
response = requests.get(url, headers=headers)
print(response.json())
```

Sample response:

```
{
"principal": {
"name": "string",
"clientId": "string",
"properties": {
"property1": "string",
"property2": "string"
},
"createTimestamp": 0,
"lastUpdateTimestamp": 0,
"entityVersion": 0
},
"credentials": {
"clientId": "string",
"clientSecret": "pa$$word"
}
}
```

Create a Principal

Create a new principal for interacting with the Polaris system.

Endpoint:

```
POST /principals
```

Sample cURL request:

```
curl -X POST \
  https://polaris.example.com/api/management/v1/principals \
  -H "Authorization: Bearer <ACCESS_TOKEN>" \
  -H "Content-Type: application/json" \
  -d '{
      "principal": {
        "name": "data_analyst",
        "clientId": "analyst321",
        "properties": {
          "team": "analytics",
          "region": "us-west"
        }
      },
      "credentialRotationRequired": true
    }'
```

Sample Python request:

```
import requests
url = "https://polaris.example.com/api/management/v1/principals"
```

```python
headers = {
    "Authorization": "Bearer <ACCESS_TOKEN>",
    "Content-Type": "application/json"
}
data = {
    "principal": {
        "name": "data_analyst",
        "clientId": "analyst321",
        "properties": {
            "team": "analytics",
            "region": "us-west"
        }
    },
    "credentialRotationRequired": True
}

response = requests.post(url, headers=headers, json=data)
print(response.json())
```

Sample response:

```json
{
  "principal": {
    "name": "data_analyst",
    "clientId": "analyst321",
    "properties": {
      "team": "analytics",
      "region": "us-west"
    },
    "createTimestamp": 1694372200000,
    "lastUpdateTimestamp": 1694372200000,
    "entityVersion": 1
  },
  "credentials": {
    "clientId": "analyst321",
    "clientSecret": "secure$Password123"
  }
}
```

Get Principal Details

Fetch details of a specific principal by name.

Endpoint:

```
GET /principals/{principalName}
```

Sample cURL request:

```
curl -X GET \
  https://polaris.example.com/api/management/v1/principals/data_analyst \
  -H "Authorization: Bearer <ACCESS_TOKEN>"
```

Sample Python request:

```python
import requests
url = "https://polaris.example.com/api/management/v1/principals/data_analyst"
headers = {"Authorization": "Bearer <ACCESS_TOKEN>"}

response = requests.get(url, headers=headers)
print(response.json())
```

Sample response:

```json
{
  "name": "data_analyst",
  "clientId": "analyst321",
  "properties": {
    "team": "analytics",
    "region": "us-west"
  },
  "createTimestamp": 1694372200000,
  "lastUpdateTimestamp": 1694378400000,
  "entityVersion": 1
}
```

Update a Principal

Update details of an existing principal, such as properties or version.

Endpoint:

```
PUT /principals/{principalName}
```

Sample cURL request:

```
curl -X PUT \
  https://polaris.example.com/api/management/v1/principals/data_analyst \
  -H "Authorization: Bearer <ACCESS_TOKEN>" \
  -H "Content-Type: application/json" \
  -d '{
        "currentEntityVersion": 1,
        "properties": {
          "team": "analytics",
          "region": "us-east",
          "project": "forecasting"
        }
      }'
```

Sample Python request:

```python
import requests
url = "https://polaris.example.com/api/management/v1/principals/data_analyst"
headers = {
    "Authorization": "Bearer <ACCESS_TOKEN>",
    "Content-Type": "application/json"
}
```

```python
data = {
    "currentEntityVersion": 1,
    "properties": {
        "team": "analytics",
        "region": "us-east",
        "project": "forecasting"
    }
}

response = requests.put(url, headers=headers, json=data)
print(response.json())
```

Sample response:

```json
{
  "name": "data_analyst",
  "clientId": "analyst321",
  "properties": {
    "team": "analytics",
    "region": "us-east",
    "project": "forecasting"
  },
  "createTimestamp": 1694372200000,
  "lastUpdateTimestamp": 1694378400000,
  "entityVersion": 2
}
```

Delete a Principal

Delete an existing principal from the system.

Endpoint:

```
DELETE /principals/{principalName}
```

Sample cURL request:

```
curl -X DELETE \
  https://polaris.example.com/api/management/v1/principals/data_analyst \
  -H "Authorization: Bearer <ACCESS_TOKEN>"
```

Sample Python request:

```python
import requests
url = "https://polaris.example.com/api/management/v1/principals/data_analyst"
headers = {"Authorization": "Bearer <ACCESS_TOKEN>>"}

response = requests.delete(url, headers=headers)
print(response.status_code)
```

If successful, this request will have an empty response.

Rotate Principal Credentials

Rotate credentials for a specific principal and return the new credentials.

Endpoint:

```
POST /principals/{principalName}/rotate
```

Sample cURL request:

```
curl -X POST \
  https://polaris.example.com/api/management/v1/principals/data_analyst/rotate \
  -H "Authorization: Bearer <YOUR_ACCESS_TOKEN>"
```

Sample Python request:

```python
import requests
url = "https://polaris.example.com/api/management/v1/principals
/data_analyst/rotate"
headers = {"Authorization": "Bearer <ACCESS_TOKEN>"}

response = requests.post(url, headers=headers)
print(response.json())
```

Sample response:

```json
{
  "principal": {
    "name": "data_analyst",
    "clientId": "analyst321",
    "properties": {
      "team": "analytics",
      "region": "us-east",
      "project": "forecasting"
    },
    "createTimestamp": 1694372200000,
    "lastUpdateTimestamp": 1694378400000,
    "entityVersion": 2
  },
  "credentials": {
    "clientId": "analyst321",
    "clientSecret": "new$Password456"
  }
}
```

These endpoints provide everything needed to create, update, delete and list principals in Apache Polaris.

Managing Roles

Apache Polaris provides a set of APIs to manage permissions between catalogs and principals. These APIs allow you to grant, list, and revoke privileges, ensuring secure and efficient access management across your data lakehouse. This section outlines each endpoint with detailed descriptions, sample requests, and responses.

Create a Catalog Role

Create a new role within a catalog.

Endpoint:

```
POST /catalogs/{catalogName}/catalog-roles
```

Sample cURL request:

```
curl -X POST \
  https://polaris.example.com/api/management/v1/catalogs/finance_catalog
  /catalog-roles \
  -H "Authorization: Bearer <ACCESS_TOKEN>" \
  -H "Content-Type: application/json" \
  -d '{
      "catalogRole": {
        "name": "viewer",
        "properties": {
          "permissions": "read_only"
        }
      }
    }'
```

Create a Principal Role

Create a new principal role.

Endpoint:

```
POST /principal-roles
```

Sample cURL request:

```
curl -X POST \
  https://polaris.example.com/api/management/v1/principal-roles \
  -H "Authorization: Bearer <ACCESS_TOKEN>" \
  -H "Content-Type: application/json" \
  -d '{
      "principalRole": {
        "name": "report_viewer",
        "properties": {
          "access_scope": "read_only"
        }
      }
    }'
```

List Catalog Roles

List all roles within a catalog.

Endpoint:

```
GET /catalogs/{catalogName}/catalog-roles
```

Sample cURL request:

```
curl -X GET \
  https://polaris.example.com/api/management/v1/catalogs/finance_catalog
  /catalog-roles \
  -H "Authorization: Bearer <ACCESS_TOKEN>"
```

List Roles Assigned to a Principal

Retrieve all roles assigned to a specific principal.

Endpoint:

```
GET /principals/{principalName}/principal-roles
```

Sample cURL request:

```
curl -X GET \
  https://polaris.example.com/api/management/v1/principals/john_doe
  /principal-roles \
  -H "Authorization: Bearer <ACCESS_TOKEN>"
```

List All Principal Roles

Retrieve a list of all principal roles in the system.

Endpoint:

```
GET /principal-roles
```

Sample cURL request:

```
curl -X GET \
  https://polaris.example.com/api/management/v1/principal-roles \
  -H "Authorization: Bearer <ACCESS_TOKEN>"
```

List Principals Assigned to a Principal Role

Retrieve a list of principals who are assigned a specific principal role.

Endpoint:

```
GET /principal-roles/{principalRoleName}/principals
```

Sample cURL request:

```
curl -X GET \
  https://polaris.example.com/api/management/v1/principal-roles/report_viewer
  /principals \
  -H "Authorization: Bearer <ACCESS_TOKEN>"
```

Get Catalog Roles Mapped to a Principal Role

Retrieve catalog roles mapped to a specific principal role for a catalog.

Endpoint:

```
GET /principal-roles/{principalRoleName}/catalog-roles/{catalogName}
```

Sample cURL request:

```
curl -X GET \
  https://polaris.example.com/api/management/v1/principal-roles/report_viewer
  /catalog-roles/finance_catalog \
  -H "Authorization: Bearer <ACCESS_TOKEN>"
```

Get Details of a Principal Role

Retrieve details of a specific principal role.

Endpoint:

```
GET /principal-roles/{principalRoleName}
```

Sample cURL request:

```
curl -X GET \
  https://polaris.example.com/api/management/v1/principal-roles/report_viewer \
  -H "Authorization: Bearer <ACCESS_TOKEN>"
```

Add a Grant to a Catalog Role

Add a permissions grant to a catalog, determining the kind of access to the catalog's assets.

Endpoint:

```
PUT /catalogs/{catalogName}/catalog-roles/{catalogRoleName}/grants
```

Sample cURL request:

```
curl -X PUT "https://polaris.example.com/api/management/v1/catalogs/finance
/catalog-roles/analyst/grants" \
-H "Authorization: Bearer <ACCESS_TOKEN>" \
-H "Content-Type: application/json" \
-d '{
  "grant": {
    "type": "catalog",
```

```
    "privilege": "CATALOG_MANAGE_CONTENT"
  }
}'
```

Revoke a Grant from a Catalog Role

Revoke permissions from a particular Catalog Role.

Endpoint:

```
DELETE /catalogs/{catalogName}/catalog-roles/{catalogRoleName/grants
```

Example cURL Request:

```
curl -X DELETE "https://polaris.example.com/api/management/v1/catalogs/finance
/catalog-roles/analyst/grants?cascade=true" \
-H "Authorization: Bearer <ACCESS_TOKEN>" \
-H "Content-Type: application/json" \
-d '{
  "grant": {
    "type": "catalog",
    "privilege": "CATALOG_MANAGE_CONTENT"
  }
}'
```

Assign a Catalog Role to a Principal Role

Assign a catalog role to a principal role within a catalog.

Endpoint:

```
PUT /principal-roles/{principalRoleName}/catalog-roles/{catalogName}
```

Sample cURL request:

```
curl -X PUT \
  https://polaris.example.com/api/management/v1/principal-roles/report_viewer
  /catalog-roles/finance_catalog \
  -H "Authorization: Bearer <ACCESS_TOKEN>" \
  -H "Content-Type: application/json" \
  -d '{
      "catalogRole": {
        "name": "editor",
        "properties": {
          "edit_scope": "limited"
        }
      }
    }'
```

Assign a Role to a Principal

Assign a specific role to a principal.

Endpoint:

```
PUT /principals/{principalName}/principal-roles
```

Sample cURL request:

```
curl -X PUT \
  https://polaris.example.com/api/management/v1/principals/john_doe
  /principal-roles \
  -H "Authorization: Bearer <ACCESS_TOKEN>" \
  -H "Content-Type: application/json" \
  -d '{
      "principalRole": {
        "name": "data_admin",
        "properties": {
          "access_level": "full"
        }
      }
    }'
```

Update a Principal Role

Update the details of an existing principal role.

Endpoint:

```
PUT /principal-roles/{principalRoleName}
```

Sample cURL request:

```
curl -X PUT \
  https://polaris.example.com/api/management/v1/principal-roles/report_viewer \
  -H "Authorization: Bearer <ACCESS_TOKEN>" \
  -H "Content-Type: application/json" \
  -d '{
      "currentEntityVersion": 2,
      "properties": {
        "access_scope": "write_enabled"
      }
    }'
```

Revoke a Role from a Principal

Remove a specific role from a principal.

Endpoint:

```
DELETE /principals/{principalName}/principal-roles/{principalRoleName}
```

Sample cURL request:

```
curl -X DELETE \
  https://polaris.example.com/api/management/v1/principals/john_doe
  /principal-roles/data_admin \
  -H "Authorization: Bearer <ACCESS_TOKEN>"
```

Revoke a Catalog Role from a Principal Role

Remove a catalog role from a principal role within a catalog.

Endpoint:

```
DELETE /principal-roles/{principalRoleName}/catalog-roles/{catalogName}/{catalogRoleName}
```

Sample cURL request:

```
curl -X DELETE \
  https://polaris.example.com/api/management/v1/principal-roles/report_viewer
  /catalog-roles/finance_catalog/editor \
  -H "Authorization: Bearer <ACCESS_TOKEN>"
```

Delete a Principal Role

Delete an existing principal role.

Endpoint:

```
DELETE /principal-roles/{principalRoleName}
```

Sample cURL request:

```
curl -X DELETE \
  https://polaris.example.com/api/management/v1/principal-roles/report_viewer \
  -H "Authorization: Bearer <ACCESS_TOKEN>"
```

Delete a Catalog Role

Delete an existing catalog role.

Endpoint:

```
DELETE /catalogs/{catalogName}/catalog-roles/{catalogRoleName}
```

Sample cURL request:

```
curl -X DELETE \
 https://polaris.example.com/api/management/v1/catalogs/finance_catalog
 /catalog-roles/viewer \
  -H "Authorization: Bearer <ACCESS_TOKEN>"
```

These are the endpoints for managing catalog and principal roles, ensuring users can handle their access control effectively in Apache Polaris.

Apache Iceberg REST Catalog Endpoints

This section covers the endpoints provided by Apache Polaris that implement the Apache Iceberg REST Catalog Specification (*https://oreil.ly/g7Zgv*). These endpoints allow clients to interact with catalogs, namespaces, tables, and views in a standardized and interoperable way.

Each endpoint is prefixed by `/api/catalog/` in Polaris. For example, the Iceberg spec's `/v1/config` would be accessed as `/api/catalog/v1/config` in Polaris.

These APIs are designed for compatibility with tools and engines that speak the Iceberg REST standard, enabling advanced catalog operations like schema management, table creation, and view control. While Polaris also provides its own management API (covered in Sections 5.1 through 5.3), the Iceberg REST Catalog endpoints enable broader ecosystem interoperability and integration with external engines.

The following subsections describe each group of endpoints, beginning with a short summary of its purpose, followed by the corresponding API definitions.

The latest version of Apache Iceberg REST Catalog Spec can be found here:

https://github.com/apache/iceberg/blob/main/open-api/rest-catalog-open-api.yaml

Configuration API

Retrieve server-supplied default and override configuration properties for initializing and managing Iceberg catalog clients.

Endpoint:

```
GET /v1/config
```

Clients should call this endpoint first to obtain default and override properties that determine how the catalog client should behave. The response includes:

Defaults
Settings applied before client configuration

Overrides
Settings applied after client configuration

Optional endpoints list
Enumerates which Iceberg REST routes are supported

These values guide client behavior such as pooling size, endpoint routing, and warehouse location. Learn more in the Iceberg documentation on catalog properties (*https://oreil.ly/xDqBj*).

Sample cURL request:

```
curl -X GET https://polaris.example.com/api/catalog/v1/config \
    -H "Authorization: Bearer <ACCESS_TOKEN>" \
    -H "Content-Type: application/json"
```

Sample Python request:

```python
import requests

url = "https://polaris.example.com/api/catalog/v1/config"
headers = {
    "Authorization": "Bearer <ACCESS_TOKEN>",
    "Content-Type": "application/json"
}

response = requests.get(url, headers=headers)
print(response.json())
```

Sample response:

```json
{
  "defaults": {
    "client.pool.size": "4",
    "catalog.name": "main"
  },
  "overrides": {
    "warehouse": "s3://bucket/warehouse/"
  },
  "endpoints": [
    "GET /v1/{prefix}/namespaces",
    "POST /v1/{prefix}/namespaces",
    "GET /v1/{prefix}/namespaces/{namespace}",
    "DELETE /v1/{prefix}/namespaces/{namespace}",
    "GET /v1/{prefix}/namespaces/{namespace}/tables"
  ]
}
```

OAuth2 API

Exchange credentials or tokens using the OAuth 2.0 client credentials or token exchange flows.

This endpoint is deprecated and will be removed; it is not recommended for new implementations. Use the `oauth2-server-uri` configuration property instead to integrate with external identity providers.

Endpoint:

```
POST /v1/oauth/tokens
```

This endpoint was originally designed to support three flows:

Client Credentials Flow
Exchange client ID and secret for an access token.

Token Exchange Flow (Actor + Subject)
Exchange a client token and identity token for a new access token with user context.

Token Refresh Flow
Exchange an expiring token for a new one with a refreshed expiration.

These capabilities are being phased out in favor of more secure, explicitly configured OAuth integration patterns.

Sample cURL Request (Client Credentials Flow):

```
curl -X POST https://polaris.example.com/api/catalog/v1/oauth/tokens \
    -H "Content-Type: application/x-www-form-urlencoded" \
    -d 'grant_type=client_credentials&client_id=your-client-
    id&client_secret=your-client-secret'
```

Sample Python request:

```
import requests

url = "https://polaris.example.com/api/catalog/v1/oauth/tokens"
headers = {
    "Content-Type": "application/x-www-form-urlencoded"
}
payload = {
    "grant_type": "client_credentials",
    "client_id": "your-client-id",
    "client_secret": "your-client-secret"
}

response = requests.post(url, headers=headers, data=payload)
print(response.json())
```

Sample response:

```
{
  "access_token": "eyJhbGciOiJIUzI1NiIsInR5cCI6IkpXVCJ9...",
  "token_type": "Bearer",
  "expires_in": 3600
}
```

Table API

Perform operations to create, register, update, load, delete, and rename Iceberg tables in the catalog.

Base Endpoint Prefix:

```
/v1/{prefix}/namespaces/{namespace}/tables
```

The Table API allows clients to manage the full lifecycle of Iceberg tables program-matically. This includes creating new tables, registering existing ones by metadata location, committing schema or snapshot changes, and retrieving table metadata. These endpoints enable automation and integration with ingestion pipelines, CI/CD workflows, and schema management tools.

List Table Identifiers

Retrieve all table identifiers under a specified namespace.

Endpoint:

```
GET /v1/{prefix}/namespaces/{namespace}/tables
```

This endpoint returns a list of all Iceberg tables within the given namespace. It is useful for discovery and inventory tasks, such as enumerating datasets for a team or validating ingestion pipelines. Results may be paginated using `page-size` and `page-token` query parameters.

Sample cURL request:

```
curl -X GET https://polaris.example.com/api/catalog/v1/dev_team/namespaces
/analytics/tables \
        -H "Authorization: Bearer <ACCESS_TOKEN>" \
        -H "Content-Type: application/json"
```

Sample Python request:

```
import requests
url = "https://polaris.example.com/api/catalog/v1/dev_team/namespaces
/analytics/tables"
headers = {
    "Authorization": "Bearer <ACCESS_TOKEN>",
    "Content-Type": "application/json"
}

response = requests.get(url, headers=headers)
print(response.json())
```

Sample response:

```
{
  "identifiers": [
    {
      "namespace": ["analytics"],
      "name": "monthly_sales"
    },
    {
      "namespace": ["analytics"],
```

```
      "name": "user_events"
    },
    {
      "namespace": ["analytics"],
      "name": "product_catalog"
    }
  ]
}
```

Create a Namespace

Create a new namespace with optional metadata properties.

Endpoint:

```
POST /v1/{prefix}/namespaces
```

This endpoint creates a new logical namespace for organizing tables and views within the catalog. Namespaces can represent teams, domains, or business units. You may optionally supply metadata properties (such as owner or description). If the namespace already exists, the request will fail with a conflict response.

Sample cURL request:

```
curl -X POST https://polaris.example.com/api/catalog/v1/dev_team/namespaces \
    -H "Authorization: Bearer <ACCESS_TOKEN>" \
    -H "Content-Type: application/json" \
    -d '{
          "namespace": ["analytics"],
          "properties": {
            "owner": "data.platform@company.com",
            "created_by": "automation_pipeline"
          }
        }'
```

Sample Python request:

```
import requests

url = "https://polaris.example.com/api/catalog/v1/dev_team/namespaces"
headers = {
    "Authorization": "Bearer <ACCESS_TOKEN>",
    "Content-Type": "application/json"
}
payload = {
    "namespace": ["analytics"],
    "properties": {
        "owner": "data.platform@company.com",
        "created_by": "automation_pipeline"
    }
}

response = requests.post(url, headers=headers, json=payload)
```

```
print(response.json())
```

Sample response:

```
{
  "namespace": ["analytics"],
  "properties": {
    "owner": "data.platform@company.com",
    "created_by": "automation_pipeline",
    "last_modified_time": "2025-06-20T13:45:00Z"
  }
}
```

Load Namespace Properties

Retrieve all stored metadata properties for a given namespace.

Endpoint:

```
GET /v1/{prefix}/namespaces/{namespace}
```

This endpoint fetches metadata properties associated with a specific namespace. Properties may include custom fields, such as owner, description, creation metadata, or system-managed values, like the last modified time. This is useful for managing schema boundaries, auditing ownership, or integrating namespace metadata into external tooling.

Sample cURL request:

```
curl -X GET https://polaris.example.com/api/catalog/v1/dev_team/namespaces
/analytics \
     -H "Authorization: Bearer <ACCESS_TOKEN>" \
     -H "Content-Type: application/json"
```

Sample Python request:

```
import requests

url = "https://polaris.example.com/api/catalog/v1/dev_team/namespaces/analytics"
headers = {
    "Authorization": "Bearer <ACCESS_TOKEN>",
    "Content-Type": "application/json"
}

response = requests.get(url, headers=headers)
print(response.json())
```

Sample response:

```
{
  "namespace": ["analytics"],
  "properties": {
    "owner": "data.platform@company.com",
```

```
    "description": "Namespace for analytics tables and dashboards",
    "last_modified_time": "2025-06-20T14:10:00Z"
  }
}
```

Check Namespace Existence

Verify whether a specific namespace exists in the catalog.

Endpoint:

```
HEAD /v1/{prefix}/namespaces/{namespace}
```

This lightweight endpoint allows you to check if a namespace exists without retrieving its metadata. It returns HTTP 204 No Content if the namespace exists or 404 Not Found if it does not. This is useful for validation steps in automation scripts or provisioning workflows.

Sample cURL request:

```
curl -I -X HEAD https://polaris.example.com/api/catalog/v1/dev_team/namespaces
/analytics \
        -H "Authorization: Bearer <ACCESS_TOKEN>"
```

Sample Python request:

```
import requests

url = "https://polaris.example.com/api/catalog/v1/dev_team/namespaces/analytics"
headers = {
    "Authorization": "Bearer <ACCESS_TOKEN>"
}

response = requests.head(url, headers=headers)
print(response.status_code)  # 204 if exists, 404 if not
```

Sample response:

- `204 No Content`: Namespace exists
- `404 Not Found`: Namespace does not exist

Drop a Namespace

Remove a namespace from the catalog. The namespace must be empty before deletion.

Endpoint:

```
DELETE /v1/{prefix}/namespaces/{namespace}
```

This endpoint deletes a namespace and its associated metadata. The namespace must not contain any tables, views, or child namespaces. Attempting to delete a non-empty namespace will result in a conflict error. This operation is typically used for cleanup or when decommissioning a data domain.

Sample cURL request:

```
curl -X DELETE https://polaris.example.com/api/catalog/v1/dev_team/namespaces
/analytics \
    -H "Authorization: Bearer <ACCESS_TOKEN>" \
    -H "Content-Type: application/json"
```

Sample Python request:

```
import requests

url = "https://polaris.example.com/api/catalog/v1/dev_team/namespaces/analytics"
headers = {
    "Authorization": "Bearer <ACCESS_TOKEN>",
    "Content-Type": "application/json"
}

response = requests.delete(url, headers=headers)
print(response.status_code)  # 204 if successful, 409 if namespace not empty
```

Sample response:

- `204 No Content`: Namespace successfully deleted

- `404 Not Found`: Namespace does not exist

- `409 Conflict`: Namespace is not empty

Set or Remove Namespace Properties

Update or delete properties on an existing namespace.

Endpoint:

```
POST /v1/{prefix}/namespaces/{namespace}/properties
```

This endpoint allows clients to modify metadata for a namespace by setting new key-value pairs and/or removing existing ones. Only the properties specified in the request will be changed; unspecified properties remain untouched. This is useful for updating ownership, lifecycle tags, or automation-related flags.

Not all catalog implementations are required to support namespace properties.

Sample cURL request:

```
curl -X POST https://polaris.example.com/api/catalog/v1/dev_team/namespaces
/analytics/properties \
    -H "Authorization: Bearer <ACCESS_TOKEN>" \
    -H "Content-Type: application/json" \
```

```
    -d '{
        "updates": {
          "owner": "dataops@company.com",
          "environment": "production"
        },
        "removals": ["created_by"]
```

Sample Python request:

```python
import requests

url = "https://polaris.example.com/api/catalog/v1/dev_team/namespaces
/analytics/properties"
headers = {
    "Authorization": "Bearer <ACCESS_TOKEN>",
    "Content-Type": "application/json"
}
payload = {
    "updates": {
        "owner": "dataops@company.com",
        "environment": "production"
    },
    "removals": ["created_by"]
}

response = requests.post(url, headers=headers, json=payload)
print(response.json())
```

Sample response:

```
{
  "namespace": ["analytics"],
  "properties": {
    "owner": "dataops@company.com",
    "environment": "production"
  }
}
```

Create a Table

Create a new Iceberg table within the specified namespace.

Endpoint:

```
POST /v1/{prefix}/namespaces/{namespace}/tables
```

This endpoint creates a new Iceberg table with an initial schema and optional configuration properties. You can either make the table immediately (stage-create: false) or initiate a staged transaction for committing later (stage-create: true).

Use staged creation if your workflow involves multiple operations (e.g., schema, sort order, partitioning) that should be committed atomically. The response includes the metadata needed to complete the transaction using the "Commit Updates to a Table" endpoint.

Sample cURL Request (Immediate Creation):

```
curl -X POST https://polaris.example.com/api/catalog/v1/dev/namespaces
/analytics/tables \
    -H "Authorization: Bearer <ACCESS_TOKEN>" \
    -H "Content-Type: application/json" \
    -d '{
        "name": "customer_profiles",
        "schema": {
          "type": "struct",
          "fields": [
            { "id": 1, "name": "customer_id", "required": true, "type":
            "long" },
            { "id": 2, "name": "email", "required": false, "type":
            "string" },
            { "id": 3, "name": "created_at", "required": true, "type":
            "timestamp" }
          ]
        },
        "spec": { "fields": [ { "source-id": 3, "transform": "day", "name":
        "day_created" } ] },
        "stage-create": false
      }'
```

Sample Python request:

```
import requests

url = "https://polaris.example.com/api/catalog/v1/dev/namespaces/analytics
/tables"
headers = {
    "Authorization": "Bearer <ACCESS_TOKEN>",
    "Content-Type": "application/json"
}
payload = {
    "name": "customer_profiles",
    "schema": {
        "type": "struct",
        "fields": [
            { "id": 1, "name": "customer_id", "required": True, "type": "long" },
            { "id": 2, "name": "email", "required": False, "type": "string" },
            { "id": 3, "name": "created_at", "required": True, "type":
            "timestamp" }
        ]
    },
    "spec": {
        "fields": [
            { "source-id": 3, "transform": "day", "name": "day_created" }
        ]
    },
```

```
    "stage-create": False
}

response = requests.post(url, headers=headers, json=payload)
print(response.json())
```

Sample response:

```
{
  "metadata-location": "s3://warehouse/analytics/customer_profiles
  /metadata/00000.metadata.json",
  "table-uuid": "9bde37b3-fc9e-4b32-9b9e-abc123def456"
}
```

Register a Table

Register an existing Iceberg table in the catalog using its metadata location.

Endpoint:

```
POST /v1/{prefix}/namespaces/{namespace}/register
```

This endpoint allows clients to register a preexisting Iceberg table by specifying the full path to its metadata JSON file. This is commonly used when migrating or recovering tables from storage that were created outside of the catalog, such as those bootstrapped manually or recovered after system failure.

Once registered, the table becomes fully managed and queryable via the catalog.

Sample cURL request:

```
curl -X POST https://polaris.example.com/api/catalog/v1/dev/namespaces
/analytics/register \
    -H "Authorization: Bearer <ACCESS_TOKEN>" \
    -H "Content-Type: application/json" \
    -d '{
        "name": "recovered_events",
        "metadata-location": "s3://warehouse/analytics/recovered_events
        /metadata/00000.metadata.json"
      }'
```

Sample Python request:

```
import requests

url = "https://polaris.example.com/api/catalog/v1/dev/namespaces
/analytics/register"
headers = {
    "Authorization": "Bearer <ACCESS_TOKEN>",
    "Content-Type": "application/json"
}
payload = {
    "name": "recovered_events",
```

```
    "metadata-location": "s3://warehouse/analytics/recovered_events
    /metadata/00000.metadata.json"
}

response = requests.post(url, headers=headers, json=payload)
print(response.json())
```

Sample response:

```
{
  "metadata-location": "s3://warehouse/analytics/recovered_events
  /metadata/00000.metadata.json",
  "table-uuid": "52f7ab2e-47d1-4d96-9f5c-d6e12a77de2a"
}
```

Load Table Metadata

Retrieve the full metadata and optional configuration for a specific Iceberg table.

Endpoint:

```
GET /v1/{prefix}/namespaces/{namespace}/tables/{table}
```

This endpoint loads the metadata of an Iceberg table, including its schema, partition specification, properties, and configuration overrides. The returned metadata can be used for planning queries, validating schema versions, or understanding a table's structure and lifecycle.

Clients may optionally include an If-None-Match header to return HTTP 304 Not Modified if the metadata hasn't changed since the last load. You may also use the snapshots query parameter to control which snapshots are returned (all or refs).

Sample cURL request:

```
curl -X GET https://polaris.example.com/api/catalog/v1/dev/namespaces
/analytics/tables/customer_profiles \
    -H "Authorization: Bearer <ACCESS_TOKEN>" \
    -H "Content-Type: application/json"
```

Sample Python request:

```
import requests

url = "https://polaris.example.com/api/catalog/v1/dev/namespaces/analytics
/tables/customer_profiles"
headers = {
    "Authorization": "Bearer <ACCESS_TOKEN>",
    "Content-Type": "application/json"
}

response = requests.get(url, headers=headers)
print(response.json())
```

Sample response:

```
{
  "metadata-location": "s3://warehouse/analytics/customer_profiles
  /metadata/00001.metadata.json",
  "table-uuid": "9bde37b3-fc9e-4b32-9b9e-abc123def456",
  "schema": {
    "type": "struct",
    "fields": [
      { "id": 1, "name": "customer_id", "required": true, "type": "long" },
      { "id": 2, "name": "email", "required": false, "type": "string" },
      { "id": 3, "name": "created_at", "required": true, "type": "timestamp" }
    ]
  },
  "spec": {
    "fields": [
      { "source-id": 3, "transform": "day", "name": "day_created" }
    ]
  },
  "last-sequence-number": 7,
  "last-snapshot-id": 7452913019,
  "snapshots": [
    {
      "snapshot-id": 7452913019,
      "timestamp-ms": 1721234567890,
      "operation": "append",
      "manifest-list": "s3://.../manifests/manifest-list.avro"
    }
  ]
}
```

Commit Updates to a Table

Commit changes to an Iceberg table, such as appending data files, updating schemas, or completing staged creation.

Endpoint:

```
POST /v1/{prefix}/namespaces/{namespace}/tables/{table}
```

This endpoint applies changes to an existing table, including new snapshots (e.g., appends or overwrites), updated schemas, or updated table metadata. It is also used to finalize a staged table created earlier using stage-create: true. The request must include the current table metadata location and a new version of the metadata file that reflects the desired changes.

Concurrency is managed via *optimistic locking*: the commit will succeed only if the provided base metadata location matches the current state of the table.

Sample cURL request:

```
curl -X POST https://polaris.example.com/api/catalog/v1/dev/namespaces
/analytics/tables/customer_profiles \
    -H "Authorization: Bearer <ACCESS_TOKEN>" \
    -H "Content-Type: application/json" \
    -d '{
          "updates": {
            "metadata-location": "s3://warehouse/analytics
            /customer_profiles/metadata/00002.metadata.json",
            "base": "s3://warehouse/analytics/customer_profiles
            /metadata/00001.metadata.json"
          }
        }'
```

Sample Python request:

```
import requests

url = "https://polaris.example.com/api/catalog/v1/dev/namespaces/analytics/tables
/customer_profiles"
headers = {
    "Authorization": "Bearer <ACCESS_TOKEN>",
    "Content-Type": "application/json"
}
payload = {
    "updates": {
        "metadata-location": "s3://warehouse/analytics/customer_profiles
        /metadata/00002.metadata.json",
        "base": "s3://warehouse/analytics/customer_profiles/metadata
        /00001.metadata.json"
    }
}

response = requests.post(url, headers=headers, json=payload)
print(response.status_code)
```

Sample response:

```
{
  "metadata-location": "s3://warehouse/analytics/customer_profiles
  /metadata/00002.metadata.json",
  "table-uuid": "9bde37b3-fc9e-4b32-9b9e-abc123def456"
}
```

Drop a Table

Delete an Iceberg table from the catalog, with the option to purge data.

Endpoint:

```
DELETE /v1/{prefix}/namespaces/{namespace}/tables/{table}
```

This endpoint removes a table from the catalog. By default, this deletes only the catalog entry, preserving the underlying data files. To also purge the data (e.g., metadata files, manifests, and data files), include the query parameter `purgeRequested=true`.

Use this operation with care in production environments, especially when using `purgeRequested=true`, as it will permanently delete storage assets managed by the table.

Sample cURL Request (catalog only):

```
curl -X DELETE https://polaris.example.com/api/catalog/v1/dev/namespaces
/analytics/tables/customer_profiles \
    -H "Authorization: Bearer <ACCESS_TOKEN>"
```

Sample cURL Request (catalog + data purge):

```
curl -X DELETE "https://polaris.example.com/api/catalog/v1/dev/namespaces
/analytics/tables/customer_profiles?purgeRequested=true" \
    -H "Authorization: Bearer <ACCESS_TOKEN>"
```

Sample Python Request (with purge):

```
import requests

url = "https://polaris.example.com/api/catalog/v1/dev/namespaces/analytics
/tables/customer_profiles?purgeRequested=true"
headers = {
    "Authorization": "Bearer <ACCESS_TOKEN>"
}

response = requests.delete(url, headers=headers)
print(response.status_code)
```

Sample response:

- `204 No Content`: Table deleted successfully
- `404 Not Found`: Table not found
- `409 Conflict`: Table cannot be deleted (e.g., in use or write conflict)

Check Table Existence

Verify whether a specific table exists in the catalog.

Endpoint:

```
HEAD /v1/{prefix}/namespaces/{namespace}/tables/{table}
```

This lightweight endpoint checks whether a given Iceberg table exists in the specified namespace. It does not return any metadata or payload; it only returns an HTTP status code. This is useful for validation in automation workflows, such as confirming table creation before inserting data or avoiding accidental overwrites.

Sample cURL request:

```
curl -I -X HEAD https://polaris.example.com/api/catalog/v1/dev/namespaces
/analytics/tables/customer_profiles \
    -H "Authorization: Bearer <ACCESS_TOKEN>"
```

Sample Python request:

```
import requests

url = "https://polaris.example.com/api/catalog/v1/dev/namespaces/analytics
/tables/customer_profiles"
headers = {
    "Authorization": "Bearer <ACCESS_TOKEN>"
}

response = requests.head(url, headers=headers)
if response.status_code == 204:
    print("Table exists.")
elif response.status_code == 404:
    print("Table not found.")
else:
    print(f"Unexpected status: {response.status_code}")
```

Sample response:

- 204 No Content: Table exists
- 404 Not Found: Table does not exist

Rename a Table

Change the name of an existing Iceberg table within the same namespace or across namespaces.

Endpoint:

```
POST /v1/{prefix}/rename
```

This endpoint renames an Iceberg table by moving it from its current identifier to a new one. The source and destination identifiers can refer to the same namespace or different namespaces. The operation updates the catalog reference; the underlying metadata and data files remain unchanged.

If the target table name already exists, the request will fail with a 409 Conflict status.

Sample cURL request:

```
curl -X POST https://polaris.example.com/api/catalog/v1/dev/rename \
    -H "Authorization: Bearer <ACCESS_TOKEN>" \
    -H "Content-Type: application/json" \
    -d '{
        "source": {
          "namespace": ["analytics"],
```

```
          "name": "customer_profiles"
        },
        "destination": {
          "namespace": ["analytics"],
          "name": "customer_profiles_archive"
        }
      }'
```

Sample Python request:

```python
import requests

url = "https://polaris.example.com/api/catalog/v1/dev/rename"
headers = {
    "Authorization": "Bearer <ACCESS_TOKEN>",
    "Content-Type": "application/json"
}
payload = {
    "source": {
        "namespace": ["analytics"],
        "name": "customer_profiles"
    },
    "destination": {
        "namespace": ["analytics"],
        "name": "customer_profiles_archive"
    }
}

response = requests.post(url, headers=headers, json=payload)
print(response.status_code)
```

Sample response:

- 200 OK: Table successfully renamed

- 404 Not Found: Source table does not exist

- 409 Conflict: Destination table already exists

Submit Metrics for a Table

Submit performance, access, or operational metrics associated with a table.

Endpoint:

```
POST /v1/{prefix}/namespaces/{namespace}/tables/{table}/metrics
```

This endpoint allows clients to submit custom metrics related to an Iceberg table. These can include statistics like query latency, row counts, file sizes, or domain-specific metrics relevant to governance and optimization. Submitted metrics may be stored, monitored, or visualized depending on the catalog's capabilities.

This feature enables integration with monitoring systems and observability tooling to track table health and usage patterns over time.

Sample cURL request:

```
curl -X POST https://polaris.example.com/api/catalog/v1/dev/namespaces
/analytics/tables/customer_profiles/metrics \
    -H "Authorization: Bearer <ACCESS_TOKEN>" \
    -H "Content-Type: application/json" \
    -d '{
        "metrics": {
          "row_count": 1823947,
          "last_query_duration_ms": 231,
          "fragmentation_score": 0.75
      }
    }'
```

Sample Python request:

```
import requests

url = "https://polaris.example.com/api/catalog/v1/dev/namespaces/analytics
/tables/customer_profiles/metrics"
headers = {
    "Authorization": "Bearer <ACCESS_TOKEN>",
    "Content-Type": "application/json"
}
payload = {
    "metrics": {
        "row_count": 1823947,
        "last_query_duration_ms": 231,
        "fragmentation_score": 0.75
    }
}

response = requests.post(url, headers=headers, json=payload)
print(response.status_code)
```

Sample response:

- `200 OK`: Metrics successfully submitted

- `404 Not Found`: Table does not exist

- `400 Bad Request`: Invalid metric format

Send Table Notifications

Send a lightweight custom notification event for a table.

Endpoint:

```
POST /v1/{prefix}/namespaces/{namespace}/tables/{table}/notifications
```

This endpoint allows systems or users to send implementation-specific notification events related to a table. These events may be used to trigger downstream processes, communicate lifecycle changes (e.g., compaction complete), or signal state transitions to observability tools.

The catalog implementation determines how notifications are handled, storing them, forwarding them to consumers, or using them for auditing or orchestration purposes.

Sample cURL request:

```
curl -X POST https://polaris.example.com/api/catalog/v1/dev/namespaces
/analytics/tables/customer_profiles/notifications \
    -H "Authorization: Bearer <ACCESS_TOKEN>" \
    -H "Content-Type: application/json" \
    -d '{
        "notification": {
          "event_type": "compaction_complete",
          "summary": "Compaction job finished for June partition",
          "timestamp": "2025-06-20T13:45:00Z"
        }
      }'
```

Sample Python request:

```python
import requests

url = "https://polaris.example.com/api/catalog/v1/dev/namespaces
/analytics/tables/customer_profiles/notifications"
headers = {
    "Authorization": "Bearer <ACCESS_TOKEN>",
    "Content-Type": "application/json"
}
payload = {
    "notification": {
        "event_type": "compaction_complete",
        "summary": "Compaction job finished for June partition",
        "timestamp": "2025-06-20T13:45:00Z"
    }
}

response = requests.post(url, headers=headers, json=payload)
print(response.status_code)
```

Sample response:

- 200 OK: Notification accepted

- 404 Not Found: Table not found

- 400 Bad Request: Malformed or unsupported notification payload

Commit Updates to Multiple Tables

Atomically commit metadata updates across multiple Iceberg tables using a single transaction.

Endpoint:

```
POST /v1/{prefix}/transactions/commit
```

This endpoint performs a multi-table commit operation, allowing you to update the metadata of multiple Iceberg tables in a single atomic transaction. This ensures that either all updates succeed together or none are applied, preventing partial state changes and preserving catalog consistency.

This operation is ideal for orchestrated schema updates, partitioning adjustments, or any workflow where consistency across tables is critical.

Sample cURL request:

```
curl -X POST https://polaris.example.com/api/catalog/v1/dev/transactions/commit \
    -H "Authorization: Bearer <ACCESS_TOKEN>" \
    -H "Content-Type: application/json" \
    -d '{
        "updates": [
          {
            "identifier": {
              "namespace": ["analytics"],
              "name": "customer_profiles"
            },
            "base": "s3://warehouse/analytics/customer_profiles
            /metadata/00001.metadata.json",
            "metadata-location": "s3://warehouse/analytics/customer_profiles
            /metadata/00002.metadata.json"
          },
          {
            "identifier": {
              "namespace": ["analytics"],
              "name": "sales_summary"
            },
            "base": "s3://warehouse/analytics/sales_summary
            /metadata/00005.metadata.json",
            "metadata-location": "s3://warehouse/analytics/sales_summary
            /metadata/00006.metadata.json"
          }
        ]
      }'
```

Sample Python request:

```
import requests

url = "https://polaris.example.com/api/catalog/v1/dev/transactions/commit"
headers = {
```

```
        "Authorization": "Bearer <ACCESS_TOKEN>",
        "Content-Type": "application/json"
    }
    payload = {
        "updates": [
            {
                "identifier": {
                    "namespace": ["analytics"],
                    "name": "customer_profiles"
                },
                "base": "s3://warehouse/analytics/customer_profiles
                /metadata/00001.metadata.json",
                "metadata-location": "s3://warehouse/analytics/customer_profiles
                /metadata/00002.metadata.json"
            },
            {
                "identifier": {
                    "namespace": ["analytics"],
                    "name": "sales_summary"
                },
                "base": "s3://warehouse/analytics/sales_summary
                /metadata/00005.metadata.json",
                "metadata-location": "s3://warehouse/analytics/sales_summary
                /metadata/00006.metadata.json"
            }
        ]
    }

    response = requests.post(url, headers=headers, json=payload)
    print(response.json())
```

Sample response:

```
{
  "results": [
    {
      "identifier": {
        "namespace": ["analytics"],
        "name": "customer_profiles"
      },
      "metadata-location": "s3://warehouse/analytics/customer_profiles/metadata
      /00002.metadata.json",
      "table-uuid": "9bde37b3-fc9e-4b32-9b9e-abc123def456"
    },
    {
      "identifier": {
        "namespace": ["analytics"],
        "name": "sales_summary"
      },
      "metadata-location": "s3://warehouse/analytics/sales_summary/metadata
      /00006.metadata.json",
      "table-uuid": "2c51aa91-13fd-4404-874c-b0df41ec83d8"
    }
```

```
      ]
    }
```

Error Handling:

- `409 Conflict`: One or more updates failed validation (e.g., base metadata no longer matches); entire transaction aborted
- `400 Bad Request`: Malformed request payload
- `200 OK`: All updates applied successfully and atomically

View API

The View API provides endpoints for managing SQL-based views within a Polaris catalog namespace.

Views in Apache Iceberg are named, versioned objects that encapsulate SQL query logic. They can reference tables or other views and are stored in the catalog alongside physical datasets. These endpoints enable clients to list, create, inspect, and delete views programmatically.

Each view has a unique identifier consisting of a namespace and view name. Views are immutable once created and can be replaced atomically to create new versions with updated definitions. This enables safe evolution of business logic without disrupting dependent consumers.

The endpoints in this section mirror the structure of the Table API and include support for standard operations like checking existence, retrieving metadata, and managing lifecycle.

List View Identifiers

Retrieve a list of all views in a given namespace.

Endpoint:

```
GET /v1/{prefix}/namespaces/{namespace}/views
```

This endpoint returns a list of all views defined within the specified namespace. The response includes the identifiers (namespace and name) for each view, allowing clients to enumerate existing view objects in the catalog. This is useful for user interfaces, discovery tools, or orchestration systems that need to browse available views.

Sample cURL request:

```
curl -X GET https://polaris.example.com/api/catalog/v1/dev/namespaces
/analytics/views \
    -H "Authorization: Bearer <ACCESS_TOKEN>"
```

Sample Python request:

```python
import requests

url = "https://polaris.example.com/api/catalog/v1/dev/namespaces/analytics/views"
headers = {
    "Authorization": "Bearer <ACCESS_TOKEN>"
}

response = requests.get(url, headers=headers)
print(response.json())
```

Sample response:

```json
{
  "identifiers": [
    {
      "namespace": ["analytics"],
      "name": "customer_summary"
    },
    {
      "namespace": ["analytics"],
      "name": "daily_revenue"
    }
  ]
}
```

Error Handling:

- `404 Not Found`: Namespace does not exist
- `200 OK`: List of views returned successfully

Create a View

Define or update an SQL-based view in the specified namespace.

Endpoint:

```
POST /v1/{prefix}/namespaces/{namespace}/views
```

This endpoint creates a new view or replaces an existing one in the specified namespace. An SQL SELECT statement defines a view, and clients must provide both the view's identifier and its SQL definition in the request body. If a view with the same name already exists, it will be atomically replaced.

Each view is versioned internally by the catalog, enabling safe updates to analytical logic over time without disrupting consumers.

Sample cURL request:

```
curl -X POST https://polaris.example.com/api/catalog/v1/dev/namespaces
/analytics/views \
```

```
            -H "Authorization: Bearer <ACCESS_TOKEN>" \
            -H "Content-Type: application/json" \
            -d '{
                  "view-version": {
                    "version-id": "v1",
                    "schema-id": 1,
                    "sql": "SELECT customer_id, COUNT(*) AS orders FROM orders
                    GROUP BY customer_id"
                  },
                  "identifier": {
                    "namespace": ["analytics"],
                    "name": "customer_order_summary"
                  }
                }'
```

Sample Python request:

```python
import requests

url = "https://polaris.example.com/api/catalog/v1/dev/namespaces/analytics/views"
headers = {
    "Authorization": "Bearer <ACCESS_TOKEN>",
    "Content-Type": "application/json"
}
payload = {
    "view-version": {
        "version-id": "v1",
        "schema-id": 1,
        "sql": "SELECT customer_id, COUNT(*) AS orders FROM orders
        GROUP BY customer_id"
    },
    "identifier": {
        "namespace": ["analytics"],
        "name": "customer_order_summary"
    }
}

response = requests.post(url, headers=headers, json=payload)
print(response.status_code)
```

Sample response:

- `200 OK`: View created or replaced successfully

- `400 Bad Request`: Invalid SQL or missing required fields

- `409 Conflict`: View version conflict (e.g., immutable update violation)

Load View Metadata

Retrieve metadata for a specific view, including its SQL definition and version.

Endpoint:

```
GET /v1/{prefix}/namespaces/{namespace}/views/{view}
```

This endpoint fetches the full metadata for a given view, including its SQL definition, schema ID, and version identifier. It can be used by query engines, UI clients, or orchestration tools to display or process the view definition. The response includes the SQL query text that defines the view and other metadata associated with the current version.

Sample cURL request:

```
curl -X GET https://polaris.example.com/api/catalog/v1/dev/namespaces
/analytics/views/customer_order_summary \
    -H "Authorization: Bearer <ACCESS_TOKEN>"
```

Sample Python request:

```python
import requests

url = "https://polaris.example.com/api/catalog/v1/dev/namespaces/analytics
/views/customer_order_summary"
headers = {
    "Authorization": "Bearer <ACCESS_TOKEN>"
}

response = requests.get(url, headers=headers)
print(response.json())
```

Sample response:

```json
{
  "identifier": {
    "namespace": ["analytics"],
    "name": "customer_order_summary"
  },
  "view-version": {
    "version-id": "v1",
    "schema-id": 1,
    "sql": "SELECT customer_id, COUNT(*) AS orders FROM orders
    GROUP BY customer_id"
  }
}
```

Error Handling:

- `404 Not Found`: View does not exist

- `200 OK`: View metadata returned successfully

Replace a View

Atomically replace an existing view with a new SQL definition.

Endpoint:

```
POST /v1/{prefix}/namespaces/{namespace}/views
```

This endpoint is used to replace an existing view by providing a new SQL definition. It uses the same request structure as view creation, and if the view already exists, the new version will overwrite the current one atomically.

Replacing a view allows teams to evolve their business logic or analytical models safely while preserving the view's name and identity. Each replacement should include a new `version-id` to track changes over time. (Note: If the view does not exist, this call will create it.)

Sample cURL request:

```
curl -X POST https://polaris.example.com/api/catalog/v1/dev/namespaces
/analytics/views \
    -H "Authorization: Bearer <ACCESS_TOKEN>" \
    -H "Content-Type: application/json" \
    -d '{
        "view-version": {
          "version-id": "v2",
          "schema-id": 1,
          "sql": "SELECT customer_id, COUNT(*) AS orders, MAX(order_date)
          AS last_order FROM orders GROUP BY customer_id"
        },
        "identifier": {
          "namespace": ["analytics"],
          "name": "customer_order_summary"
        }
      }'
```

Sample Python request:

```
import requests

url = "https://polaris.example.com/api/catalog/v1/dev/namespaces/analytics/views"
headers = {
    "Authorization": "Bearer <ACCESS_TOKEN>",
    "Content-Type": "application/json"
}
payload = {
    "view-version": {
        "version-id": "v2",
        "schema-id": 1,
        "sql": "SELECT customer_id, COUNT(*) AS orders, MAX(order_date)
        AS last_order FROM orders GROUP BY customer_id"
    },
    "identifier": {
        "namespace": ["analytics"],
        "name": "customer_order_summary"
    }
}
```

```
response = requests.post(url, headers=headers, json=payload)
print(response.status_code)
```

Sample response:

- `200 OK`: View replaced successfully
- `400 Bad Request`: SQL is invalid or missing required fields
- `409 Conflict`: Conflicting version or schema constraints

Drop a View

Delete a view from the specified namespace.

Endpoint:

```
DELETE /v1/{prefix}/namespaces/{namespace}/views/{view}
```

This endpoint deletes a view by name from the given namespace. Once deleted, the view and its associated SQL definition will no longer be available to consumers. This operation is irreversible and should be used with caution, especially in environments where dashboards, pipelines, or downstream systems reference views.

The request does not require a body, and the server will return a success response if the view is successfully removed.

Sample cURL request:

```
curl -X DELETE https://polaris.example.com/api/catalog/v1/dev/namespaces
/analytics/views/customer_order_summary \
    -H "Authorization: Bearer <ACCESS_TOKEN>"
```

Sample Python request:

```
import requests

url = "https://polaris.example.com/api/catalog/v1/dev/namespaces/analytics
/views/customer_order_summary"
headers = {
    "Authorization": "Bearer <ACCESS_TOKEN>"
}

response = requests.delete(url, headers=headers)
print(response.status_code)
```

Sample response:

- `204 No Content`: View deleted successfully
- `404 Not Found`: View does not exist
- `403 Forbidden`: Insufficient permissions to delete the view

Check View Existence

Determine whether a view exists in the specified namespace.

Endpoint:

```
HEAD /v1/{prefix}/namespaces/{namespace}/views/{view}
```

This endpoint allows clients to check if a view exists without retrieving its full metadata. It returns a `200 OK` status if the view is present and a `404 Not Found` if the view does not exist. This is useful for lightweight validation in orchestration pipelines, UI navigation, or before attempting updates or deletions.

No response body is returned.

Sample cURL request:

```
curl -I https://polaris.example.com/api/catalog/v1/dev/namespaces/analytics
/views/customer_order_summary \
    -H "Authorization: Bearer <ACCESS_TOKEN>"
```

Sample Python request:

```
import requests

url = "https://polaris.example.com/api/catalog/v1/dev/namespaces/analytics
/views/customer_order_summary"
headers = {
    "Authorization": "Bearer <ACCESS_TOKEN>"
}

response = requests.head(url, headers=headers)
print(response.status_code)
```

Sample Response Status Codes:

- `200 OK`: View exists
- `404 Not Found`: View does not exist
- `403 Forbidden`: Insufficient permissions to access the view

Rename a View

Change the name of a view within or across namespaces.

Endpoint:

```
POST /v1/{prefix}/views/rename
```

This endpoint renames a view by specifying the current identifier and the new desired identifier. The operation can also move the view to a different namespace. This is useful when evolving naming conventions or organizing views by domain.

The rename is atomic and preserves the underlying view version and SQL definition. If the destination view name already exists, the operation will fail with a conflict error.

Sample cURL request:

```
curl -X POST https://polaris.example.com/api/catalog/v1/dev/views/rename \
    -H "Authorization: Bearer <ACCESS_TOKEN>" \
    -H "Content-Type: application/json" \
    -d '{
        "from": {
          "namespace": ["analytics"],
          "name": "customer_order_summary"
        },
        "to": {
          "namespace": ["sales"],
          "name": "customer_summary"
        }
      }'
```

Sample Python request:

```python
import requests

url = "https://polaris.example.com/api/catalog/v1/dev/views/rename"
headers = {
    "Authorization": "Bearer <ACCESS_TOKEN>",
    "Content-Type": "application/json"
}
payload = {
    "from": {
        "namespace": ["analytics"],
        "name": "customer_order_summary"
    },
    "to": {
        "namespace": ["sales"],
        "name": "customer_summary"
    }
}

response = requests.post(url, headers=headers, json=payload)
print(response.status_code)
```

Sample response:

- `200 OK`: View renamed successfully

- `404 Not Found`: Source view does not exist

- `409 Conflict`: Destination view already exists

- `400 Bad Request`: Invalid identifier format or namespace

These endpoints provide robust capabilities for managing catalogs, namespaces, tables, and views within the Polaris platform, ensuring administrators have the flexibility to effectively control resources.

Conclusion

In this chapter, we explored the comprehensive set of Polaris REST API endpoints that enable seamless management of catalogs, namespaces, tables, views, and more. These APIs provide the foundation for advanced catalog operations. Now that you understand the capabilities of Polaris and how it streamlines data governance and access, it's time to see it in action. The following section will delve into hands-on examples, integrating Polaris with powerful tools such as Apache Spark, Dremio, and Snowflake.

## PART III

Hands-on with Apache Polaris

In the first two sections of this book, we laid the groundwork of exploring the core concepts of lakehouses, Apache Iceberg, and Apache Polaris. We delved into the architecture, the principles of open table formats, and how Polaris serves as a cutting-edge catalog solution for managing metadata at scale. With this foundational knowledge in place, it's time to roll up our sleeves and put these concepts into action.

Part III focuses on the practical application of Apache Polaris and its integration with modern data tools. We'll start by learning how to deploy Polaris locally, enabling you to get hands-on experience with its open source version. From there, we'll explore how Polaris interacts with powerful tools such as Apache Spark, Snowflake, and Dremio. Each chapter will provide step-by-step guides to configure, query, and manage catalogs, helping you connect the theoretical concepts covered earlier to real-world workflows.

By the end of this section, you'll not only have deployed Polaris but also integrated it into a broader data ecosystem, giving you a comprehensive understanding of how lakehouse architectures operate in practice. Whether you're building an on-premise lakehouse, experimenting with open table formats, or evaluating Polaris for production use, these chapters will equip you with the skills and insights to confidently manage your data landscape.

Let's begin by setting up Polaris in your local environment and gaining a firsthand understanding of its inner workings!

Reminder that a lot of the supporting code in this chapter can be found in the Git repository: *https://github.com/developer-advocacy-dremio/apache-polaris-the-definitive-guide*.

## CHAPTER 6

Working with Apache Polaris OSS

In the previous chapters, we explored Apache Polaris, its key features, and its API in depth. Now, it's time to move beyond theory and dive into the practical aspects of deploying and working with Apache Polaris locally. This hands-on approach will help you understand how the different components work together, enabling you to apply these concepts in real-world scenarios.

While managed Polaris offerings like Snowflake Open Catalog and Dremio Catalog provide a streamlined experience for production environments—eliminating the need to deploy and maintain your own Polaris infrastructure—it's still invaluable to have a hands-on understanding of its mechanics. By deploying Apache Polaris locally, you'll gain direct insights into how catalogs, roles, and access management come together, giving you a solid foundation to appreciate and optimize managed solutions fully.

In this chapter, we'll walk through deploying Apache Polaris using Docker, setting up catalogs, creating roles, and configuring access controls. Whether you're evaluating Polaris for your organization or sharpening your understanding of its internals, this guide will give you the tools to confidently explore its potential.

Deploying Locally with Docker

Before we dive into deploying Apache Polaris locally, it's worth noting the distinction between development and production environments. In this chapter, we'll focus on spinning up Polaris using Docker for hands-on learning and experimentation—a great way to explore how Polaris works under the hood. However, when it comes time to deploy Polaris in a production setting, several additional considerations come into play: secure authentication with OAuth2, durable metadata persistence, and proper bootstrapping of service credentials. While local deployment relies on simplified defaults, such as in-memory storage and test authenticators, production environments should follow the best practices outlined in the Polaris deployment documentation to ensure stability, security, and scalability. Think of this local setup as your Polaris lab—an essential step before rolling out the real thing.

Prerequisites

Before proceeding, ensure you have the following installed on your system:

Docker
> A containerization platform

Docker Compose
> A tool for defining and running multi-container Docker applications

Git
> To clone the repository with the deployment setup

Step 1: Clone the Repository

Start by cloning the *Apache Polaris Educational Environment* repository (*https:// oreil.ly/d8bZ5*), which contains the necessary Docker Compose file and setup instructions.

```
git clone https://github.com/AlexMercedCoder/quick-test-polaris-environment
```

Then change directories into the cloned repository.

```
cd quick-test-polaris-environment
```

This repository includes everything you need to deploy Polaris and Spark locally, including the *docker-compose.yml* file.

Step 2: Configure Environment Variables

The deployment can utilize AWS credentials and other environment-specific configurations as applicable. These settings are defined through the environment variables on your host so make sure they are represented if you are using the S3 storage.

```
# Bash/ZSH
export AWS_REGION=us-east-1
export AWS_ACCESS_KEY_ID=your-aws-access-key
export AWS_SECRET_ACCESS_KEY=your-aws-secret-key
# CMD/Windows
set AWS_REGION=us-east-1
set AWS_ACCESS_KEY_ID=your-aws-access-key
set AWS_SECRET_ACCESS_KEY=your-aws-secret-key
# Powershell Windows
$env:AWS_REGION = "us-east-1"
```

```
$env:AWS_ACCESS_KEY_ID = "your-aws-access-key"
$env:AWS_SECRET_ACCESS_KEY = "your-aws-secret-key"
```

If you are not using S3 storage, you can skip this step. If this is your first time, it's better to walk through these steps with your local file system first, then try with S3.

Step 3: Understand the Docker Compose File

The *docker-compose.yml* file provided in the repository defines the services required to run Apache Polaris and Spark locally. It ensures that both services can communicate with each other seamlessly and share data through a common volume.

Here is the full content of the *docker-compose.yml* file:

```
services:
  polaris:
    image: apache/polaris:1.1.0-incubating-SNAPSHOT
    container_name: polaris
    ports:
      - "8181:8181"
      - "8182"
    networks:
      polaris-quickstart:
    volumes:
      - ./icebergdata:/data
    environment:
      AWS_REGION: $AWS_REGION
      AWS_ACCESS_KEY_ID: $AWS_ACCESS_KEY_ID
      AWS_SECRET_ACCESS_KEY: $AWS_SECRET_ACCESS_KEY
      POLARIS_BOOTSTRAP_CREDENTIALS: POLARIS,root_user,my_secret_id
      polaris.realm-context.realms: POLARIS
      quarkus.log.file.enable: "false"
      quarkus.otel.sdk.disabled: "true"
      polaris.features."DROP_WITH_PURGE_ENABLED": "true"
      polaris.features."ALLOW_INSECURE_STORAGE_TYPES": "true"
      polaris.features."SUPPORTED_CATALOG_STORAGE_TYPES": "[\"FILE\",\"S3\",
      \"GCS\",\"AZURE\"]"
      polaris.readiness.ignore-severe-issues: "true"

  spark:
    platform: linux/x86_64
    image: alexmerced/spark35nb:latest
    ports:
      - "8080:8080"  # Master Web UI
      - "7077:7077"  # Master Port
      - "8888:8888"  # Jupyter Notebook
    volumes:
      - ./icebergdata:/data
    environment:
      - AWS_REGION=us-east-1
      - AWS_ACCESS_KEY_ID=$AWS_ACCESS_KEY_ID
      - AWS_SECRET_ACCESS_KEY=$AWS_SECRET_ACCESS_KEY
```

```
    container_name: spark
    networks:
      polaris-quickstart:

  networks:
    polaris-quickstart:
```

This file defines two services, Polaris and Spark, which are connected via a shared Docker network and utilize a standard data volume for interoperability.

Polaris service

The Polaris service acts as our Iceberg Catalog.

- Image:
    — Uses `apache/polaris:1.1.0-incubating-SNAPSHOT`, an official snapshot build of Apache Polaris.
- Ports:
    — `8181:8181`: Exposes Polaris's primary REST API.
    — `8182`: An internal port used by Polaris; no external mapping is needed.
- Volumes:
    — Mounts the local *./icebergdata* directory to */data* in the container, serving as the shared location for catalog data and metadata.
- Environment variables:
    — Reads AWS credentials and region from the host environment (or *.env* file).
    — Configures Polaris bootstrap credentials, enables support for multiple storage backends, including `FILE`, and disables telemetry and file-based logging.
- Configuration:
    — Polaris is bootstrapped with the `POLARIS_BOOTSTRAP_CREDENTIALS` and runs using its default internal configuration. Features like `DROP_WITH_PURGE_ENABLED` and `ALLOW_INSECURE_STORAGE_TYPES` are explicitly enabled to facilitate local experimentation with the `FILE` storage type.

Spark service

The Spark service acts as our environment for running queries against our Iceberg Catalog.

- Image:
    — `alexmerced/spark35nb:latest`, a custom Docker image that includes Spark 3.5, Iceberg, PySpark, JupyterLab, and additional data tools.

- Ports:
    - 8080:8080: Spark Master Web UI.
    - 7077:7077: Spark Master port for worker communication.
    - 8888:8888: Jupyter Notebook interface for interactive use.
- Volumes:
    - Shares the *./icebergdata* directory with Polaris, allowing Spark to read/write from the same physical storage path, which is essential when using local FILE storage catalogs.
- Environment variables:
    - Sets the AWS region and credentials for accessing object storage, if needed.
- Platform:
    - The linux/x86_64 platform flag ensures compatibility in environments requiring a specific architecture.

Shared network

Both services are attached to the polaris-quickstart Docker network, which enables internal communication between containers using their service names (polaris and spark).

Step 3 summary

This setup enables Apache Polaris to function as a REST-based Iceberg catalog, while Spark serves as the processing engine. They share a standard file system (*./icebergdata*), making it easy to experiment with Iceberg tables in a self-contained environment.

This configuration is designed for educational and development use cases. For production or cloud-based environments, consider adapting it to use secure object storage (e.g., S3, GCS) and managed authentication mechanisms.

Step 4: Starting the Environment

To deploy the Polaris learning environment, start the services defined in the *docker-compose.yml* file. The docker-compose command starts, stops, and manages the environment.

Open a terminal in the directory where the *docker-compose.yml* file is located. Run the following command to start the environment:

```
docker compose up
```

The docker compose up command:

- Builds and starts the services (`polaris` and `spark`) defined in the *docker-compose.yml* file.
- Outputs logs from the running containers directly to your terminal.

Once the environment is running, verify that both services are up by running:

```
docker ps
```

This will list all running containers, including `polaris` and `spark`.

Step 5: Stopping the Environment

When you are done using the Polaris learning environment, it's important to stop and clean up the running containers to free up system resources.

To stop the services but keep the containers and their states intact, run:

```
docker compose stop
```

This command halts the containers but keeps them in a paused state, so they can be restarted quickly with `docker compose start`.

To stop and remove the containers thoroughly, use the following command:

```
docker compose down
```

This command stops the services and removes the containers, networks, and any other resources defined in the *docker-compose.yml* file.

If you also want to remove the associated volumes (including the *./icebergdata* directory), add the `--volumes` flag:

```
docker compose down --volumes
```

Be cautious with this command, as it deletes all persistent data stored in the volumes. The different commands for starting Docker Compose environments can be seen in Table 6-1.

Table 6-1. Docker commands for starting and stopping Docker Compose environments

Command	Action
`docker compose up`	Starts the services and outputs logs to the terminal
`docker compose up -d`	Starts the services in detached mode (runs in the background)
`docker compose stop`	Stops the containers but retains their state, making it faster to restart
`docker compose down`	Stops and removes the containers, networks, and other resources defined in the *docker-compose.yml* file
`docker compose down --volumes`	Stops and removes containers along with their volumes, deleting any stored data

Creating Catalogs

Now that the Polaris environment is running, the first step is to create a catalog. Catalogs are the foundation of Polaris, as they store metadata about tables and other resources. We will use set names for our catalogs, principles, and roles. While you can name these whatever you want, we'll name them so they can match the Apache Spark code snippets in the next chapter.

This particular environment has your root credentials preconfigured via environmental variables:

```
POLARIS_BOOTSTRAP_CREDENTIALS: POLARIS,root_user,my_secret_id
```

For the "POLARIS" realm, the root user's ID is "root_user" and the secret is "my_secret_id". In this environment, there is a Python file that will run all the bootstrapping requests for you, and in the Polaris repo, there is a CLI you can use as well. To get acquainted with the Polaris Catalog management API, let's make raw requests to the Polaris server.

Next, use the root credentials provided in the container logs to generate a bearer token:

```
curl -i -X POST \
  http://localhost:8181/api/catalog/v1/oauth/tokens \
  -d 'grant_type=client_credentials&client_id=<ID>&client_secret=
<SECRET>&scope=PRINCIPAL_ROLE:ALL'
```

The response will include a bearer token. Copy this token for use in subsequent requests. Use the bearer token to send a POST request to create a catalog. You can choose between using the local file system or S3 storage. If this is your first time working with Polaris, for educational purposes we suggest choosing a local file system:

```
curl -i -X POST -H "Authorization: Bearer <YOUR_TOKEN>" \
  -H 'Accept: application/json' -H 'Content-Type: application/json' \
  http://localhost:8181/api/management/v1/catalogs \
  -d '{"name": "polariscatalog", "type": "INTERNAL", "properties": {
      "default-base-location": "file:///data"
    },"storageConfigInfo": {
      "storageType": "FILE",
      "allowedLocations": [
          "file:///data"
      ]
  } }'
```

For S3 storage, replace the placeholder values with your AWS configuration:

```
curl -i -X POST -H "Authorization: Bearer <YOUR_TOKEN>" \
  -H 'Accept: application/json' -H 'Content-Type: application/json' \
  http://localhost:8181/api/management/v1/catalogs \
  -d '{"name": "polariscatalog", "type": "INTERNAL", "properties": {
```

```
        "default-base-location": "s3://my/s3/path"
    },"storageConfigInfo": {
        "roleArn": "arn:aws:iam::xxxxxxxxx:role/polaris-storage",
        "storageType": "S3",
        "allowedLocations": [
            "s3://my/s3/path"
        ]
    } }'
```

Make sure to replace "xxxxxxxxx" with your actual AWS account number if using AWS.

Verify that the catalog was created successfully:

```
curl -X GET "http://localhost:8181/api/management/v1/catalogs" \
    -H "Authorization: Bearer <YOUR_TOKEN>" \
    -H "Accept: application/json"
```

When to Create a Catalog

While creating a catalog in Polaris is a straightforward operation, deciding when to make a catalog and how to organize datasets across catalogs requires more strategic thinking. Catalogs are the highest level of isolation within a Realm in Polaris. Each catalog has its own set of namespaces, tables, views, and associated security controls. Making wise choices about catalog boundaries early on can lead to better performance, more effective governance, and easier operations at scale.

When to create a new catalog

You should consider creating a new catalog when:

You need hard security boundaries between datasets or teams.
    Catalog-level access control prevents users from even listing what exists in a catalog unless explicitly granted permission.

You are managing staging and production environments within the same Polaris deployment.
    Separate catalogs for each environment reduce the risk of accidental data access or privilege escalation.

You need to enforce different storage backends or IAM roles.
    Each catalog defines its own storage configuration, making it the correct boundary for differing file systems or authentication models.

When not to create a new catalog

Avoid creating unnecessary catalogs if:

You simply want to group related tables.
Use *namespaces* instead. Namespaces offer a more lightweight form of logical organization within a catalog.

You are managing datasets that share the same governance and storage policies.
Creating too many catalogs can lead to administrative overhead without providing real benefits.

Recommended catalog strategies

By department or business unit
When working in large enterprises, it often makes sense to map one catalog to each business unit (e.g., `sales`, `marketing`). This aligns governance boundaries with organizational structure.

By environment
Create separate catalogs for `dev`, `staging`, and `prod` to isolate workloads and simplify deployment pipelines.

By use case
For data platforms serving different user personas, separate catalogs for analytics, data science, and ML feature stores can help clarify ownership and policy models.

Long-term considerations

Catalogs are relatively static. They are not designed for frequent creation and deletion. As such, make catalog design a deliberate architectural decision rather than a convenience for short-term organization. It is easier to manage and evolve namespaces and roles within a catalog than to migrate entities between catalogs later.

By designing catalogs thoughtfully, you ensure that Polaris remains scalable, secure, and easy to govern as your lakehouse grows.

Creating Catalog Roles

Catalog roles control access to catalogs and their contents. Use the bearer token created earlier to create a catalog role within the previously created catalog:

```
curl -X POST "http://localhost:8181/api/management/v1/catalogs/polariscatalog
/catalog-roles" \
  -H "Authorization: Bearer <YOUR_TOKEN>" \
  -H "Content-Type: application/json" \
  -d '{"catalogRole": {"name": "polariscatalogrole"}}'
```

List the catalog roles to ensure the role was created:

```
curl -X GET "http://localhost:8181/api/management/v1/catalogs/polariscatalog
/catalog-roles" \
    -H "Authorization: Bearer <YOUR_TOKEN>" \
    -H "Accept: application/json"
```

When to Create Catalog Roles

Catalog roles in Polaris act as the main access control unit within a catalog, determining what operations users and services can perform. While creating catalog roles is technically straightforward, designing them with long-term usability and governance in mind can make a substantial difference in how scalable, secure, and understandable your access model becomes.

This section outlines best practices for creating and managing catalog roles effectively, with a focus on clarity, security, and maintainability.

Use roles to reflect real-world responsibilities

The most effective catalog roles mirror the responsibilities of actual personas in your organization. Instead of assigning privileges directly to individual users (principals), define catalog roles that describe what a user *should be able to do*—then grant those to principal roles. This keeps your permissions model modular and easier to audit. For example:

- A `data_reader` role may be granted table and view read privileges.
- A `data_engineer` role might have broader permissions, including table creation, update, and delete.
- A `catalog_admin` role may include privileges to manage schemas, views, and catalog-level configurations.

This alignment ensures that when team responsibilities change or expand, access can be updated centrally by adjusting catalog roles rather than updating individual permissions.

Favor least privilege

When in doubt, grant fewer privileges. Catalog roles should only include the exact set of actions needed for a user or service to complete their task. This reduces the risk of accidental changes, data exposure, or abuse of access.

Start with minimal roles (e.g., read-only), and layer on additional permissions as necessary. Avoid giving `CATALOG_MANAGE_PRIVILEGES` or `TABLE_DELETE` unless required by the use case.

Reuse and generalize where possible

Avoid creating overly specific catalog roles for one-off use cases. If every user or dataset is assigned a unique role, your governance model becomes challenging to manage and audit. Instead:

- Create reusable roles for typical access patterns.
- Use namespace-specific privilege grants to restrict access without needing new roles.
- Tag roles with properties (e.g., `env=prod`, `purpose=analytics`) to help you identify intent and scope over time.

Limit catalog roles by scope and policy

While catalog roles are defined per catalog, they should not necessarily have access to everything within it. Use privilege grants at the namespace, table, or view level to constrain what a role can see or modify.

Document ownership and purpose

Take advantage of catalog role properties to store metadata about each role. For example:

```
--property owner=finance_team
--property sensitivity=internal_only
```

This helps automate governance workflows, enhances discoverability, and supports internal audits or reviews.

Periodically review and rotate

Catalog roles aren't static. Over time, roles may become obsolete, overly permissive, or redundant. Build regular access reviews into your governance process:

- Identify roles that are no longer used.
- Audit which principal roles are attached to high-privilege catalog roles.
- Remove or refactor overly broad or duplicative roles.

By applying these best practices, you ensure your access model remains robust, understandable, and secure, without slowing down the agility that Polaris is designed to deliver.

Creating Principals

A principal represents a user or a service account that can access Polaris resources. Use the bearer token to create a principal:

```
curl -X POST "http://localhost:8181/api/management/v1/principals" \
  -H "Authorization: Bearer <YOUR_TOKEN>" \
  -H "Content-Type: application/json" \
  -d '{"name": "polarisuser", "type": "user"}'
```

Confirm the principal was created:

```
curl -X GET "http://localhost:8181/api/management/v1/principals" \
      -H "Authorization: Bearer <YOUR_TOKEN>" \
      -H "Accept: application/json"
```

Creating Principal Roles

Principal roles define access privileges for a principal.

1. Create a role for the *polarisuser* principal:

   ```
   curl -X POST "http://localhost:8181/api/management/v1/principal-roles" \
       -H "Authorization: Bearer <YOUR_TOKEN>" \
       -H "Content-Type: application/json" \
       -d '{"principalRole": {"name": "polarisuserrole"}}'
   ```

2. Assign the principal role to the principal:

   ```
   curl -X PUT "http://localhost:8181/api/management/v1/principals
   /polarisuser/principal-roles" \
       -H "Authorization: Bearer <YOUR_TOKEN>" \
       -H "Content-Type: application/json" \
       -d '{"principalRole": {"name": "polarisuserrole"}}'
   ```

3. Verify the role assignment:

   ```
   curl -X GET "http://localhost:8181/api/management/v1/principals
   /polarisuser/principal-roles" \
         -H "Authorization: Bearer <YOUR_TOKEN>" \
   -H "Accept: application/json"
   ```

When to Create a Principal Role

Principal roles in Polaris serve as a scalable mechanism for managing access across users, service accounts, and automated processes. Rather than granting catalog roles or privileges to each principal individually, you will assign them to principal roles, creating a reusable and auditable layer of abstraction.

Designing principal roles well ensures that your access model is easier to manage, secure, and adaptable as your team and architecture evolve.

When to create a new principal role

You should create a new principal role when:

- A distinct group of users or services needs the same set of privileges across one or more catalogs.
- You want to separate duties between job functions—for example, analysts vs. data engineers.
- A team, department, or business unit operates in its own domain and needs clearly scoped access.
- You're introducing automation or third-party integrations that require programmatic access under defined security constraints.
- Compliance or governance policies require explicit access tracking by function or region.

Each principal role becomes a single point of truth about what that group can access, making it easier to rotate credentials, revoke access, or understand the blast radius of a permission change.

Map roles to real organizational units

Align principal roles with actual teams or responsibilities in your organization. This improves clarity and simplifies onboarding. For example:

- `data_engineers_team_a`
- `analytics_readonly`
- `etl_jobs`
- `third_party_integration_salesforce`

Using a naming convention that reflects function or ownership makes it easier to audit and manage over time.

Reuse roles across environments

Rather than duplicating roles for dev, staging, and prod, consider designing roles to be environment-agnostic, then use environment-specific catalogs to scope access appropriately. This approach simplifies governance while maintaining separation between environments.

Keep roles manageable

Avoid role sprawl. If every principal gets a custom role, you'll lose the benefits of abstraction. Instead:

- Create roles for shared access patterns.
- Use metadata tags (`--property team=finance`, `--property env=prod`) to capture additional detail.
- Revisit existing roles periodically to consolidate or deprecate as needs evolve.

Audit and review

Make principal role management part of your regular security and governance process:

- Review who has which roles.
- Track usage and rotate credentials as needed.
- Revoke roles that are no longer necessary.

A well-maintained set of principal roles becomes a powerful tool for securing and scaling access in Polaris, especially as the number of users, services, and catalogs grows. By following these best practices, you can ensure your access model remains clear, consistent, and compliant.

Assigning the Catalog Role to the Principal Role and Setting Permissions on the Catalog

Once you have created the catalog, catalog role, principal, and principal role, the next step is to assign the catalog role to the principal role. This step ensures that the principal can interact with the catalog. Additionally, you'll set the necessary permissions on the catalog role to define what actions the assigned principal can perform.

1. Assign the catalog role to the principal role using the bearer token:

   ```
   curl -X PUT "http://localhost:8181/api/management/v1/principal-roles
   /polarisuserrole/catalog-roles/polariscatalog" \
     -H "Authorization: Bearer <YOUR_TOKEN>" \
     -H "Content-Type: application/json" \
     -d '{"catalogRole": {"name": "polariscatalogrole"}}'
   ```

2. Grant privileges to the catalog role. Define the permissions that the catalog role has over the catalog. For example, you can grant the CATALOG_MANAGE_CONTENT privilege:

```
curl -X PUT "http://localhost:8181/api/management/v1/catalogs
/polariscatalog/catalog-roles/polariscatalogrole/grants" \
  -H "Authorization: Bearer <YOUR_TOKEN>" \
  -H "Content-Type: application/json" \
  -d '{"grant": {"type": "catalog", "privilege": "CATALOG_MANAGE_CONTENT"}}'
```

3. Verify the granted permissions and check that the permissions have been successfully applied to the catalog role:

```
curl -X GET "http://localhost:8181/api/management/v1/catalogs
/polariscatalog/catalog-roles/polariscatalogrole/grants" \
    -H "Authorization: Bearer <YOUR_TOKEN>" \
    -H "Accept: application/json"
```

Summary

By assigning the catalog role to the principal role and setting permissions, you've
completed the foundational access hierarchy in Polaris. This setup ensures secure and
organized management of catalogs and resources, creating a robust framework for
collaboration and data governance. With this environment now configured, you're
ready to move beyond setup and into application. In the next chapter, we'll integrate
this Polaris environment with a Python Spark environment, enabling you to query
and interact with your data programmatically. This hands-on exploration will bring
everything together, showcasing the power of Polaris in real-world scenarios.

## CHAPTER 7

Using Apache Polaris with Apache Spark

With your experimental Apache Polaris environment successfully set up on your laptop, you're now ready to start exploring its integration with Apache Spark. If you've followed the previous chapter, you should have your environment running and be able to access Jupyter Notebook at *http://localhost:8888*. While we will be working in this local setup, the steps and concepts covered in this chapter are equally applicable to any Spark environment, whether it's a local cluster or a cloud-based setup.

Apache Spark is a powerful, open source, unified analytics engine for processing large-scale data. Its in-memory computation and distributed architecture make it incredibly fast and efficient for handling complex workloads, from batch processing to real-time analytics and machine learning tasks.

In this chapter, we'll dive into the practical steps to connect your Polaris catalog to Spark, explore the Spark DataFrame API, execute SQL queries on Polaris-managed data, and even use Spark Streaming to interact with Polaris in real-time. By the end of this chapter, you'll have a comprehensive understanding of how to harness the combined power of Apache Polaris and Apache Spark in your data workflows. Let's get started!

You can see all these code snippets as well in the book's GitHub repository:

https://github.com/developer-advocacy-dremio/apache-polaris-the-definitive-guide.

Connecting Your Apache Polaris Catalog to Apache Spark

To use Apache Polaris with Apache Spark, you must configure your Spark session to recognize Polaris as a catalog. This setup involves configuring how Spark communicates with your Polaris catalog. These configurations include the catalog type, URI, credentials, and other related properties.

The following is a step-by-step guide to configure Apache Spark for using Polaris as an Iceberg catalog.

To connect Spark to Polaris, you need to set several configuration properties. These properties specify the catalog implementation, credentials, and other details required to access Polaris.

Here's a Python script that illustrates how to configure the Spark session for Polaris:

```
import pyspark
from pyspark.sql import SparkSession

# Define sensitive variables
POLARIS_URI = 'http://polaris:8181/api/catalog'
POLARIS_CATALOG_NAME = 'polariscatalog'
POLARIS_CREDENTIALS = '<principal_clientId>:<principal_clientSecret>'
POLARIS_SCOPE = 'PRINCIPAL_ROLE:ALL'
```

This PySpark snippet initializes some key configuration values needed to connect to a Polaris data catalog. It begins by importing the necessary PySpark modules and creating a SparkSession, which is the entry point for using DataFrame and SQL functionality in Spark. The script then defines several variables that hold sensitive information required to access the Polaris catalog API. POLARIS_URI specifies the endpoint where the Polaris API can be reached, while POLARIS_CATALOG_NAME designates the name of the target catalog. POLARIS_CREDENTIALS contains the client ID and secret for authentication, and POLARIS_SCOPE defines the access scope for the principal.

```
# Set up Spark configuration
conf = (
    pyspark.SparkConf()
        .setAppName('PolarisSparkApp')
        # Add necessary JARs
        .set('spark.jars.packages', 'org.apache.iceberg:iceberg-spark-runtime-
3.5_2.12:1.5.2,org.apache.hadoop:hadoop-aws:3.4.0') ❶
        # Enable Iceberg SQL extensions
        .set('spark.sql.extensions', 'org.apache.iceberg.spark.extensions.
IcebergSparkSessionExtensions') ❷
        # Configure the Polaris catalog
        .set('spark.sql.catalog.polaris',
            'org.apache.iceberg.spark.SparkCatalog') ❸
        .set('spark.sql.catalog.polaris.warehouse', POLARIS_CATALOG_NAME) ❹
        .set('spark.sql.catalog.polaris.catalog-impl',
            'org.apache.iceberg.rest.RESTCatalog') ❺
        .set('spark.sql.catalog.polaris.uri', POLARIS_URI) ❻
        .set('spark.sql.catalog.polaris.credential', POLARIS_CREDENTIALS) ❼
        .set('spark.sql.catalog.polaris.scope', POLARIS_SCOPE) ❽
```

```
        .set('spark.sql.catalog.polaris.token-refresh-enabled', 'true') ❾
)
```

Here's an explanation of the key configuration properties used in the script:

❶ `spark.jars.packages` specifies the required dependencies for Iceberg integration with Spark. This includes the Iceberg runtime library and Hadoop AWS library (if using S3).

❷ `spark.sql.extensions` enables the Iceberg SQL extensions to work with Iceberg tables and namespaces.

❸ `spark.sql.catalog.polaris` defines the catalog name used in SQL queries (e.g., `polaris`).

❹ `Spark.sql.catalog.polaris.warehouse` stores the data that is tracked in the catalog. We will pass the catalog name as the value.

❺ `spark.sql.catalog.polaris.catalog-impl` indicates the catalog implementation type, which is `org.apache.iceberg.rest.RESTCatalog` for Polaris since it is a REST Catalog supporting catalog.

❻ `spark.sql.catalog.polaris.uri` is the REST API endpoint of the Polaris catalog.

❼ `spark.sql.catalog.polaris.credential` is the credentials to authenticate with Polaris. These are principal credentials given in the API response when you create a principal.

❽ `spark.sql.catalog.polaris.scope` specifies the access scope for the credentials.

❾ `spark.sql.catalog.polaris.token-refresh-enabled` automatically refreshes the authentication token as needed.

This portion of the code kicks off the actual execution environment by initializing the Spark session using a predefined configuration object (conf). This configuration likely includes all the necessary settings, such as the Polaris URI, credentials, and catalog name, that were previously set up.

```
# Start the Spark session
spark = SparkSession.builder.config(conf=conf).getOrCreate()
print("Spark session configured for Polaris is running.")

# Test the connection
```

```
print("Listing all available namespaces:")
spark.sql("SHOW NAMESPACES IN polaris").show()
```

By calling `.getOrCreate()`, it either starts a new session or reuses an existing one. Once the session is active, the script prints a confirmation message to indicate that Spark is ready and configured to work with Polaris. To validate the connection, it runs a simple SQL command to list all available namespaces (similar to databases or schemas) within the Polaris catalog, displaying the results in the console. This serves as a quick, effective check to ensure the integration is working correctly.

After starting the Spark session, you can verify the connection to Polaris by running basic SQL commands:

```
# Show all namespaces in the Polaris catalog
spark.sql("SHOW NAMESPACES IN polaris").show()

# Create a new namespace
spark.sql("CREATE NAMESPACE IF NOT EXISTS polaris.db").show()

# List tables in a namespace
spark.sql("SHOW TABLES IN polaris.db").show()
```

If the configuration is correct, these commands will interact with the Polaris catalog and display the corresponding results.

Your Spark session is now connected to Apache Polaris. You can use the Spark DataFrame API and SparkSQL to interact with Polaris-managed data. In the next section, we'll explore how to leverage the Spark DataFrame API for data processing with Polaris.

Using Spark Dataframe API with Apache Polaris (Incubating)

The Spark DataFrame API is a powerful tool for working with structured data, enabling you to create, read, update, and delete tables programmatically. With Apache Polaris configured as a catalog, the DataFrame API makes it easy to interact with your Polaris-managed Iceberg tables. This section walks through these key operations step by step.

Creating a Table

You can create a table programmatically using the DataFrame API. This method lets you define the schema, specify partitioning, and optionally include table properties.

```
# Example: Creating a table using Spark DataFrameWriterV2 API
from pyspark.sql import SparkSession
from pyspark.sql.functions import col, lit
```

```
## ... code for initializing spark session
## & configuring catalog

# Define a DataFrame
data = [
    (1, "Alice", "2023-01-01"),
    (2, "Bob", "2023-01-02"),
    (3, "Charlie", "2023-01-03"),
]
columns = ["id", "name", "event_date"]
df = spark.createDataFrame(data, columns)

# Write the DataFrame to create a new table in Polaris
df.writeTo("polaris.db.events") \
  .partitionedBy("event_date") \
  .tableProperty("write.format.default", "parquet") \
  .create()
```

This code creates a new table, events in the db namespace, partitioned by the event_date column. Data is written in Parquet format by default, as specified in the table properties.

Querying a Table

After creating a table, you can query it using the DataFrame API to perform analytics or retrieve data.

```
# Example: Querying a table
df = spark.table("polaris.db.events")

# Perform operations on the DataFrame
df.show()

# Filter rows based on a condition
filtered_df = df.filter(col("event_date") > lit("2023-01-01"))
filtered_df.show()
```

The spark.table method loads the table as a DataFrame, enabling you to apply filters, transformations, and aggregations.

Updating a Table

You can use the MERGE INTO operation to update rows in a table. This operation enables row-level updates and inserts based on a condition.

```
# Example: Updating a table with MERGE INTO
updates = [
    (1, "Alice Updated", "2023-01-01"),
    (4, "David", "2023-01-04"),
]
updates_df = spark.createDataFrame(updates, columns)
```

```
updates_df.createOrReplaceTempView("updates")

# Perform MERGE INTO operation
spark.sql("""
    MERGE INTO polaris.db.events t
    USING updates u
    ON t.id = u.id
    WHEN MATCHED THEN UPDATE SET t.name = u.name
    WHEN NOT MATCHED THEN INSERT (id, name, event_date) VALUES (u.id, u.name,
    u.event_date)
""")
```

In this example, existing rows are updated, and new rows are inserted if no match is found.

Deleting Rows

Iceberg supports row-level deletion, allowing you to delete rows based on a condition.

```
# Example: Deleting rows from a table
spark.sql("""
    DELETE FROM polaris.db.events
    WHERE event_date < '2023-01-02'
""")
```

This deletes all rows where event_date is earlier than January 2, 2023.

Appending Data

To add new rows to an existing table, use the append method of the DataFrame API.

```
# Example: Appending data to a table
new_data = [
    (5, "Eve", "2023-01-05"),
    (6, "Frank", "2023-01-06"),
]
new_df = spark.createDataFrame(new_data, columns)

new_df.writeTo("polaris.db.events").append()
```

This appends new rows to the events table without modifying existing data.

Reading Metadata Tables

Iceberg tables expose rich metadata through special metadata tables. These can be queried using the DataFrame API for insights into table snapshots, history, and more.

```
# Example: Querying the snapshots metadata table
snapshots_df = spark.table("polaris.db.events.snapshots")
snapshots_df.show()
```

```
# Example: Querying the history metadata table
history_df = spark.table("polaris.db.events.history")
history_df.show()
```

Following these examples, you can effectively manage your Polaris-backed Iceberg tables using the Spark DataFrame API. These operations demonstrate the flexibility and ease of handling data in a Spark environment with a Polaris catalog.

Using SparkSQL with Apache Polaris

SparkSQL provides a declarative way to interact with Apache Polaris-backed Iceberg tables, allowing you to run SQL queries to create, update, delete, and query tables. In this section, we'll explore using the spark.sql function in Python to perform various SQL operations with your Polaris catalog.

Creating a Table

You can create a table in Polaris using the CREATE TABLE SQL statement. This allows you to define a table's schema, partitioning, and table properties.

```
# Example: Creating a table with SparkSQL
spark.sql("""
    CREATE TABLE polaris.db.events (
        id BIGINT,
        name STRING,
        event_date DATE
    )
    USING iceberg
    PARTITIONED BY (event_date)
    TBLPROPERTIES ('write.format.default' = 'parquet')
""")
```

This creates a table events in the db namespace, partitioned by the event_date column and stored in Parquet format.

Querying a Table

With SparkSQL, you can easily query tables to retrieve and analyze data. Use the SELECT statement to fetch data from your Polaris-backed tables.

```
# Example: Querying a table
spark.sql("""
    SELECT *
    FROM polaris.db.events
""").show()

# Example: Querying with filters and aggregations
spark.sql("""
    SELECT event_date, COUNT(*) AS event_count
```

```
    FROM polaris.db.events
    WHERE event_date > '2023-01-01'
    GROUP BY event_date
    ORDER BY event_date
""").show()
```

The show() method displays the query results in the console.

Inserting Data

You can insert data into a table using the INSERT INTO statement.

```
# Example: Inserting data into a table
spark.sql("""
    INSERT INTO polaris.db.events
    VALUES
        (1, 'Alice', '2023-01-01'),
        (2, 'Bob', '2023-01-02'),
        (3, 'Charlie', '2023-01-03')
""")
```

This appends the specified rows to the events table.

Updating Data

To modify existing rows, use the UPDATE statement with a condition.

```
# Example: Updating rows in a table
spark.sql("""
    UPDATE polaris.db.events
    SET name = 'Alice Updated'
    WHERE id = 1
""")
```

This updates the name column for the row where id = 1.

Deleting Data

To remove specific rows from a table, use the DELETE statement.

```
# Example: Deleting rows from a table
spark.sql("""
    DELETE FROM polaris.db.events
    WHERE event_date < '2023-01-02'
""")
```

This deletes all rows where event_date is earlier than January 2, 2023.

Merging Data

The MERGE INTO statement allows you to perform upserts by updating or inserting rows based on a condition.

```
# Example: Merging data into a table
spark.sql("""
    MERGE INTO polaris.db.events t
    USING (
        SELECT 1 AS id, 'Alice Updated' AS name, '2023-01-01' AS event_date
        UNION ALL
        SELECT 4, 'David', '2023-01-04'
    ) u
    ON t.id = u.id
    WHEN MATCHED THEN UPDATE SET t.name = u.name
    WHEN NOT MATCHED THEN INSERT (id, name, event_date) VALUES (u.id, u.name,
    u.event_date)
""")
```

This updates rows with matching `id` values and inserts new rows where no match is found.

Reading Metadata Tables

Polaris-backed Iceberg tables expose metadata tables that provide insights into the table's snapshots, history, lists of data files, partitions and more.

```
# Example: Querying the snapshots metadata table
spark.sql("""
    SELECT *
    FROM polaris.db.events.snapshots
""").show()
```

```
# Example: Querying the history metadata table
spark.sql("""
    SELECT *
    FROM polaris.db.events.history
""").show()
```

These queries allow you to inspect the table's historical changes and snapshots.

Time Travel Queries

Iceberg supports time travel queries, enabling you to access data as it existed at a specific point in time or snapshot.

```
# Example: Querying a table at a specific timestamp
spark.sql("""
    SELECT *
    FROM polaris.db.events
    TIMESTAMP AS OF '2023-01-02 12:00:00'
""").show()
```

```
# Example: Querying a table at a specific snapshot
spark.sql("""
    SELECT *
    FROM polaris.db.events
```

```
    VERSION AS OF 10963874102873
""").show()
```

By using SparkSQL with Polaris, you can leverage the full power of SQL to interact with your Iceberg-backed tables. SparkSQL offers a concise, expressive way to work with your data, whether you're creating tables, querying data, or managing snapshots.

Using Spark Streaming with Apache Polaris

Apache Spark Streaming allows you to process and analyze data in real time. With Apache Polaris (incubating) backing your Iceberg tables, you can ingest streaming data and write it to your Polaris catalog for efficient storage and querying. This section will explore using Spark Structured Streaming with Polaris to perform streaming reads and writes.

Setting Up Spark Streaming with Polaris

To enable Spark Streaming with Polaris, you need to configure the streaming Data-FrameReader and DataFrameWriter appropriately as illustrated in the following code snippets. The configurations will point to your Polaris catalog and specify how streaming data is read and written.

Streaming Reads from Polaris

Iceberg supports incremental data reads from tables, allowing you to process appended data in real time. Use the readStream method to set up a streaming query.

```
# Example: Streaming reads from a Polaris-backed table
from pyspark.sql import SparkSession

# Start a streaming query to read incremental data
streaming_df = (
    spark.readStream
        .format("iceberg")
        .option("stream-from-timestamp", "1640995200000") ❶
  # Start from a specific timestamp (epoch in milliseconds)
        .load("polaris.db.events") ❷
)

# Process the streaming data
query = (
    streaming_df
        .select("id", "name", "event_date")
        .writeStream
        .format("console") ❸
        .outputMode("append")
        .start()
)
```

```
query.awaitTermination()
```

❶ `stream-from-timestamp` specifies the starting point for the stream in epoch milliseconds.

❷ The streaming DataFrame processes appended data in the events table.

❸ The results are displayed in the console.

Streaming Writes to Polaris

Iceberg allows streaming writes to append data to a table. Use the `writeStream` method with the appropriate configuration to persist the data into a Polaris-backed Iceberg table.

```
# Example: Streaming writes to a Polaris-backed table
from pyspark.sql import SparkSession
from pyspark.sql.functions import current_timestamp

# Generate a streaming DataFrame with simulated data
input_stream = (
    spark.readStream
        .format("rate") ❶
        # Simulate 10 rows per second
        .option("rowsPerSecond", 10)
        .load()
        .withColumn("name", lit("Simulated Name"))
        .withColumn("event_date", current_timestamp())
)

# Write the streaming data to a Polaris-backed table
query = (
    input_stream
        .selectExpr("value AS id", "name", "event_date")
        .writeStream ❷
        .format("iceberg")
        .outputMode("append")
        .option("checkpointLocation", "/tmp/checkpoints/events") ❸
        .toTable("polaris.db.events")
)

query.awaitTermination()
```

❶ `rate` is used to simulate a streaming data source, generating rows at a specified rate.

❷ The `writeStream` method appends the processed data into the events table.

③ `checkpointLocation`ensures fault tolerance by storing the streaming job's state.

Handling Deletes and Overwrites

By default, Iceberg does not support processing delete or overwrite snapshots in streaming jobs. However, you can configure Spark to skip these operations by setting specific options:

```
# Example: Handling overwrite and delete snapshots in streaming reads
streaming_df = (
    spark.readStream
        .format("iceberg")
        .option("stream-from-timestamp", "1640995200000")
        .option("streaming-skip-overwrite-snapshots", "true")
        .option("streaming-skip-delete-snapshots", "true")
        .load("polaris.db.events")
)
```

These options ensure that the stream processes only append snapshots, avoiding overwrite or delete operations conflicts.

Using Partitioned Tables

For partitioned Iceberg tables, Spark requires that data is sorted by partition before being written. This ensures efficient storage and metadata handling. You can enable fanout writing to simplify partition management in streaming workloads.

```
# Example: Streaming writes to a partitioned table with fanout
query = (
    input_stream
        .selectExpr("value AS id", "name", "event_date")
        .writeStream
        .format("iceberg")
        .outputMode("append")
        .option("fanout-enabled", "true")  # Automatically handle partitions
        .option("checkpointLocation", "/tmp/checkpoints/partitioned_events")
        .toTable("polaris.db.partitioned_events")
)

query.awaitTermination()
```

Maintaining Streaming Tables

Streaming writes can generate many small files, leading to metadata bloat and decreased query performance. To mitigate this, you should:

Compact small files
    Use the `rewrite_data_files` procedure to merge small files.

Expire old snapshots
> Regularly clean up unnecessary snapshots using snapshot expiration.

Optimize metadata
> Use the `rewrite_manifests` procedure to compact manifest files.

Conclusion

By leveraging Spark Structured Streaming with Polaris, you can seamlessly process and store real-time data in Iceberg-backed tables.

In the next chapter, we'll explore the usage of Apache Polaris with Snowflake whether connecting an externally managed Polaris table or using Snowflake's managed Polaris service, Open Catalog.

## CHAPTER 8

Using Apache Polaris with Snowflake

In this chapter, we explore how to integrate Apache Polaris with Snowflake to query Iceberg tables from Snowflake's platform. We'll walk through setting up Snowflake to connect to a Polaris catalog (either a self-hosted Polaris OSS instance or Snowflake's managed Polaris service, Open Catalog), configuring the necessary external resources, running SQL queries on Polaris-managed Iceberg tables from Snowflake, and understanding the differences between Polaris-backed tables and native Snowflake tables. By the end, you will be able to query Iceberg tables via Snowflake using Polaris as the metadata catalog. You can also appreciate the trade-offs between this approach and Snowflake's native table storage.

You should have a running Apache Polaris service with an Iceberg catalog and at least one table available. This can be a self-hosted Polaris instance (as set up in previous chapters) or the Snowflake Open Catalog. You will also need a Snowflake account with appropriate permissions (ACCOUNTADMIN or ORGADMIN role to create integrations) and access to the cloud storage where the Iceberg data resides.

Establishing Connectivity Between Snowflake and Polaris

To allow Snowflake to query data managed by Apache Polaris, it needs to connect to Polaris's REST Catalog API. Snowflake treats Polaris as an external Iceberg catalog, retrieving table metadata and reading data files from cloud storage. This integration is achieved via two Snowflake objects:

External volume

> An object configuring access to the external cloud storage (e.g., an S3 bucket or Azure Blob container) where the Iceberg table's data and metadata files are stored. The external volume holds the storage location URL and any necessary cloud IAM roles or credentials for Snowflake to access that storage.

Catalog integration

An object that tells Snowflake how to reach the external catalog's REST endpoint and how to authenticate to it. In our case, this integration will point to the Polaris REST API and use OAuth credentials (a *client ID* and *client secret*) for a Polaris service principal. The integration also specifies an *-*/allowed scope* for the OAuth token, which in Polaris defines what access roles the token grants.

Before creating these objects, it is critical to ensure network connectivity from Snowflake to your Polaris service. If you are using Snowflake Open Catalog, Snowflake's Polaris is hosted on Snowflake's infrastructure, so connectivity is handled internally. But if you are connecting to a self-managed Polaris OSS instance, Snowflake must be able to reach Polaris's REST endpoint. This typically means your Polaris API must be accessible over the public internet (e.g., a public EC2 IP or domain or via a public API Gateway). Snowflake cannot directly reach into a private VPC without special networking setups. Some users employ AWS PrivateLink endpoints or similar mechanisms for private connectivity. Still, as of 2025, Snowflake's external catalog integrations generally require a public endpoint unless using SigV4 with an API Gateway for AWS-hosted Polaris. For simplicity, we assume your Polaris API (port 8181) is publicly reachable over HTTPS.

Configuring an External Volume

The first step is to create an external volume in Snowflake. This object represents the cloud storage location of your Iceberg table's data and metadata. You will need the URI of the storage and the appropriate cloud IAM role or keys that Snowflake can use to access it. For example, if your Iceberg data (managed by Polaris) is stored in an Amazon S3 bucket, you might have an AWS IAM role that grants read access to that bucket.

The following code is an example of an S3 bucket (for other clouds, the syntax is similar but uses storage integration or container names as needed). This example requires ACCOUNTADMIN or similar privileges.

```
CREATE OR REPLACE EXTERNAL VOLUME my_iceberg_ext_volume

  STORAGE_LOCATIONS = (

    (

      NAME = 'polaris_s3_storage',
      STORAGE_PROVIDER = 'S3',

      STORAGE_BASE_URL = 's3://<your-bucket-name>/<optional-path-prefix>/',

      STORAGE_AWS_ROLE_ARN = '<ARN-of-IAM-role-with-access>'
```

```
      )
    );
```

This creates an external volume named `my_iceberg_ext_volume` (names are case-insensitive but usually uppercase in Snowflake). The `STORAGE_BASE_URL` points Snowflake to the root folder of the Iceberg dataset in the bucket. The `STOR` `AGE_AWS_ROLE_ARN` is an IAM role Snowflake will assume to access that bucket (Snowflake must have been configured as a trusted principal in that role). On Azure or GCS, you would specify `STORAGE_PROVIDER = 'AZURE'` or `'GCS'` and the corresponding credentials (such as SAS tokens or service account keys) as needed.

Once this is created, you can verify the external volume with a `DESCRIBE` command or by listing it.

```
DESC EXTERNAL VOLUME my_iceberg_ext_volume;
```

```
SHOW EXTERNAL VOLUMES;
```

Make sure the status of the external volume is valid. A common issue is a misconfigured cloud role or a bucket name containing dots ("."), which Snowflake does not support in S3 bucket names due to SSL limitations. Double-check the bucket name and IAM role if you encounter an error at this stage.

Creating a Polaris Catalog Integration

Next, create a *catalog integration* in Snowflake to connect to the Polaris REST Catalog. The integration will store the Polaris endpoint URL and the OAuth client credentials for authentication. You should have the following information from your Polaris setup:

The Catalog REST URI for Polaris
> If you are using Snowflake Open Catalog, this will be a Snowflake domain like *https://<org>.<account>.snowflakecomputing.com/polaris/api/catalog*. If you are using self-hosted Polaris it will be your server's URL (e.g., *https://<your-host>:8181/api/catalog*). Always use HTTPS in production for security.

The Client ID and Client Secret of a Polaris principal that Snowflake will use
> In Snowflake Open Catalog, the client ID/secret corresponds to a *service connection* you create in the Open Catalog UI for Snowflake to use. When self-hosted Polaris starts in dev mode, it prints a root principal's credentials `<client-id>:<client-secret>` in the logs. Creating a dedicated *service principal* in Polaris for Snowflake with limited privileges is recommended.

The OAuth scopes that Snowflake should request
> Polaris uses OAuth 2.0 client credentials flow. The scopes determine what privileges the issued token will have. In Polaris, scopes often tie to principal roles. For example, `'PRINCIPAL_ROLE: ALL'` is a special scope that grants all

roles assigned to that principal. Using `ALL` allows full access to the principal, which is convenient for a read-write service principal. You could also specify a particular principal role name to restrict scope. For our example, we'll use `'PRINCIPAL_ROLE:ALL'` to ensure Snowflake can read all tables the Polaris principal is allowed to.

(Optional) The catalog name or namespace in Polaris that you want Snowflake to use
Polaris can host multiple catalogs internally. If your Polaris server has a single catalog (as in our local OSS setup from Chapter 6), you might not need to specify a name (the integration can default to the *namespace* level).

However, Snowflake's integration supports specifying both `CATALOG_NAME` and `CATALOG_NAMESPACE`:

`CATALOG_NAME`
This is the Polaris catalog identifier (if Polaris has named catalogs).

`CATALOG_NAMESPACE`
This is the default namespace (like a database or schema path) within that catalog to scope operations. If a default is not provided, Snowflake requires fully qualified table names when referencing tables.

```
CREATE OR REPLACE CATALOG INTEGRATION polaris_catalog_int

  CATALOG_SOURCE = POLARIS

  TABLE_FORMAT = ICEBERG

  CATALOG_NAMESPACE = 'default'
  -- If your Polaris has a specific catalog name, you can include:

  -- REST_CONFIG = ( CATALOG_URI = 'https://<polaris-host>/api/catalog',
     CATALOG_NAME = '<yourCatalogName>' )

  REST_CONFIG = (

    CATALOG_URI = 'https://<polaris-host>/api/catalog'  -- Polaris REST endpoint

      -- If using Snowflake Open Catalog, your URI would be
         'https://<org>.<account>.snowflakecomputing.com/polaris/api/catalog'

      -- For Snowflake Open Catalog, also include
         CATALOG_NAME = '<OpenCatalogName>' as provided by Snowflake.

  )

  REST_AUTHENTICATION = (

    TYPE = OAUTH,
```

```
    OAUTH_CLIENT_ID = '<Polaris_client_ID>',

    OAUTH_CLIENT_SECRET = '<Polaris_client_secret>',

    OAUTH_ALLOWED_SCOPES = ( 'PRINCIPAL_ROLE:ALL' )

  )

  ENABLED = TRUE;
```

A few things to note in this command:

- We set `CATALOG_SOURCE = POLARIS` to indicate this integration uses Apache Polaris (Iceberg REST) as the source. Snowflake recognizes Polaris specifically as a type of Iceberg REST catalog.

- `TABLE_FORMAT = ICEBERG` confirms we are dealing with Iceberg table format.

- We provided a `CATALOG_URI` pointing to Polaris. If you are not using the Snowflake-hosted Open Catalog, ensure this is a publicly reachable URL for your Polaris service. Suppose Polaris is running locally (e.g., `localhost:8181`). In that case, Snowflake *will not* be able to reach that: it needs an address to which Snowflake's cloud can connect (consider deploying Polaris on a cloud VM with a public IP or using a tunneling solution for testing).

- We left `CATALOG_NAMESPACE = 'default'` as an example. If your Polaris catalog organizes tables under specific top-level namespaces (like a database name), you could put that here. Otherwise, you can omit `CATALOG_NAMESPACE` and specify the namespace when registering tables (we will show an example in the section Querying Iceberg Tables via Snowflake and Polaris). If using Snowflake Open Catalog, you might set this to the top-level namespace of your Open Catalog (which could be your organization or project name as configured).

- The `OAUTH_CLIENT_ID` and `OAUTH_CLIENT_SECRET` are the credentials Snowflake will use to obtain an OAuth token from Polaris. Snowflake will automatically call Polaris's token endpoint (`/oauth/tokens`) using these credentials to get a bearer token. It will include the `OAUTH_ALLOWED_SCOPES` in that request, so Polaris knows which scopes to grant. Ensure the principal (client) on the Polaris side is configured with the necessary roles and privileges to read the catalog. For read-only access to all tables, the principal should have a Polaris role with `TABLE_LIST` and `TABLE_READ_DATA` privileges on the catalog.

After running the above, you will create a Snowflake integration object. Users with the ACCOUNTADMIN or a custom role with a `CREATE INTEGRATION` privilege can do this. Once created, grant usage on the integration to the role that will query the tables. For example, if you plan to use the SYSADMIN role for querying, run:

```
GRANT USAGE ON INTEGRATION polaris_catalog_int TO ROLE SYSADMIN;
```

Without this grant, if a lesser role tries to use the integration, you might encounter an "SQL access control error: Insufficient privileges to operate on integra tion 'POLARIS_CATALOG_INT'". Granting usage ensures Snowflake roles can utilize the credentials in the integration to access Polaris.

At this point, Snowflake has what it needs to connect to Polaris: knowledge of *where* the Polaris API is and *how* to authenticate it, as well as knowledge of *where* the data files are stored (the external volume). Now, we can proceed to query Iceberg tables through this setup.

A note about security in production: Never use or document development mode cre dentials in production. When Polaris runs in development mode with the in-memory metastore, it prints root credentials as [client-id]:[client-secret]. These cre dentials are for testing only and pose a security risk if used in production.

Follow these steps to configure Polaris for production.

1. Replace Development Defaults to align with production best practices:

```
# Metastore (REQUIRED - replace in-memory)
metaStoreManager:
  type: eclipse-link  # or relational-jdbc

# Storage
defaultRealms:
  - name: production-realm
    allowedLocations:
      - type: s3  # Only S3, GCS, or AZURE
        allowed-locations: ["s3://your-bucket"]

# Authentication
authenticator:
  class: org.apache.polaris.service.auth.DefaultPolarisAuthenticator

# OAuth2
oauth2:
  type: default
```

2. Create a dedicated service principal for Snowflake:

```
# Create service principal
./polaris principals create snowflake_service

# Create roles and grant minimal required privileges
./polaris principal-roles create snowflake_reader
./polaris catalog-roles create --catalog prod_catalog catalog_reader
./polaris privileges --catalog prod_catalog --catalog-role catalog_reader \
  catalog grant TABLE_LIST TABLE_READ_DATA
```

3. Configure Snowflake integration:

```
CREATE CATALOG INTEGRATION polaris_integration
  CATALOG_SOURCE = POLARIS
  TABLE_FORMAT = ICEBERG
  REST_CONFIG = (
    CATALOG_URI = 'https://your-polaris-api.com/api/catalog'
    CATALOG_NAME = 'production_catalog'
  )
  REST_AUTHENTICATION = (
    TYPE = OAUTH
    OAUTH_CLIENT_ID = 'snowflake_service_clientid'
    OAUTH_CLIENT_SECRET = 'secure_client_secret'
    OAUTH_ALLOWED_SCOPES = ('PRINCIPAL_ROLE:snowflake_reader')
  )
  ENABLED = TRUE;
```

Next, you need to configure network security. In this case, we'll use the default public internet access.

1. Get Snowflake IP ranges:

```
SELECT * FROM TABLE(SYSTEM$ALLOWLIST());
```

2. Configure firewall rules:

   - Allow inbound HTTPS (port 443) from Snowflake IPs
   - Implement rate limiting
   - Use valid TLS certificates

3. Monitor changes:

   - Snowflake IP ranges are dynamic and region-specific
   - Regularly update firewall rules

Secure credential management is crucial in production. Make sure to follow these practices:

1. Store credentials in secure vaults (AWS Secrets Manager, Azure Key Vault)

2. Enable credential rotation: `ENFORCE_PRINCIPAL_CREDENTIAL_ROTATION_` `REQUIRED_CHECKING: true`

3. Never log OAuth secrets or bearer tokens

4. Use unique service principals per external service

Finally, you need to configure OAuth2:

```
featureConfiguration:
  ENFORCE_PRINCIPAL_CREDENTIAL_ROTATION_REQUIRED_CHECKING: true
  TOKEN_EXPIRATION_SECONDS: 3600  # 1 hour
```

```
tokenBroker:
  type: symmetric-key  # or asymmetric for RSA
```

Congratulations! You've successfully configured the catalog.

Querying Iceberg Tables via Snowflake and Polaris

With the external volume and catalog integration in place, we can create *Iceberg table references* in Snowflake that use Polaris for metadata. Snowflake's CREATE ICEBERG TABLE command will create a new table or register an existing Iceberg table. In our scenario, we assume the Iceberg tables already exist and are managed by Polaris (Polaris is the source of truth for the metadata). Thus, we will create Snowflake objects pointing to Polaris's tables.

Before creating the table in Snowflake, ensure you have selected a database and schema where the Snowflake table reference will live:

```
USE ROLE SYSADMIN;

USE DATABASE MY_POLARIS_DB;

CREATE SCHEMA IF NOT EXISTS POLARIS_DEMO;

USE SCHEMA POLARIS_DEMO;
```

The database and schema here are in Snowflake and serve as a container for the external Iceberg table reference. You can name them to reflect the Polaris catalog or project you are working with (in this example, MY_POLARIS_DB.POLARIS_DEMO).

Registering an Existing Polaris Table in Snowflake

Let's say the Polaris catalog we connected via the integration contains a table of events in namespace db (as we created in Chapter 7's Spark examples). We want to query this events table in Snowflake. Because Polaris manages this table, Snowflake must know how to access it. We do this by creating an Iceberg table in Snowflake with the CATALOG = 'polaris_catalog_int' (our integration) and linking it to the actual table name in Polaris.

```
CREATE OR REPLACE ICEBERG TABLE events_external

  CATALOG = 'POLARIS_CATALOG_INT'              -- use the Polaris
                                                  catalog integration

  EXTERNAL_VOLUME = 'MY_ICEBERG_EXT_VOLUME'    -- use the external volume for
                                                  storage access

  CATALOG_TABLE_NAME = 'db.events';
```

In this command, `events_external` is the name of the Snowflake table we create (under `MY_POLARIS_DB.POLARIS_DEMO` as set by our USE schema). We could also make it with the same name as the Polaris table (e.g., `events`), but we use the suffix `_external` to distinguish it here. The crucial part is `CATALOG_TABLE_NAME = 'db.events'`. This string should match the namespace and table name in the Polaris catalog.

In Polaris, fully qualified table names are typically `<namespace>.<table>`. If Polaris's catalog has multiple levels of namespace (like `analytics.db.events`), include the full path. If we had specified a `CATALOG_NAMESPACE` in the integration, that namespace would be prepended or assumed. For example, since we used `CATALOG_NAMESPACE = 'default'` in the integration, Snowflake will look for `default.db.events` in Polaris unless the `default` was a top namespace already. To avoid confusion, you can omit `CATALOG_NAMESPACE` in the integration and instead provide the full path here.

Snowflake will contact Polaris via the integration to fetch the table's metadata (schema, partition info, etc.) when this statement runs. It will also verify that the `EXTERNAL_VOLUME` points to the correct storage. If everything is configured correctly, the table will be created quickly. If there is a mismatch or another issue, you may get errors. Some possible errors include:

Table not found
> Snowflake might report it cannot find the specified table in the external catalog. This means either the name is wrong or the Polaris principal used by Snowflake doesn't have access to that table. Double-check the `CATA LOG_TABLE_NAME` and Polaris permissions. Using functions like `SYSTEM$LIST_ICE BERG_TABLES_FROM_CATALOG('POLARIS_CATALOG_INT')` can help list what Polaris tables Snowflake can see.

Region or connectivity errors
> If the external volume's region doesn't match Snowflake's region (Snowflake currently requires the cloud storage to be in the same cloud region for Iceberg tables), creation can fail. Similarly, if the Polaris API is not reachable due to network issues, Snowflake will timeout or error out.

Duplicate or invalid data files
> If Polaris's metadata contains any inconsistencies (such as duplicate data file entries in a manifest), Snowflake may throw an error upon table creation. In such cases, you'd need to fix the data on the Polaris side.

Once the `CREATE ICEBERG TABLE` succeeds, Snowflake will register the external table. *No data is copied* into Snowflake; it's simply a pointer. You can verify the table in Snowflake:

```
SHOW TABLES LIKE 'EVENTS_EXTERNAL';
```

Or, you can check that its table type is Iceberg and externally managed:

```
DESCRIBE TABLE events_external;
```

The output will indicate it's an Iceberg table and list the catalog integration and external volume in the table properties.

Querying the External Iceberg Table

Now comes the fun part: running queries. Since the table is now a first-class table in Snowflake (albeit externally managed), you can run standard SQL queries on it:

```
SELECT

FROM events_external

LIMIT 5;
```

This query will cause Snowflake to plan a query on the Iceberg table. Behind the scenes, Snowflake uses the metadata from Polaris to determine which Parquet files to read, then reads them from the S3 bucket via the external volume. If this is the first query, Snowflake will scan the data from S3. Subsequent queries may benefit from Snowflake's SSD cache of remote data, meaning the performance can improve for repeated access (Snowflake's "use of warehouse cache" is supported for both Snowflake-managed and externally managed Iceberg tables).

You can filter, aggregate, and join external Iceberg tables just like any Snowflake table, as long as the operations are supported. For example:

```
SELECT event_date, COUNT() AS num_events

FROM events_external

WHERE event_date >= '2025-01-01'

GROUP BY event_date

ORDER BY event_date;
```

Snowflake will push down predicates and read only necessary data thanks to Iceberg's metadata (file pruning via manifests). The results are computed by Snowflake's warehouse and returned to you as usual.

One powerful feature to highlight is time travel. You can query historical data because Iceberg and Polaris maintain snapshots. For Snowflake-managed Iceberg tables, Snowflake maintains snapshots itself. Snowflake will know about new snapshots for externally managed tables only when you refresh the table (more on refresh below). If Polaris has snapshots that Snowflake hasn't seen yet, Snowflake can't time travel to them until a refresh syncs them. However, for demonstration, if the table had multiple snapshots and we registered it after several commits, we can do the following.

Suppose we know the snapshot ID or timestamp from Polaris:

```
SELECT

FROM events_external AT (OFFSET => <snapshot-id>);
```

This would retrieve data as it existed in the Iceberg snapshot (if available). If you attempt to time travel to a snapshot that predates Snowflake's knowledge (e.g., older than when you created the table in Snowflake and not yet refreshed), Snowflake might error or return no data.

Automated versus manual metadata refresh

By default, an externally managed Iceberg table in Snowflake does not automatically know about new data appended outside of Snowflake. For example, suppose a Spark job writes new events into the Polaris events table after we create the Snowflake reference. In that case, Snowflake's events_external table will not see those rows until we *refresh* the metadata. You can refresh manually:

```
ALTER ICEBERG TABLE events_external REFRESH;
```

This tells Snowflake to call Polaris and update the table metadata (pull any new snapshots, schema changes, etc.). After a refresh, new data becomes visible to queries. Snowflake has also introduced an AUTO_REFRESH = TRUE table property to let Snowflake periodically refresh the external table in the background, sparing you from manual intervention. This is useful for keeping data in sync, but be mindful of the slight lag and potential cost of repeated metadata fetches.

Read-only behavior of external tables

Understanding that Snowflake *cannot modify data in a Polaris-managed table* is crucial. Any Iceberg table using an external catalog (Polaris, Glue, etc.) is *read-only* from Snowflake's perspective. No INSERT, UPDATE, MERGE, or DELETE SQL statements are allowed on events_external. If you try, you'll get an error. For example:

```
INSERT INTO events_external VALUES (999, 'Test User', '2025-04-01');
```

This will fail with an error:

```
SQL compilation error: Cannot perform DML on an externally managed Iceberg table.
```

This limitation exists because Snowflake is not the system of record for this table's metadata– Polaris is. Allowing Snowflake to write could create inconsistencies. Therefore, treat events_external as a *read-only mirror* of the Polaris table. All writes must happen through Polaris or another engine using Polaris. Once new data is written via Polaris, use REFRESH in Snowflake to see it.

Snowflake's documentation explicitly notes that externally managed Iceberg tables provide limited Snowflake platform support with *read access only*. In contrast, Iceberg tables that use Snowflake as the catalog (managed Iceberg tables) allow full read/write and integrate with Snowflake features.

Querying Polaris metadata from Snowflake

Besides reading the data, you can also list catalog contents via Snowflake. As mentioned, Snowflake provides special table functions to inspect the remote catalog:

`SYSTEM$LIST_ICEBERG_TABLES_FROM_CATALOG('POLARIS_CATALOG_INT')`
    Returns a list of tables Snowflake can see in the Polaris catalog

`SYSTEM$LIST_NAMESPACES_FROM_CATALOG('POLARIS_CATALOG_INT'):`
    Returns namespaces in the Polaris catalog

These can be useful for discovering tables or verifying dynamic connectivity. For example:

```
SELECT

FROM TABLE(SYSTEM$LIST_ICEBERG_TABLES_FROM_CATALOG('POLARIS_CATALOG_INT'));
```

This might output rows with columns like `CATALOG_NAME`, `NAMESPACE`, `TABLE_NAME`, etc., showing each Iceberg table in Polaris that Snowflake has privileges to list.

Another nuance: if Polaris has multiple catalogs and you didn't specify `CATALOG_NAME` in the integration, Snowflake might only target a default one. If needed, you can create multiple integrations, each pointing at different Polaris catalogs (with different URIs or different credentials if separate).

Handling permissions and errors

When integrating across systems, permission issues can arise in multiple places. Let's recap a few and how to address them:

Snowflake integration usage
    As covered in "Creating a Polaris Catalog Integration" on page 145, ensure the Snowflake role used for queries has `USAGE` on both the external volume and the catalog integration. For example: `GRANT USAGE ON EXTERNAL VOLUME my_iceberg_ext_volume TO ROLE SYSADMIN;` and `GRANT USAGE ON INTEGRA TION polaris_catalog_int TO ROLE SYSADMIN;`. If you forget these, errors like "*SQL access control error*" appear.

Polaris OAuth 2.0 scopes and roles
    The Polaris principal's allowed scopes should correspond to a Polaris principal role that has been granted appropriate catalog roles. In Polaris, a *catalog role* defines privileges (like `TABLE_READ_DATA`, `TABLE_LIST`, etc.) at the catalog

level. The principal role that the service connection (Client ID) uses should have a catalog role granting read access to the desired tables. We used `PRINCI PAL_ROLE:ALL` to simplify, which means "grant all privileges of the principal's roles" in the token. In a production setting, you might use a narrower scope like `PRINCIPAL_ROLE:reader_role` if your Polaris admin defined a role only with read permissions.

Cloud storage access
If queries fail with storage errors, it could be that Snowflake's external volume doesn't have permission to read the files. Check that the IAM role can list and get objects on the bucket path. Snowflake provides error details if it can't open files (for example, an AWS `AccessDenied` error).

Data compatibility
Queries might error or return wrong results if the Iceberg table uses features not yet supported by Snowflake (e.g., Iceberg v2 features like row-level deletes or exotic Parquet types). Snowflake currently does not support Iceberg's row-level delete files (position/equality deletes) on external tables. If your Polaris table has such deletes, Snowflake may ignore them or throw an error. Keep an eye on Snowflake release notes for improvements in Iceberg support.

By resolving these issues proactively, you can achieve a smooth integration.

Using Snowflake Open Catalog (Managed Polaris)

Snowflake Open Catalog is essentially Snowflake's hosted version of Polaris, which is offered as a service. If you opt to use Open Catalog instead of running Polaris yourself, the process of integration is similar, with a few differences in setup:

- You would create your Open Catalog account and a catalog within it using Snowflake's UI or APIs. When making a catalog in Open Catalog, you can specify whether it's *External* (managed by another system's metadata, e.g., syncing Snowflake-managed tables to Polaris) or *Internal* (Polaris manages the metadata). In most cases, for new usage, you'll create an Internal catalog in Open Catalog to manage Iceberg metadata centrally.

- Snowflake Open Catalog provides a UI to create *Service Connections*. Each service connection in Open Catalog corresponds to a set of OAuth 2.0 Client ID/ Client secret credentials (with an associated principal role). For Snowflake itself, you would create a service connection (for example, named `snowflake_engi neer`) that Snowflake will use to interface with that catalog. The credentials from this service connection are what you put in the Snowflake integration's `OAUTH_CLIENT_ID` and `OAUTH_CLIENT_SECRET`.

- The `CATALOG_URI` for Open Catalog will be a Snowflake domain, as shown earlier, and you will include `CATALOG_NAME,` which is the name of your Open Catalog catalog resource. Also, ensure the `<orgname>` and account name in the URI are correct (these are found via Snowflake's org and account info).

- One convenient aspect of this service is if Snowflake Open Catalog is in the same Snowflake organization as your main account, network access is not an issue. Snowflake handles it internally. If it's a different region or cloud, you need to set it up accordingly (Open Catalog currently must be in AWS regions for GA).

- Snowflake Open Catalog has a credential vending feature where external engines (such as Spark and Trino) can retrieve temporary credentials to access the catalog using Snowflake as an identity broker. This is beyond our scope, but if you have data scientists who want to use Spark on the same Polaris catalog, they can get credentials without handling long-term secrets. We have already seen Snowflake using an OAuth client flow. Snowflake basically "vends" itself as a token for Polaris using the integration.

From a usage perspective in Snowflake, once the integration is set up, querying an Open Catalog table is identical to the steps in the Querying Iceberg Tables via Snowflake and Polaris section. You'd create an Iceberg table in Snowflake with `CATALOG = '<open_catalog_integration>'` and appropriate `EXTERNAL_VOLUME`. The only difference is that you might make new tables via Snowflake in Open Catalog scenarios and have them appear in Polaris (the reverse of read-only). For instance, Snowflake can create an Iceberg table with `CATALOG_SYNC` property to push it into Polaris (Open Catalog). However, Snowflake *cannot directly create tables in an external catalog* unless it's syncing a Snowflake-managed table. In Open Catalog, a common pattern is:

- Create a Snowflake-managed Iceberg table using Snowflake as a catalog, so it's writable in Snowflake.

- Alter the table to set `CATALOG_SYNC = '<your_open_catalog_integration>'`.

- Any changes Snowflake makes to that table will also appear in the Polaris catalog (Open Catalog). This effectively publishes the table to Polaris so other engines can see it.

- Conversely, suppose you want Snowflake to consume a table primarily managed by Open Catalog (like other engines). In that case, you create it as an externally managed table in Snowflake.

Open Catalog's significant advantage is simplifying governance and sharing. You have one centralized catalog (Polaris) where all Iceberg tables are registered, and Snowflake is just one of the clients (albeit a first-class one). This enables use cases like cross-engine analytics and data sharing more seamlessly. For example, an organization can produce data in Snowflake, sync it to Open Catalog, and a partner can consume it with Spark or Dremio, all while everyone is looking at the same table data and snapshots.

One thing to note: Snowflake Open Catalog (Polaris) has its own RBAC system (the Polaris roles we discussed). This is separate from Snowflake's internal RBAC. When Snowflake queries Polaris, it does so as a service principal with specific Polaris roles. Polaris can enforce different permissions if another engine uses a different service principal. This means data access control can be managed within Polaris itself across all engines.

However, Snowflake's role-based policies (like row access policies or data masking) do *not* automatically apply to data when read outside Snowflake. And vice versa, Polaris's access rules won't apply within Snowflake beyond what tables Snowflake can see. Remember this "dual security layer." Snowflake controls who can create or query an external table object, and Polaris controls which table external catalog credentials can access.

The steps to query are nearly the same, and the limitations (read-only for external tables) still apply when Snowflake is *not* the catalog. The benefit is ease of setup and integrated management if you're a Snowflake customer.

Polaris-Backed Tables vs. Native Snowflake Tables

Snowflake now supports multiple ways to manage data: the traditional Snowflake tables (with data in Snowflake's proprietary storage format), Snowflake-managed Iceberg tables, and externally managed Iceberg tables (Polaris-backed or other catalogs). It's essential to understand how Polaris-backed Iceberg tables differ from Snowflake's native tables so you can choose the right approach for your use case.

Data storage and control
> In Snowflake native tables, data is stored inside Snowflake's compressed proprietary micro-partition format. With Polaris-backed tables, data lives in an open format (Parquet) in your cloud storage. This gives you control and portability: multiple engines can read/write that data outside Snowflake. It also decouples storage from Snowflake, which can be cost-effective and avoids vendor lock-in for the data files. The tradeoff is that you are responsible for the data lifecycle (compaction, retention) since Snowflake won't manage that for external data.

Metadata catalog
> Snowflake native tables use Snowflake's internal metadata store with all the rich time-travel and optimization features Snowflake offers. A Polaris-backed table uses the Polaris catalog for metadata. You get Iceberg's capabilities (schema evolution, hidden partitioning, snapshot isolation) and Polaris's multi-engine visibility. However, Snowflake's additional features may not be supported at all.

For instance, Snowflake Time Travel (AS OF queries up to 90 days) and zero-copy cloning are not supported on external Iceberg tables. You rely on Iceberg's time travel via snapshots instead. Features like Dynamic Tables (materialized views) and database replication currently do not support external Iceberg tables. Essentially, feature parity is not 100%. Snowflake-managed tables have the edge in integration with Snowflake's ecosystem.

Write capabilities

The most significant difference is that Polaris-backed tables are read-only from Snowflake. If your workflow requires Snowflake to insert or update data routinely, an external table won't suffice. You would use Snowflake-managed Iceberg tables, which allow Snowflake to write, or write via another engine, into Polaris. This is a key factor in deciding whether to use Polaris integration. If you need a two-way street (Snowflake both reads and writes), consider Snowflake-managed Iceberg tables with CATALOG_SYNC to Polaris. That way, Snowflake can write and then share those writes via Polaris for others to read. You can also simply stick to Snowflake's native storage for heavy DML use cases.

Performance

Query performance for Polaris-backed Iceberg tables in Snowflake has been surprisingly strong. Snowflake can leverage local caching and its optimized engine to query Parquet nearly as fast as its storage in many cases. Native tables still have an advantage for small point queries and scenarios where Snowflake's optimizer can use clustering or other data statistics that external formats don't provide. Also, the first query on external data may be slower due to cold reads from cloud storage, whereas native data might already be optimized in SSD.

Maintenance and consistency

Snowflake native tables are fully managed. Snowflake handles vacuuming deleted data, clustering, and consistency. With an external Polaris catalog, you must maintain the Iceberg data (expire old snapshots to free space and compact small files if needed). Polaris provides APIs to manage these, but it's a DIY effort or requires running maintenance jobs. Additionally, with multiple writers (say Spark and Snowflake both writing to the same Polaris table via different means), you need to consider transaction isolation. Iceberg is ACID compliant, but each engine must use proper commit protocols through Polaris to avoid conflicts. Snowflake doesn't use multi-writers on an external catalog; it's essentially read-only, so consistency is primarily external.

Use cases

Use Polaris-backed tables when interoperability is a top priority, e.g., sharing lakehouse storage between Snowflake and other platforms (Spark, Flink, Presto, etc.). It shines in data-sharing scenarios across organizations using open formats and when you want to offload specific workloads from Snowflake to other engines (for cost or specialization reasons) while still querying the same source of truth. On the other hand, use Snowflake native tables when you need the full suite of Snowflake features and high concurrency of writes within Snowflake.

Apache Polaris integration brings Snowflake into the open data ecosystem: you're no longer siloed into Snowflake's storage. You can maintain an open lakehouse where Snowflake is one of many consumers and producers of data. The decision boils down to flexibility vs. simplicity. Polaris offers flexibility and openness, while Snowflake native tables offer simplicity and deeper feature integration.

Conclusion

This chapter demonstrated how to connect Snowflake with Apache Polaris (incubating) to query Iceberg tables. We covered configuring Snowflake's external volume and catalog integration for Polaris, creating external Iceberg table references, and running queries. We also touched on using Snowflake's Open Catalog service, which simplifies the setup by hosting Polaris for you. Finally, we compared Polaris-backed tables with Snowflake's native tables to clarify when each approach makes sense.

By integrating Polaris with Snowflake, you unlock open data architecture possibilities: data can be ingested by one system and analyzed by another without cumbersome export/import, all thanks to Iceberg's open format and Polaris's REST catalog. You can leverage Snowflake's powerful query engine on data that lives outside its walled garden, achieving interoperability without sacrificing performance. This is a significant step toward the lakehouse vision of unified data across platforms.

As Apache Polaris continues to evolve and Snowflake expands its Iceberg support, we expect even more capabilities to become available, such as write support, broader feature compatibility, and richer cross-engine collaboration features.

In the next chapter, we will explore using Apache Polaris with Dremio, examining how Polaris enables a consistent experience across different tools in the data ecosystem.

Using Apache Polaris with Dremio

In this chapter, we explore how to integrate Apache Polaris with Dremio, a high-performance intelligent data lakehouse platform. Dremio has robust support for Apache Polaris, being one of the co-creators of the project along with Snowflake. By connecting Dremio to Polaris, you can query and create Apache Iceberg tables managed by Polaris as the metadata authority, while Dremio serves as the execution engine accessing data on cloud storage. This enables a seamless lakehouse architecture where Polaris handles table metadata (schemas, snapshots, partition info, etc.) and Dremio handles query processing and query federation, allowing you to join your Iceberg tables with data in other databases, data lakes, and data warehouses in a governed semantic layer (as illustrated in Figure 9-1). We will cover setting up the connection in Dremio, configuring authentication and storage properties, and using Dremio SQL to work with Polaris-managed Iceberg tables. All examples assume you have a Polaris service running with a catalog created and accessible via its REST API and Dremio Enterprise Edition version 26.0 or later. You can try Dremio by visiting *https://www.dremio.com/get-started*. Dremio Enterprise Edition also has its own integrated Iceberg catalog powered by Apache Polaris, making it another option for a managed Polaris catalog along with the Snowflake Open Catalog.

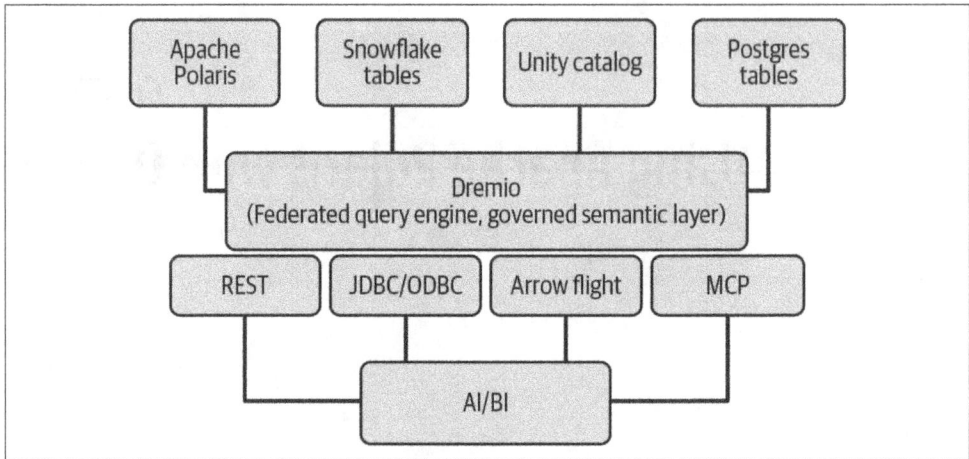

Figure 9-1. Dremio enables you to federate queries between your Polaris managed tables with data in databases, data warehouses and data lakes into a governed semantic layer accessible to all workloads

Connecting Dremio to an Apache Polaris Catalog

A key benefit of Dremio's open lakehouse architecture is its ability to openly integrate seamlessly with the vast ecosystem of Iceberg catalogs along with its own integrated Iceberg catalog. This allows Dremio to act as a powerful, high-performance query engine unifying your Apache Iceberg catalogs along with other data in databases, data warehouses and data lakes.

In this section, we'll explore how to connect Dremio to Apache Polaris in two ways, via the Apache Iceberg REST Catalog connector for self-managed Polaris and the Snowflake Open Catalog connector specifically for Snowflake's Open Catalog. These integrations enable Dremio to discover, query, and even write Iceberg tables governed by an external catalog—opening the door to federated analytics across cloud object stores, databases, and lakehouse systems. Whether you're working with Polaris OSS or Snowflake's enterprise catalog service, Dremio provides native connectors that simplify configuration and allow you to bring your Iceberg tables into a unified SQL interface.

Connecting Polaris Using the REST Catalog Connector

Before using Dremio with Polaris, ensure you have the following prerequisites ready:

Polaris service URL
> The URL where your Polaris service is running (for example, `http://<polaris-host>:8181/api/catalog`).

Polaris credentials
> A Polaris principal (client) with access to the catalog, including its Client ID and Client Secret for authentication. Dremio will use these to authenticate to Polaris's REST API.

Cloud storage access
> The Iceberg tables managed by Polaris reside in cloud object storage (e.g., AWS S3). If Polaris is not configured to vend temporary credentials for storage, you will need the storage access keys (for S3, an AWS Access Key and Secret Key) that allow Dremio to read/write the data files.

With these in hand, we can configure Dremio to connect to Polaris. Dremio introduces a generic Iceberg REST Catalog connector (there is also a dedicated connector for Snowflake's Open Catalog). This connector is found under the Lakehouse Catalogs category in Dremio's Add Source dialog.

The following sections describe how to set up the connection.

Add a new source

In the Dremio web UI, navigate to the Datasets page. Click the Add Source button (usually a + icon next to "Sources"). In the Add Data Source dialog, select Iceberg REST Catalog under the *Lakehouse Catalogs* section. This will open the *New Iceberg REST Catalog Source* configuration screen.

General settings

On the General tab, provide a Name for this source. Choose a unique, descriptive name (for example, PolarisCatalog). This name will be used as the reference in SQL queries. Next, for the Endpoint URI, enter the Polaris catalog service URL (e.g., `http://localhost:8181/api/catalog`). This URL should point to the base API endpoint of Polaris. Leave "Use vended credentials" unchecked for Polaris OSS. By default, Dremio enables "Use vended credentials", which attempts to obtain temporary storage credentials from the catalog service.

Advanced Options

Switch to the Advanced Options tab. Here we will supply the necessary catalog properties and credentials for Polaris and S3. In the Catalog Properties section, add the following key-value pairs:

- `warehouse = Polaris Catalog Name` (the name of your Polaris catalog, e.g., `my_catalog`). This tells Dremio which Polaris catalog to use for table metadata.

- `scope = PRINCIPAL_ROLE:ALL`. This property ensures Polaris grants the client full access scope. It is required by Polaris's security model to authorize the principal's role(s) for all operations.

- `fs.s3a.aws.credentials.provider = org.apache.hadoop.fs.s3a`.

- `SimpleAWSCredentialsProvider`. This setting instructs Dremio's Iceberg connector to use a simple AWS key/secret authentication for S3. It's a required property when providing static S3 keys if choosing not to use credential vending.

Advanced options: Catalog credentials

Still in Advanced Options, under Catalog Credentials, add the sensitive keys:

- `fs.s3a.access.key = Your AWS Access Key ID` (for the S3 bucket that houses the Iceberg data). Needed only if not using credential vending.

- `fs.s3a.secret.key = Your AWS Secret Access Key`. Needed only if not using vended credentials.

- `credential` = Polaris Client ID and Secret in the format `<client_id>:<client_secret>`.

> Dremio uses this combined credential string to authenticate with the Polaris REST Catalog. For example, if your Polaris client ID is `polaris_user` and the secret is `ABC123`, you would enter `polaris_user:ABC123` as the credentials. This will typically be sent as an authorization header to Polaris, such as Basic Auth or Bearer token, depending on Polaris's implementation.

Save the source

After filling in the above, click Save or Add. Dremio will attempt to connect to the Polaris service using the provided endpoint and credentials. If the configuration is correct, the source will be created successfully. You should see the new source (e.g., PolarisCatalog) in the Sources list, and you can expand it to browse the databases/namespaces and tables within the Polaris catalog.

While you can use the REST Catalog connector to connect to Snowflake Open Catalog as well, there is a dedicated connector that eliminates many of these steps. You can find more detail on this option in the Dremio documentation (*https://oreil.ly/KcAXe*).

Here is a summary example of the key Advanced settings for a Polaris OSS catalog on S3 (for illustration if you are not using vended credentials):

```
# Example Advanced Options for Dremio Iceberg REST Catalog (Polaris OSS on S3)

# Polaris catalog name
warehouse=my_catalog

# Polaris security scope for the principal
scope=PRINCIPAL_ROLE:ALL

# use access/secret keys
fs.s3a.aws.credentials.provider=org.apache.hadoop.fs.s3a.
SimpleAWSCredentialsProvider

fs.s3a.access.key=AKIA...
# AWS Access Key ID (replace with yours)
# AWS Secret Key (replace with yours)
fs.s3a.secret.key=wJalrXUtnF...

# Polaris client_id:client_secret for auth
credential=polaris_user:ABC123
```

Click "Test Connection" to ensure that the catalog is successfully added.

Make sure to replace the example values (catalog name, keys, IDs, etc.) with those from your environment. Once this configuration is saved, Dremio will establish the connection to Polaris. If Polaris requires HTTPS and valid certificates (for instance, Snowflake's managed Polaris Open Catalog requires TLS), ensure your endpoint URI and Polaris setup meet those requirements. In our example with Dremio and Polaris OSS, a local or HTTP endpoint is used for simplicity.

Connecting Snowflake's Open Catalog to Dremio

In addition to Apache Polaris, Dremio also supports connecting to Snowflake Open Catalog, Snowflake's managed Polaris service. This enables you to query Iceberg tables registered in internal or external Snowflake catalogs and write to external catalogs directly from Dremio. This integration extends the open lakehouse approach by letting you work with Iceberg metadata managed by Snowflake using Dremio's SQL interface.

Before you begin, make sure you have the following from your Snowflake environment:

- The Catalog Service URI (the REST API endpoint of the catalog)
- A Client ID and Client Secret for authentication
- (Optional) Cloud storage credentials if you're not using Snowflake's vended credentials feature

Use the steps in the following sections to connect Dremio to the Snowflake Open Catalog.

Add a new source

In the Dremio UI, navigate to the Datasets page. Under the Sources panel on the left, click the Add Source icon (typically a + symbol). In the Add Data Source dialog, choose Snowflake Open Catalog from the Lakehouse Catalogs section.

General settings

In the General tab of the configuration dialog:

- Provide a unique and descriptive name for the source, such as `Snowflake0 Catalog`. This name will be used in SQL to reference tables.

- Specify the Endpoint URI, which is the catalog service URI provided by Snowflake.

- Enter the Client ID and Client Secret. These are used for OAuth-style authentication to the Snowflake Open Catalog.

- By default, "Use vended credentials" is enabled. When enabled, Dremio requests short-lived storage access tokens from Snowflake, removing the need to manually manage cloud storage credentials.

- Optionally, you can configure Allowed Namespaces to limit which parts of the catalog Dremio will expose. Namespaces can be nested, and you can choose to include all sub-namespaces.

Advanced options

In the Advanced Options tab, you can supply catalog properties and credentials if you're not using vended credentials.

Depending on your cloud provider, use one of the supported storage authentication methods:

- Amazon S3 (static keys)
  - `fs.s3a.aws.credentials.provider = org.apache.hadoop.fs.s3a.Simple AWSCredentialsProvider`
  - `fs.s3a.access.key = <your_access_key>`
  - `fs.s3a.secret.key = <your_secret_key>`
- Amazon S3 (assumed role)
  - `fs.s3a.assumed.role.arn = arn:aws:iam::...:role/...`
  - `fs.s3a.aws.credentials.provider = com.dremio.plugins.s3.store.STS CredentialProviderV1`

- Azure Storage (OAuth)
  - `fs.azure.account.auth.type = OAuth`
  - `fs.azure.account.oauth2.client.id = <your_client_id>`
  - `fs.azure.account.oauth2.client.endpoint = https://login.microsoft online.com/<tenant_id>/oauth2/token`
  - `fs.azure.account.oauth2.client.secret = <your_client_secret>`
- Google Cloud Storage (GCS)
  - To use default credentials: `dremio.gcs.use_keyfile = false`
  - To use keyfile authentication, provide values such as `dremio.gcs.privateKey`, `projectId`, `clientEmail`, and others.

These credentials enable Dremio to read and write data files in your cloud object store if vended credentials are not used.

You can also adjust caching behavior here. Enabling asynchronous and local caching improves performance for large Parquet scans by reducing roundtrips to cloud storage.

Reflection refresh settings

Use this tab to configure Reflection refresh policies—settings that control how Dremio's *Reflections* are maintained. Reflections are Dremio's intelligent, query-accelerating materializations: they are physically optimized representations of your datasets (such as Iceberg tables) that Dremio uses to speed up query execution behind the scenes. Unlike traditional materialized views, Reflections are decoupled from your SQL and automatically substituted into queries by Dremio's optimizer when they match the logical intent of the query.

In this tab, you can define how often Reflections should be refreshed to ensure they stay up to date with the underlying data, set expiration times after which they are considered stale and purged, and configure custom schedules that align with your data update cycles. Tuning these settings helps balance performance gains from faster queries with the operational cost of maintaining fresh materializations.

Metadata settings

This tab allows you to configure metadata discovery intervals and dataset detail refresh timing. You can define how often Dremio checks for new tables or updates schema information. By default, Dremio fetches object names every hour and expires metadata after three hours.

Privileges

Optionally, grant privileges to specific users or roles. This defines who can query or manage the Snowflake Open Catalog source in Dremio. Use the UI to add users or roles and assign the appropriate checkboxes for access control.

Save and validate

Once all the required fields are filled in, click Save. Dremio will attempt to connect to the catalog using the provided credentials. If successful, the Snowflake Open Catalog will appear in the list of sources. You can now expand it to browse namespaces and query Iceberg tables using SQL. For example:

```
SELECT *
FROM SnowflakeOCatalog.analytics.customers
LIMIT 10;
```

Note that Dremio requires fully qualified table references: `<Source>.<Namespace>.<Table>`.

Updating and deleting a source

To update the configuration, right-click the source name in the Sources panel and choose Settings, or open the source and click the gear icon. You can modify most settings except the source name.

To delete a source, right-click it and choose Delete. Be aware that deleting a source breaks any views or dashboards that reference its tables.

Using Snowflake Open Catalog with Dremio allows you to bring governed Iceberg metadata from Snowflake into your federated lakehouse environment. This setup promotes interoperability, lets you read and write Iceberg tables via a common REST interface, and ensures consistent data access across engines like Dremio, Spark, and others.

For more details, see the official Dremio documentation on Snowflake Open Catalog (*https://oreil.ly/ExM3_*).

Why Disable Use Vended Credentials?

When Dremio v26 or later connects to a Polaris OSS catalog, leave the use vended credentials setting turned on. In that mode, Polaris follows the Iceberg REST specification and returns two things in the same API call: the table's metadata and a short-lived, table-scoped storage token (for example, an AWS STS credential). Dremio consumes this token to read the data files, then discards it when it expires, eliminating any need to store long-term S3 keys in the engine. The switch should be disabled only when you must work with a client or operation that does not yet understand vended tokens.

Using Dremio SQL with Apache Polaris

After successfully adding Polaris as an Iceberg REST Catalog source in Dremio, you can interact with Polaris-managed tables through Dremio's SQL interface. In the Dremio UI, the Polaris source will appear much like any other source: you can expand it to see namespaces and the tables within them. This section covers how to work with your Polaris managed Apache Iceberg tables in Dremio SQL. We will emphasize the importance of fully qualified names and clarify what operations are supported.

Querying Iceberg Tables via Polaris

Once connected, Dremio can query Iceberg tables registered in Polaris just as it would query any other table, with one key difference: you must reference the table by a *fully qualified identifier* that includes the Polaris source and namespace. Dremio does not assume a default catalog for SQL commands, so every table reference should start with the source name you gave (e.g., `PolarisCatalog`), followed by the Polaris namespace (database) and table name. The general form is:

```
<SourceName>.<Namespace>.<TableName>
```

For example, if you have an Iceberg table `customers` in namespace `sales` inside the Polaris catalog, and your Dremio source is named `PolarisCatalog`, you would query it as:

```
SELECT *
FROM PolarisCatalog.sales.customers
LIMIT 10;
```

This query will fetch data via Dremio from the `customers` table. Under the hood, Dremio asks Polaris for the table's metadata (schema, snapshot pointers, etc.) over the REST API, then reads the actual data files (Parquet/ORC) from the cloud storage location indicated by that metadata. Polaris acts purely as the metadata authority, while Dremio is the execution engine scanning the files.

You can join Polaris tables with other data sources in Dremio as well. For instance, if you have another source (say, a CSV or a different database), you could do a join between a Polaris-backed table and that source. Dremio will handle query planning and execution across these sources, giving you the ability to combine Iceberg tables with other datasets.

Querying the Iceberg Metadata Tables

While querying table data is a core part of most analytics workflows, understanding what's happening under the hood can be just as important, especially when working with Iceberg tables in a lakehouse architecture. Fortunately, Dremio provides built-in support for querying Iceberg metadata tables using special functions, allowing you to inspect snapshots, file layouts, partition stats, manifest lists, and more. This is particularly useful for debugging, optimizing query performance, auditing table history, or simply understanding how your data is evolving over time.

When using Dremio with an Apache Polaris catalog, you can take advantage of these metadata queries by referencing the Polaris-backed Iceberg tables via fully qualified names, just as you would in standard queries. The key difference is that instead of selecting from the table directly, you use Dremio's `TABLE()` function with one of the Iceberg metadata inspection functions like `table_files()`, `table_history()`, or `table_snapshot()`.

The following are several metadata views you can query, along with practical examples using a Polaris table.

Inspecting data files with table_files()

This function allows you to see every data file that makes up the current state of a table, including file paths, sizes, record counts, and min/max statistics for each column:

```
SELECT *
FROM TABLE(table_files('PolarisCatalog.sales.orders'))
```

This can be helpful for understanding how data is partitioned and distributed, especially when investigating skew or performance bottlenecks.

Viewing table history with table_history()

If you want to trace how a table evolved over time, use the `table_history()` function. It shows a list of all snapshots that were committed to the table, including timestamps and snapshot lineage:

```
SELECT *
FROM TABLE(table_history('PolarisCatalog.sales.orders'))
```

You can filter on `snapshot_id` or `made_current_at` to see when major updates occurred, which is useful when comparing different versions of a table or implementing time travel.

Getting snapshot metadata with table_snapshot()

The `table_snapshot()` function returns detailed metadata for each snapshot, including what operation was performed (e.g., append, overwrite), and the associated manifest list:

```
SELECT *
FROM TABLE(table_snapshot('PolarisCatalog.sales.orders'))
```

Pair this with `AT SNAPSHOT` or `AT TIMESTAMP` queries to perform reproducible point-in-time analytics on Polaris-managed Iceberg tables.

Listing manifest files with table_manifests()

To go one level deeper and inspect how data files are grouped and referenced in the table's metadata, use the `table_manifests()` function:

```
SELECT *
FROM TABLE(table_manifests('PolarisCatalog.sales.orders'))
```

Manifest files are the building blocks of Iceberg metadata trees, and analyzing them helps reveal how incremental changes (like new inserts or deletes) affect metadata size and structure.

Analyzing partitions with table_partitions()

Use this function to get record counts, file counts, and partition values for each partition in the table. It's helpful for assessing data distribution and whether partition pruning is likely to be effective during query execution:

```
SELECT *
FROM TABLE(table_partitions('PolarisCatalog.sales.orders'))
```

You can use this to identify imbalanced partitions, unused partition columns, or unnecessary small files.

Monitoring table clustering with clustering_information()

For Iceberg tables that have been optimized with clustering, Dremio can report on clustering health using this function:

```
SELECT *
FROM TABLE(clustering_information('PolarisCatalog.sales.orders'))
```

This output includes clustering keys and a clustering depth metric, which reflects how well the data aligns with your clustering strategy. Lower values (approaching 1) suggest more efficient clustering.

Together, these metadata functions allow you to treat Iceberg tables not just as sources of data but also as transparent, inspectable objects. WithPolaris managing your table metadata and Dremio acting as the query engine, the resulting level of observability makes it easier to diagnose issues, monitor table health, and tune your data layout for performance—all using SQL.

In practice, these queries are especially useful for:

- Auditing changes and understanding snapshot lineage
- Identifying problematic files or skewed partitions

- Debugging unexpected query performance issues
- Validating creating tables as the result of a query or ingestion workflows
- Implementing time travel or rollback logic

Because Polaris is Iceberg REST-compliant, Dremio's metadata query support applies seamlessly, offering the same metadata inspection tools you would expect from any Iceberg-native environment.

Creating Tables and CTAS in Polaris via Dremio

One of the powerful features of Dremio is that it reads not only Polaris-managed tables but also creates new tables in the Polaris catalog. Dremio supports creating empty tables and creating tables as the result of a query when using an Iceberg REST Catalog source. You can use Dremio's SQL to define new Iceberg tables in Polaris or ingest data from other sources into Polaris-managed Iceberg format.

Creating an empty table

You can create an Iceberg table in Polaris by running a standard `CREATE TABLE` command in Dremio, with the fully qualified name of the target table. For example, to create a new table called `new_orders` in the `sales` namespace of Polaris:

```
CREATE TABLE PolarisCatalog.sales.new_orders (
    order_id BIGINT,
    customer_id INT,
    order_date DATE,
    total_amount DOUBLE
);
```

This will instruct Polaris to create a new Iceberg table named `new_orders` with the specified schema. No data is inserted yet—the table is empty. You should see this table appear in the Dremio source browser under `PolarisCatalog > sales > new_orders`. The metadata for `new_orders` lives in Polaris (and its backing metastore/database), and if you check your S3 bucket, Polaris will have created a directory for this table's data and metadata (even though no data files exist yet, there will be an Iceberg metadata file and folder structure).

Create Table as Select (CTAS)

Dremio also allows creating a new Polaris table from the results of a query. This is done with the `CREATE TABLE ... AS SELECT ...` syntax. For instance, suppose you have an existing dataset called `orders` in Polaris (or even in another Dremio source) and you want to create a summarized table in Polaris. You could run:

```
CREATE TABLE PolarisCatalog.sales.high_value_orders AS
SELECT customer_id, COUNT(*) as order_count, MAX(total_amount) as max_order
```

```
FROM PolarisCatalog.sales.orders
WHERE total_amount > 1000
GROUP BY customer_id;
```

This single SQL statement will perform a query filtering orders for high-value orders and aggregating by customer and write the results into a new Iceberg table called high_value_orders in the sales namespace, managed by Polaris. Under the covers, Dremio executes the SELECT portion, then commits the output as a new Iceberg table via Polaris's REST API. The new table's files (Parquet data files and Iceberg metadata) will be written to the cloud storage location defined by Polaris for the sales.high_value_orders table. After completion, high_value_orders is an Iceberg table fully tracked in Polaris—any engine connected to the same Polaris catalog (Spark, Trino, etc.) could now also see this new table and query it.

Dremio's support for CTAS on Iceberg REST catalogs means you can use it to ingest data into your Polaris catalog from a variety of sources. For example, you might use Dremio to pull data from an external SQL database or a JSON file and then use CTAS to land it as an Iceberg table via Polaris. This can be a convenient way to populate your data lakehouse tables.

Adding Data from Files to a Table Using Copy Into

In many data lakehouse workflows, raw files, whether CSVs from partners, JSON logs from applications, or Parquet files from upstream processes, must be ingested into structured Iceberg tables. With Dremio, you can use the COPY INTO SQL command to load data directly into Iceberg tables in any catalog from files cloud object storage. This eliminates the need for external Spark jobs or ETL tools for simple data loading tasks.

The COPY INTO command works with any Iceberg table registered in a REST catalog, including those managed by Apache Polaris. You specify the target table, the source location (within a Dremio-connected source), and optional file-level filters, format declarations, or transformation clauses.

Let's see an example:

```
COPY INTO PolarisCatalog.sales.my_table
FROM '@MySource/path/to/files/'
FILE_FORMAT 'csv'
```

This will scan all files in the specified directory and attempt to insert the data into the my_table table registered in the Polaris catalog. You can also specify file names, regular expression (regex) patterns, format-specific options, and transformation logic to fine-tune the ingestion process.

Practical examples

The following sections provide some practical examples.

Load all files in a folder (e.g., JSON logs).   In this example we see all JSON files in a particular folder get loaded into the `web_events` table:

```
COPY INTO PolarisCatalog.logs.web_events
FROM '@CloudSource/logs/2024-01/'
FILE_FORMAT 'json'
```

Load a subset of files using a regex.   You don't always need to load every file in a folder into a table; you can specify only certain files by using a regular expression (regex) to allow Dremio to know which files to use based on the filename pattern:

```
COPY INTO PolarisCatalog.sales.daily_orders
FROM '@S3Data/orders/2023/'
REGEX '.*_2023-12-.*\\.csv'
FILE_FORMAT 'csv'
```

Specify CSV format options and error handling.   CSV files can have diverse delimiters or inconsistent formatting. To deal with this, the COPY INTO command has different commands to customize how CSV files are read such as "what is the delimiter?" and how to handle errors in the file formatting:

```
COPY INTO PolarisCatalog.hr.employees
FROM '@S3Bucket/hr_data/'
FILES ('new_hires.csv')
(FILE_FORMAT 'csv', FIELD_DELIMITER '|', ON_ERROR 'continue', NULL_IF ('NA'))
```

Transform and reorder fields during ingest.   This example parses a CSV file and maps columns to the target Iceberg table's schema, performing inline transformations using standard SQL expressions:

```
COPY INTO PolarisCatalog.sales.transactions(city, zip, sale_date, price)
FROM (
  SELECT SUBSTR(t.$2, 1, 20), t.$1, t.$5, CAST(t.$4 AS DOUBLE)
  FROM '@S3Bucket/sales/jan2024/sales.csv' t
)
FILE_FORMAT 'csv'
```

Supported file formats and options

Dremio supports ingesting data from files in CSV, JSON, or Parquet formats. The file format can be auto-detected from extensions or explicitly defined using the `FILE_FORMAT` clause. Each format supports its own set of parsing and error-handling options, such as:

- FIELD_DELIMITER, QUOTE_CHAR, and ESCAPE_CHAR for CSV
- NULL_IF, EMPTY_AS_NULL, and TRIM_SPACE for both CSV and JSON
- ON_ERROR behavior for all formats (abort, continue, or skip_file)

These options let you gracefully handle messy or inconsistent data files without failing the entire ingestion job.

Monitoring and debugging COPY INTO jobs

After running a COPY INTO command, Dremio will report the number of rows inserted and any rejected records. You can view the ingestion job history and error details using Dremio's built-in system tables.

To inspect rejected records, query the job history for errors:

```
SELECT *
FROM sys.copy_errors_history
WHERE table_name = 'sales.transactions'
Then, drill into a specific job using the copy_errors() function:
SELECT *
FROM TABLE(copy_errors('PolarisCatalog.sales.transactions', 'job_id_here'))
```

This ability to easily view failed records helps troubleshoot ingest problems without rerunning large loads or manually parsing log files.

Maintaining Your Iceberg Tables with Dremio

Like any data system, Apache Iceberg tables require regular maintenance to stay performant and cost efficient. Over time, as tables accumulate new snapshots and increasing numbers of small files, queries can slow down and storage usage can grow unnecessarily. Dremio provides two SQL-based commands, VACUUM and OPTIMIZE, to help you manage the lifecycle and layout of your Iceberg tables directly from within your SQL interface.

If you're using a self-managed Polaris catalog or connecting to Snowflake Open Catalog, you can manually run these maintenance operations at any time. However, if your table is managed through Dremio's integrated catalog (powered by Polaris), these tasks can be automated behind the scenes, making maintenance nearly effortless.

Reclaiming storage with VACUUM

Iceberg's design as an append-only format means that every change (e.g., inserts, overwrites) creates a new snapshot. While this enables powerful features like time travel and rollback, old snapshots and their associated metadata can accumulate quickly, resulting in unused files and increased storage costs.

Dremio's VACUUM TABLE command helps you clean up by expiring old snapshots and removing unreferenced data files. You can control the expiration policy based on snapshot age and retention count. Following are examples of different options available using VACUUM TABLE.

Remove snapshots selectively.   In this example we expire all snapshots earlier than a particular snapshot (in this case, older than April 20, 2023) but retain the last 20 snapshots regardless of their age:

```
VACUUM TABLE PolarisCatalog.sales.orders
EXPIRE SNAPSHOTS older_than '2023-04-20 00:00:00.000' retain_last 20;
```

Retain most recent snapshots.   In this example, we maintain the last 100 snapshots, regardless of age, and expire all others:

```
VACUUM TABLE PolarisCatalog.sales.orders
    EXPIRE SNAPSHOTS retain_last 100;
```

Use default settings.   This example uses the default settings, which expire any snapshots over than 5 days but always makes sure to maintain at least 1 snapshot:

```
VACUUM TABLE PolarisCatalog.sales.orders
    EXPIRE SNAPSHOTS;
```

These operations reduce the clutter in your S3 or cloud storage layer while preserving the table's integrity and rollback capabilities.

Improving query performance with OPTIMIZE

Another common performance issue in Iceberg tables is file fragmentation, many small data files resulting from streaming ingest, CTAS operations, or COPY INTO jobs. These small files can slow down scans and increase query planning overhead.

The OPTIMIZE TABLE command rewrites data and manifest files to a more optimal size using a bin-packing strategy, combining small files or splitting overly large ones. It also supports clustering, ensuring that records are physically reordered along defined clustering keys.

Default optimization with bin-packing.   This uses the default settings, compacting the entire table. This process can be time consuming for very large tables and is fine if compaction is periodic. For more frequent compaction, in particular for streaming data, trying to define the narrowest compactions possible will allow them to complete quickly and avoid collisions with streaming ingestion:

```
OPTIMIZE TABLE PolarisCatalog.sales.orders
```

Tune file sizes and thresholds manually.   One way to tune the scope of an OPTIMIZE job is determining which files are considered for being rewritten. For streaming ingestion you may want to tolerate a lower minimum file size so fewer files are rewritten and only the smallest files will be rewritten, thus balancing performance improvement with the length of the compaction jobs:

```
OPTIMIZE TABLE PolarisCatalog.sales.orders
    REWRITE DATA USING BIN_PACK (
        TARGET_FILE_SIZE_MB = 256,
        MIN_FILE_SIZE_MB = 100,
        MAX_FILE_SIZE_MB = 1000,
        MIN_INPUT_FILES = 10
    );
```

Optimize only specific partitions. When you know new data and updates have occurred only in particular partitions, you can run a better scoped OPTIMIZE job by targeting just those partitions:

```
OPTIMIZE TABLE PolarisCatalog.sales.orders
    REWRITE DATA USING BIN_PACK
    FOR PARTITIONS order_date >= '2024-01-01'
```

Rewrite manifest files to control metadata bloat. Sometimes the issue isn't the file sizes of your data files but the number of manifests that track all these data files. Sometimes you may want to rewrite only the manifests so more files can be tracked per manifest:

```
OPTIMIZE TABLE PolarisCatalog.sales.orders
    REWRITE MANIFESTS
```

The OPTIMIZE TABLE operation improves query efficiency by reducing the number of files scanned during query execution and shrinking the size of manifest lists. It's especially beneficial after bulk ingests or large updates.

Dremio Automates Optimization

If you're using Dremio's integrated catalog—such as when creating tables via the Dremio UI or SQL without explicitly pointing to an external catalog—Dremio can automatically manage optimization in the background.

This means that for many common use cases—like running a CTAS or COPY INTO into a Polaris-backed table—you don't need to manually run OPTIMIZE or VACUUM unless you want to force a specific policy or optimize on demand.

Maintaining your Iceberg tables is crucial to keeping your lakehouse performant and cost-effective. With Dremio's VACUUM and OPTIMIZE commands, you have full control when needed, and you can automate table hygiene if this high level of control is not necessary. Whether you're working in a self-managed Polaris setup or leveraging Dremio's integrated catalog, these operations make it easy to keep your Iceberg tables clean, efficient, and fast.

Showing table properties

Understanding how an Iceberg table is configured can be critical when diagnosing behavior, tuning performance, or validating ingestion and optimization settings. Fortunately, Dremio supports the `SHOW TBLPROPERTIES` command, which allows you to inspect all the metadata properties associated with a given Iceberg table.

Table properties in Iceberg control a variety of behaviors, from how deletes are handled, to snapshot retention policies, to optimization thresholds. When your table is managed by Apache Polaris, these properties are stored as part of the table's metadata and surfaced through the REST catalog interface. Using Dremio, you can view these settings directly via SQL.

Here is the basic syntax to pull up the properties of an Iceberg table in Dremio:

```
SHOW TBLPROPERTIES <table_name>
```

Here, `<table_name>` must be the *fully qualified name* of your table in the form of `<Source>.<Namespace>.<Table>`. This is especially important when querying Polaris-managed tables, as Dremio does not assume a default catalog.

To view the properties of a Polaris table named `high_value_orders` in the `sales` namespace:

```
SHOW TBLPROPERTIES PolarisCatalog.sales.high_value_orders;
```

This command returns a result set with two columns.

table_property_name	table_property_value
write.metadata.delete-after-commit.enabled	true
read.split.target-size	134217728
commit.retry.num-retries	3
...	...

Each row corresponds to a property set on the table, either explicitly by the user or inherited from defaults. These properties are typically set during table creation or updated through operations like `ALTER TABLE`.

Common use cases for `SHOW TBLPROPERTIES` include:

- Auditing table configuration before ingesting or querying
- Verifying optimization thresholds such as target file sizes
- Debugging time-travel or snapshot retention issues by checking snapshot-related properties

- Checking for clustering settings if using the OPTIMIZE command with clustering keys
- Ensuring compatibility across engines (e.g., when using Spark, Trino, and Dremio with the same Polaris catalog)

> Keep in mind that SHOW TBLPROPERTIES returns *only Iceberg-level table properties*. It does not show Dremio-specific configurations like Reflections or catalog-level storage settings. For those, you'll need to consult the source configuration UI or system tables.

Conclusion

Bringing together the power of Apache Iceberg and Apache Polaris with Dremio creates a foundation for building an open, flexible, and high-performance lakehouse architecture. In this chapter, we walked through how to connect Dremio to Polaris, whether you're running a self-managed OSS catalog or working with Snowflake's Open Catalog, and we explored the full lifecycle of working with Iceberg tables in that environment. From querying and creating tables to inspecting metadata, ingesting files, and maintaining performance through VACUUM and OPTIMIZE, Dremio empowers data teams to manage their lakehouse with ease and transparency.

One thing to note is Dremio's integrated Polaris catalog, which is built directly into the platform. This gives users the option to leverage a fully managed Iceberg REST catalog without any external dependencies, offering all the benefits of Polaris while simplifying deployment. Whether you're integrating with external catalogs or using Dremio's native one, you get the same standards-based experience backed by Iceberg's table format and Polaris's robust metadata model.

Perhaps even Dremio more powerful is how Dremio extends beyond simply querying Polaris-backed tables. With its semantic layer, Dremio enables teams to define business-friendly views and access controls across multiple sources, including databases, data warehouses, data lakes, and Polaris-managed Iceberg tables, all in one place. This unified abstraction not only democratizes access to data for BI and AI workloads, but it also enforces governance and performance optimizations through features like Reflections, caching, and federated execution planning.

Advanced Polaris Configuration and CLI Management

As you've seen in earlier chapters, Apache Polaris offers a powerful foundation for managing Iceberg table metadata in distributed, multi-tenant data lakehouse environments. But as with any production-grade system, truly unlocking its potential—and running it reliably at scale— requires a deeper understanding of its advanced features and operational tools.

This chapter goes beyond day-to-day usage and explores how to manage Polaris effectively in real-world deployments. We'll start by introducing the Polaris command-line interface (CLI), a flexible tool for scripting and automation. From there, we'll cover critical administrative concepts like realms, observability, logging, and production configuration. Whether you're spinning up new environments, debugging permission issues, or integrating with enterprise infrastructure, this chapter will equip you with the knowledge and tools to operate Polaris with confidence.

We'll also take a close look at how Polaris handles metadata persistence via metastores, the various options for metrics and tracing, and how to configure Polaris in containerized or cloud-native environments. By the end, you'll have a complete view of what it takes to run Polaris securely and efficiently in production.

Using the Polaris CLI

While much of Polaris's functionality is exposed via its REST API, the Polaris command-line interface (CLI) offers a more approachable and scriptable way to interact with the system, especially for administrators and data engineers managing metadata workflows, debugging issues, or automating catalog operations. The CLI wraps many common API calls into concise, human-friendly commands that support managing catalogs, principals, roles, privileges, and more.

In this section, we'll walk through the core structure of the Polaris CLI, how authentication works, and how to use it effectively in both local and remote environments. Whether you're quickly creating a catalog, rotating credentials, or granting privileges across logical boundaries, the CLI provides a flexible and efficient way to interact with Polaris, without writing raw HTTP requests or custom scripts. You'll also see how commands can be scoped to specific realms, which Polaris uses to isolate tenants, teams, or environments within a single deployment.

CLI Structure, Authentication, and Profiles

The Polaris CLI is designed for flexibility and ease of use, mirroring the structure of the REST API while offering a more compact and user-friendly interface. Every command begins with the `polaris` keyword, followed by one or more *commands* and *subcommands*, with optional flags and arguments.

Here's a quick look at the basic pattern:

```
polaris [global-options] <command> <subcommand> [action] [options and arguments]
```

For example:

```
polaris principals list
polaris catalogs create --storage-type s3 --default-base-location
s3://my-bucket my_catalog
```

Authentication options

The CLI supports multiple methods for authentication. At a minimum, you'll need to authenticate using either:

- A client ID and secret:

```
polaris --client-id <your-client-id> --client-secret <your-client-secret> ...
```

- Or a bearer access token:

```
polaris --access-token <your-access-token> ...
```

You *cannot* use both `--client-id`/`--client-secret` and `--access-token` in the same command.

If you omit credentials on the command line, the CLI will fall back to environment variables (to avoid the command being part of your shell command history, start the command with a space):

```
export CLIENT_ID=<your-client-id>
export CLIENT_SECRET=<your-client-secret>
```

Profiles for convenience

To simplify repeated use, Polaris supports *CLI profiles* that store authentication and connection settings. This is especially useful when working with multiple environments or switching between realms.

To create a profile, use:

```
polaris profiles create dev
```

You can then use the `--profile` flag to invoke it:

```
polaris --profile dev catalogs list
```

Alternatively, set it as an environment default:

```
export CLIENT_PROFILE=dev
```

Profiles store information like the host, port, access token, or client credentials, so you don't have to re-enter them every time. This is especially useful when automating tasks or using the CLI in scripts or CI pipelines.

Connecting to Polaris

By default, the CLI connects to `localhost:8181`. If your Polaris server is running on a different host or port, you can set it manually using the following:

```
--host my.polaris.server --port 8181
```

Or you can use the `--base-url` flag instead to supply a full URL path:

```
--base-url https://my-polaris.example.com/api/catalog/v1
```

You should only provide one of `--host`/`--port` *or* `--base-url` per command.

Managing Entities with the CLI

At its core, Polaris is a metadata platform built around a handful of key entities: catalogs, principals, roles, namespaces, and privileges. The CLI exposes intuitive commands to manage each of these, making it easy to create and inspect metadata structures or automate governance tasks. This section walks through how to work with each of these entity types using real examples.

Catalogs

Catalogs are the foundation of Polaris—they define where Iceberg tables live and how they're organized. With the CLI, you can create, list, update, and delete catalogs.

To create a simple file-backed catalog:

```
polaris catalogs create \
  --storage-type file \
  --default-base-location file:///tmp/polaris \
  my_catalog
For cloud storage, specify the relevant credentials:
polaris catalogs create \
  --storage-type s3 \
  --default-base-location s3://my-bucket/polaris-data \
  --role-arn arn:aws:iam::1234567890:role/my-polaris-role \
  my_cloud_catalog
```

To list all catalogs:

```
polaris catalogs list
```

And to update a catalog's properties:

```
polaris catalogs update my_catalog --property environment=dev
```

Principals

Principals represent users or service accounts. You'll typically create one for each data user or application that needs access to Polaris.

To create a principal:

```
polaris principals create data_engineer_1
```

You can also attach metadata to principals using properties:

```
polaris principals create --property team=analytics data_scientist_1
```

To rotate credentials:

```
polaris principals rotate-credentials data_engineer_1
```

List or inspect principals:

```
polaris principals list
polaris principals get data_engineer_1
```

Roles: principal and catalog

Roles in Polaris come in two flavors: *principal roles*, which define high-level access policies across catalogs, and *catalog roles*, which govern access within a specific catalog.

To create a principal role:

```
polaris principal-roles create analyst_role
```

Then assign it to a user:

```
polaris principal-roles grant --principal data_scientist_1 analyst_role
```

To create a catalog role within a catalog:

```
polaris catalog-roles create --catalog my_catalog limited_reader
```

Then grant it to a principal role:

```
polaris catalog-roles grant \
  --catalog my_catalog \
  --principal-role analyst_role \
  limited_reader
```

These layers let you decouple identity (who the user is) from access scope (what they can see or modify), making access policies easier to manage at scale.

Namespaces

Namespaces act like folders within a catalog. Use them to hierarchically organize tables.

To create a namespace:

```
polaris namespaces create --catalog my_catalog analytics.q1
```

To list them:

```
polaris namespaces list --catalog my_catalog
```

Privileges

Once roles are assigned, you can grant or revoke fine-grained privileges—on catalogs, namespaces, tables, or views.

Example: granting catalog-level content management:

```
polaris privileges catalog grant \
  --catalog my_catalog \
  --catalog-role limited_reader \
  CATALOG_MANAGE_CONTENT
```

Or granting read access to a specific table:

```
polaris privileges table grant \
  --catalog my_catalog \
  --catalog-role limited_reader \
  --namespace analytics.q1 \
  --table sales_data \
  TABLE_READ_DATA
```

Use the revoke subcommand with `--cascade` to remove dependent permissions:

```
polaris privileges table revoke \
  --catalog my_catalog \
  --catalog-role limited_reader \
  --namespace analytics.q1 \
  --table sales_data \
  --cascade \
  TABLE_READ_DATA
```

Each of these commands maps closely to the REST API, but with syntax that's friendlier for human operators and automation scripts. In the next section, we'll explore how Polaris uses realms to provide multi-tenant isolation and how to manage that context from the CLI and configuration.

Understanding Realms

Polaris supports *multi-tenant isolation* out of the box through a construct called a *realm*. A realm is a logical partition of Polaris's metadata layer that allows different teams, business units, or environments (e.g., dev, staging, prod) to operate in complete isolation, even if they share the same Polaris server instance. Understanding how realms work is essential for anyone deploying Polaris at scale, especially in organizations with strict data boundaries or compliance requirements.

What is a realm?

A realm in Polaris is a top-level boundary that encapsulates its catalogs, roles, principals, and metadata. When a user authenticates into a realm, typically by including the realm name in a configuration file or API request header, all subsequent actions (such as creating catalogs, assigning roles, or querying metadata) are scoped strictly within that realm. This ensures complete separation of privileges and data across tenants or environments. Administrators define realms during deployment or bootstrap; they are not created dynamically through the API. Identifiers like `my_team_realm` must be explicitly configured in Polaris's startup settings (e.g., in `application.properties`) to be recognized and used.

Think of realms as lightweight, secure sandboxes within Polaris:

- Multiple business units can share infrastructure but manage their own policies.
- Service providers can host Polaris for customers without cross-contamination.

How realm context works

In Polaris, realm context refers to how the system determines which realm a request belongs to. This context is critical for enforcing isolation and ensuring that metadata operations, such as catalog creation, role assignments, or table queries, are executed

---

within the correct security and governance boundary. Every request to Polaris must include enough information for the server to resolve the appropriate realm.

Determining realm using the Polaris-Realm HTTP header (default)

By default, Polaris resolves realm context using a special HTTP header. Clients include the name of the target realm in the request using the Polaris-Realm header. This approach is common when interacting with Polaris through its REST API.

For example:

```
Polaris-Realm: my_team_realm
```

This tells Polaris that the request, whether it's to list catalogs or grant privileges, should be scoped to the my_team_realm realm. If this header is omitted and no default realm is configured, the request will fail with a realm resolution error.

Realm-aware authentication and bootstrapping

Authentication in Polaris is *realm-scoped*. Each realm has its own root principal, whose credentials are required to bootstrap and manage the realm. When setting up a realm in a production environment, you'll usually:

- Configure the realm in your application.properties or via environmental variables.
- Bootstrap the realm using the CLI or `java -jar` command.
- Issue tokens specific to that realm's root principal.

Example environment variables to set root credentials (the initial user you can use to create initial principals and catalogs):

```
export POLARIS_BOOTSTRAP_MY_REALM_ROOT_CLIENT_ID=my-client-id
export POLARIS_BOOTSTRAP_MY_REALM_ROOT_CLIENT_SECRET=my-secret
```

Then bootstrap the realm:

```
java -jar runtime/admin/build/quarkus-app/quarkus-run.jar bootstrap --help
```

To specify the credentials to be created in the command would look like this:

```
java -jar runtime/admin/build/quarkus-app/quarkus-run.jar bootstrap
-r my_realm -c my_realm,client-id,my-secret
```

The -r flag specifies which realm to bootstrap and -c specifies the credentials.

Once bootstrapped, the realm is fully operational and ready for catalog provisioning and role setup.

Realm isolation in practice

Behind the scenes, Polaris uses realm context to enforce a higher level of isolation that sits above individual catalogs. While Chapter 3 discussed how catalogs are isolated from one another, meaning metadata, roles, and permissions within one catalog do not affect another, realms introduce a broader boundary. A realm isolates entire groups of catalogs, along with their associated principals, roles, grants, and metadata, into a logically separate domain. This allows different teams, business units, or tenants to operate independently within the same Polaris deployment, without any risk of cross-access or configuration leakage. Realm isolation is enforced through scoped authentication, separate database connections, and realm-specific context resolution at runtime, providing a strong multi-tenancy model that complements catalog-level boundaries.

Polaris uses the realm context to isolate metadata at multiple levels:

Metastore
> Separate storage backends or schemas per realm.

Security
> Distinct principals, roles, and policies.

Logging and tracing
> Realm identifiers are attached to log entries and telemetry spans, making it easier to debug and audit activity per realm.

This isolation makes realms ideal for SaaS-style multi-tenancy, hybrid cloud environments, and any scenario where firm boundaries between users or systems are required, compared to the isolation of governance and logical organization of catalogs within a realm (if you are a company providing catalogs as a SaaS, each customer would have a realm, while that customer maintains many catalogs within that Realm).

Next, we'll explore how to observe and troubleshoot Polaris using built-in metrics, traces, and logs—critical tools for production deployments and root-cause analysis.

Observability: Metrics, Tracing, and Logging

Running Polaris in production means more than just standing it up—it requires visibility into what's happening under the hood. Whether you're tracking API performance, debugging a failed request, or auditing access across realms, observability is key to operating Polaris with confidence and control.

Polaris provides a robust observability layer out of the box, including:

Metrics
> Exposed via Micrometer and ready to be scraped by Prometheus

Distributed traces
Published using OpenTelemetry for deep request-level visibility

Structured logging
Powered by Quarkus and enriched with context like request IDs, trace IDs, and realm identifiers

Tracing
To help make troubleshooting much easier

In this section, you'll learn how to configure and consume Polaris's observability signals in both development and production environments. We'll walk through how to expose and customize metrics, enable traces for distributed debugging, and tailor logging behavior to fit your operational workflows. If you're responsible for running Polaris at scale—or need to troubleshoot complex behaviors—this is where you'll find the tools to do it effectively.

Metrics with Micrometer and Prometheus

Polaris exposes a comprehensive set of runtime metrics using Micrometer, a vendor-neutral instrumentation library that integrates seamlessly with monitoring tools like Prometheus, Datadog, and others. These metrics provide in-depth visibility into system health and behavior, including request volumes, response latencies, error rates, and resource utilization. For example, you can track API request counts by HTTP status code, monitor memory consumption and garbage collection performance, or set alerts when request latencies exceed defined thresholds. Polaris also supports custom metric tags, allowing you to filter and aggregate metrics by realm, region, catalog, or deployment environment, making it easier to pinpoint issues and analyze trends in complex, multi-tenant deployments.

Accessing metrics

Polaris publishes metrics through its management interface, typically served on port 8282. You can access them via a browser or use a Prometheus-compatible scraper: *http://<your-polaris-host>:8282/q/metrics*

If you're running Polaris locally, that might look like: http://localhost:8282/q/metrics

This endpoint returns a plaintext stream of metrics in Prometheus format, including system stats (CPU, memory, HTTP response codes) as well as Polaris-specific counters and gauges.

Scraping with Prometheus

To integrate with Prometheus, just add Polaris as a scrape target in your Prometheus configuration:

```
scrape_configs:
  - job_name: 'polaris'
    metrics_path: '/q/metrics'
    static_configs:
      - targets: ['localhost:8282']
```

You can now create Grafana dashboards or alerts based on Polaris's performance and usage.

Customizing metric tags

You can enrich your Polaris metrics with custom tags to distinguish between services, environments, or deployments. Polaris supports tagging via configuration properties like:

```
polaris.metrics.tags.environment=prod
polaris.metrics.tags.service=metadata-api
polaris.metrics.tags.region=us-west-2
```

These tags are automatically appended to every metric, making it easy to break down metrics across environments or filter them in dashboards.

By default, Polaris includes:

```
polaris.metrics.tags.application=Polaris
```

You can override it by setting:

```
polaris.metrics.tags.application=my-polaris-instance
```

> The /q/metrics endpoint should be exposed only to trusted infra-structure, such as internal monitoring systems, especially in production environments. Use a firewall, reverse proxy, or Kubernetes ingress rules to control access.

Tracing with OpenTelemetry

While metrics offer a broad overview of Polaris's health and performance, tracing provides a more detailed, request-level view of what's happening inside the system. With distributed tracing via OpenTelemetry, Polaris can emit spans that help you follow individual requests as they move through components, services, and realms. This level of visibility is beneficial when debugging high-latency requests, investigating intermittent timeouts, or understanding behavior across multi-realm or multi-service environments. Tracing also becomes essential when coordinating with external systems, such as Spark, Kafka, or cloud-native services, that emit their own OpenTelemetry traces. By default, tracing is disabled in Polaris, so you'll need to explicitly enable it and configure an OTLP (OpenTelemetry Protocol) collector to capture and analyze these signals.

Enabling tracing

To enable tracing, set the following property in your Polaris configuration (e.g., in `application.properties` or via environment variables):

```
quarkus.otel.sdk.disabled=false
```

Then, specify the collector endpoint where traces should be sent. This must be a valid HTTP or HTTPS URL pointing to a compatible OpenTelemetry collector:

```
quarkus.otel.exporter.otlp.traces.endpoint=http://otlp-collector:4317
```

The endpoint must support the OTLP gRPC protocol, and the default port is typically 4317.

Customizing trace metadata

Polaris automatically attaches helpful metadata to every trace:

`service.name`
> Defaults to Apache Polaris Server (incubating)

`service.version`
> The current Polaris release version

`polaris.realm`
> The realm ID for the request

`polaris.request.id`
> If the client provides a Polaris-Request-Id header

You can override or extend these attributes using:

```
quarkus.otel.resource.attributes=service.name=polaris,deployment.environment=prod
```

Alternatively, you can use the indexed syntax:

```
quarkus.otel.resource.attributes[0]=service.name=polaris
quarkus.otel.resource.attributes[1]=deployment.environment=prod
```

This is useful when running multiple Polaris services (e.g., per team or region) and you want to break down trace data by context.

Troubleshooting trace export

If Polaris fails to send traces, you may see logs like:

```
SEVERE [io.ope.exp.int.grp.OkHttpGrpcExporter] ... Failed to export spans.
The request could not be executed. Full error message: Failed to connect
to localhost:4317
```

This typically means:

- The collector isn't running
- The endpoint URL is incorrect
- The port is blocked or misconfigured

Double-check your configuration and ensure the OpenTelemetry collector is reachable from the Polaris container or host.

With Polaris emitting structured, span-level traces, you can plug into any OTEL-compatible backend like Jaeger, Grafana Tempo, or Honeycomb to get full visibility into your lakehouse metadata layer.

Logging and Debugging with Quarkus

Logging is the foundation of any good observability stack—and Polaris offers a flexible, extensible logging system built on top of Quarkus. Whether you're troubleshooting a failed request, auditing user behavior across realms, or tuning performance, Polaris's logs give you detailed insight into what the system is doing and why.

By default, Polaris logs to both the console and a rotating file in the *./logs* directory. You can customize everything from log format and level to contextual metadata like request IDs and realms.

Basic logging behavior

Polaris outputs logs in a human-readable format and rotates log files daily. Each file is capped at 10MB with a maximum of 14 backups retained. This default setup works well for development, but production environments will typically want to forward logs to a centralized logging solution (e.g., Fluentd, Logstash, or cloud-native log services).

Setting log levels

You can globally adjust the log verbosity, which controls how much detail is included in the logs, using:

```
quarkus.log.level=INFO
```

To fine-tune specific components, define per-package log levels:

```
quarkus.log.category."org.apache.polaris".level=DEBUG
```

This is especially helpful when debugging Polaris internals or observing authentication flows.

Debugging configuration issues

To troubleshoot startup or configuration problems, increase verbosity for the config loader:

```
quarkus.log.console.level=DEBUG
quarkus.log.category."io.smallrye.config".level=DEBUG
```

> Increasing the verbosity for the config loader may expose sensitive values such as credentials or tokens. Do not enable verbosity in production unless absolutely necessary.

Enabling JSON logs

If you're ingesting Polaris logs into a structured logging system (e.g., Elasticsearch), enable JSON-formatted output:

```
quarkus.log.console.json=true
quarkus.log.file.json=true
```

JSON logs make it easier to parse, search, and correlate logs across services and time windows.

Using MDC for contextual logging

Polaris automatically includes Mapped Diagnostic Context (MDC) entries in every log message, enriching them with request-level context:

requestId
> From the `Polaris-Request-Id` header

realmId
> The realm in which the request is operating

traceId, parentId, *and* spanId
> From OpenTelemetry, if tracing is enabled

sampled
> Whether the trace was sampled

Log output includes these fields in the default pattern:

```
%d{yyyy-MM-dd HH:mm:ss,SSS} %-5p [%c{3.}] [%X{requestId},%X{realmId}]
[%X{traceId},%X{parentId},%X{spanId},%X{sampled}] (%t) %s%e%n
```

Adding custom MDC keys

You can add your own contextual metadata to every log by setting additional MDC properties:

```
polaris.log.mdc.environment=prod
polaris.log.mdc.region=us-west-2
```

These tags appear in every log line and are especially useful in multi-region or multi-realm deployments where filtering by environment or location is critical.

Together with metrics and traces, Polaris's logging system forms a complete observability stack that supports both real-time monitoring and in-depth forensic analysis. With flexible formats, structured context, and easy integration into your existing tools, logs become a first-class tool for operating your data lakehouse infrastructure.

Configuring Polaris for Production

Deploying Polaris in production requires more than just standing up the service—you'll need to think through security, durability, multi-tenancy, and scalability from the ground up. While Polaris provides a streamlined developer experience out of the box, its default configuration is specifically designed for local experimentation and testing. To safely run Polaris in a real-world environment, you'll need to replace in-memory components, harden authentication flows, and carefully configure persistence and network settings.

In this section, we'll walk through the key areas you'll want to review and adjust before moving to production. These include:

- Enabling secure authentication and OAuth2 token brokers
- Configuring durable metadata storage using relational metastores
- Bootstrapping realms and root principals safely
- Disabling test features and tightening default privileges
- Setting concurrency and rate limits to protect against overload

By the end, you'll have a clear roadmap for turning Polaris from a local development sandbox into a secure, robust, and multi-tenant production catalog service.

Security and Authentication Configuration

In production environments, robust authentication is essential. Polaris provides flexible, pluggable mechanisms for securing access to metadata APIs; however, its default development configuration utilizes a test authenticator that's not intended for real-world use. Transitioning to a secure authentication setup is one of the first and most critical steps in preparing Polaris for production.

Configure OAuth2 and token brokers

Polaris supports OAuth2-based authentication flows, which allow service accounts or users to request access tokens tied to a specific principal and realm. You can configure Polaris to issue tokens via a token broker, which can use either symmetric keys or asymmetric RSA key pairs.

To configure the token broker with symmetric key encryption:

```
polaris.authentication.token-broker.type=symmetric-key
polaris.authentication.token-broker.symmetric-key.file=/secrets/symmetric.key
```

Or, configure the token broker using RSA keys:

```
polaris.authentication.token-broker.type=rsa-key-pair
polaris.authentication.token-broker.rsa-key-pair.public-key-file=
/secrets/public.key
polaris.authentication.token-broker.rsa-key-pair.private-key-file=
/secrets/private.key
```

> The `token-broker` settings must match in both the `oauth2` and `authenticator` configurations. Mismatched values will cause authentication failures.

Bootstrap root credentials for a realm

When deploying Polaris with persistent metadata (e.g., using a metastore), you'll need to bootstrap the system to initialize realm-level credentials and infrastructure. As part of the bootstrap process, you can provide a custom `client_id` and `client_secret` for the realm's root principal.

Set these via environment variables:

```
export POLARIS_BOOTSTRAP_MY_REALM_ROOT_CLIENT_ID=my-client-id
export POLARIS_BOOTSTRAP_MY_REALM_ROOT_CLIENT_SECRET=my-client-secret
```

Then run:

```
java -jar polaris-service-all.jar bootstrap polaris-server.yml
```

For Docker-based deployments:

```
bin/polaris-service bootstrap config/polaris-server.yml
```

This process creates the root principal and stores hashed credentials in the metastore backend.

For bootstrapping the default realm, environment variables *must* be prefixed exactly as shown:

```
env POLARIS_BOOTSTRAP_DEFAULT-REALM_ROOT_CLIENT_ID=my-client-id \
    POLARIS_BOOTSTRAP_DEFAULT-REALM_ROOT_CLIENT_SECRET=my-secret \
    <bootstrap command>
```

Token issuance example.   Once bootstrapping is completed, you can request a token:

```
curl -X POST http://localhost:8181/api/catalog/v1/oauth/tokens \
    -d "grant_type=client_credentials&client_id=my-client-id
    &client_secret=my-secret&scope=PRINCIPAL_ROLE:ALL"
```

For non-default realms, include the realm HTTP header:

```
-H 'realm: my_custom_realm'
```

Best practices for production.   Here are some best practices for when in production:

Store secrets securely
Never hardcode credentials or keys in source code or container images.

Rotate credentials periodically
Polaris supports credential rotation via CLI.

Scope tokens tightly
Use specific scopes (e.g., CATALOG_LIST, TABLE_READ_DATA) rather than blanket access.

Durable Metadata with Metastores

In development, Polaris defaults to an in-memory metastore for fast iteration and simplicity. But in production, this setup is not suitable—it's ephemeral and non-durable. Using an in-memory metastore means:

- Metadata is lost on restart
- There's no way to persist configuration between sessions
- Multiple nodes can't coordinate access to shared state

In production, these limitations are unacceptable. Durable metadata is essential for long-term stability, auditing, multi-node deployment, and compliance. For real-world use, Polaris must persist metadata like catalogs, roles, grants, and principals to a relational backend that ensures data integrity and durability.

Polaris supports two options for metastores: Relational JDBC (recommended) and NoSql Databases (in development). EclipseLink is deprecated; it should not be used for new development.

Using relational JDBC (recommended)

The preferred backend for production is the relational JDBC implementation. This approach leverages Quarkus's native support for database connections and integrates with PostgreSQL or H2 (for non-prod scenarios).

First, set your persistence type to relational-jdbc:

```
POLARIS_PERSISTENCE_TYPE=relational-jdbc
```

Next, configure the datasource using Quarkus environment variables or properties:

```
QUARKUS_DATASOURCE_DB_KIND=postgresql
QUARKUS_DATASOURCE_USERNAME=my_user
QUARKUS_DATASOURCE_PASSWORD=my_password
QUARKUS_DATASOURCE_JDBC_URL=jdbc:postgresql://mydb:5432/{realm}
```

The {realm} token in the JDBC URL allows Polaris to isolate metadata per realm, creating physical separation at the database level.

It's important to note that:

- Databases must be created manually—Polaris does not auto-create them.
- Each realm connects to its own schema or database.

You can also define the persistence backend using Polaris's application config file application.properties:

```
polaris.persistence.type=relational-jdbc
quarkus.datasource.db-kind=postgresql
quarkus.datasource.jdbc.url=jdbc:postgresql://localhost:5432/production_realm
quarkus.datasource.username=admin
quarkus.datasource.password=secret
```

Deprecated: EclipseLink metastore

While still available, the EclipseLink persistence option is deprecated and should not be used for new deployments. It requires a *persistence.xml* file to configure connection properties, which must be located at least two directories deep (e.g., /*deployments/config/persistence.xml*).

An example EclipseLink persistence configuration looks like this:

```
polaris.persistence.type=eclipse-link
polaris.persistence.eclipselink.configuration-file=/path/to/persistence.xml
polaris.persistence.eclipselink.persistence-unit=polaris
```

This setup is useful for legacy compatibility or custom use cases, but it lacks the flexibility and maintainability of the JDBC-based approach.

If you're moving from EclipseLink to JDBC, you may need to export and re-import metadata to align with schema expectations.

With a durable metastore in place, Polaris can now safely persist your metadata across restarts, deployments, and environments.

Hardening Defaults and Managing Feature Flags

Once you've configured secure authentication and a persistent metastore, the next step in productionizing Polaris is to review and harden its default behaviors. Out of the box, Polaris includes several features meant to simplify development and testing, but many of these should be disabled or tightened before going live. In production, you'll want to ensure that metadata operations are governed, storage locations are controlled, and test shortcuts are removed.

Polaris provides a flexible feature-flag system to control behavior at both global and realm-specific levels.

Disable test catalog initialization

By default, Polaris may automatically initialize a default catalog using local file-based storage. This is helpful in local testing but should be explicitly disabled in production environments to avoid accidental exposure of ungoverned storage paths.

To disable automatic catalog creation:

```
polaris.features.realm-overrides."my-realm"."INITIALIZE_DEFAULT
_CATALOG_FILEIO_FOR_TEST"=false
```

Restrict supported storage types

In development, Polaris allows catalogs to use any supported storage backend—including local file systems (FILE)—which are not suitable for production. To enforce stricter policies, use the following flag to allow only explicitly permitted catalog storage types:

```
polaris.features.defaults."SUPPORTED_CATALOG_STORAGE_TYPES"=S3,GCS,AZURE
```

Omit FILE entirely to ensure developers don't accidentally create catalogs with insecure or non-durable storage backends.

Enforce credential rotation policies

Credential hygiene is critical in multi-tenant environments. Polaris includes an optional flag to enforce that principals regularly rotate their credentials:

```
polaris.features.defaults."ENFORCE_PRINCIPAL_CREDENTIAL_
ROTATION_REQUIRED_CHECKING"=true
```

This prevents long-lived, unmanaged secrets and encourages teams to treat Polaris credentials like any other secure infrastructure credential.

Realm-specific overrides

Feature flags can be applied globally or on a per-realm basis, giving you fine-grained control over different tenants, teams, or environments.

For example, if you want to disable a feature just for the `analytics` realm:

```
polaris.features.realm-overrides."analytics"."SKIP_CREDENTIAL_
SUBSCOPING_INDIRECTION"=false
```

This level of control is particularly useful in hybrid setups, where some realms may be experimental or isolated, while others are tightly regulated.

Review logs for flag behavior

If you"e unsure which flags are active, or you want to confirm that test defaults are disabled, enable debug logging for Polaris's configuration subsystem as noted in "Debugging configuration issues" on page 193:

```
quarkus.log.category."io.smallrye.config".level=DEBUG
```

This may expose sensitive configuration values. Use with caution and only in trusted environments.

By locking down permissive defaults and activating relevant feature flags, you make Polaris safer, more predictable, and easier to operate in a compliance-sensitive production setting.

Scaling, Concurrency, and Rate Limits

With security configured and metadata durability ensured, the final step in preparing Polaris for production is tuning its performance characteristics. While earlier sections focused on setting up secure authentication and persistent metastores, they also laid the groundwork for governance, including defining realms, setting up role-based access control, and applying privilege-based restrictions at the catalog, namespace, and table levels. These governance features ensure that users can only interact with the data they're authorized to access, and that metadata operations are traceable and auditable.

Polaris is designed to serve metadata requests at scale, from multiple compute engines, concurrent users, and across many realms and catalogs. To maintain predictable performance and protect against overload, Polaris provides configuration options for managing concurrency, task queues, and request rate limits. These settings are especially important in multi-tenant or cloud-native environments, where sudden traffic surges or uneven usage patterns can strain shared infrastructure.

Task concurrency

Polaris processes metadata operations (such as creating tables or listing namespaces) as internal tasks. By default, it supports up to 100 concurrent tasks and queues up to 1,000 additional tasks.

You can tune these thresholds to match your deployment size and workload:

```
polaris.tasks.max-concurrent-tasks=200
polaris.tasks.max-queued-tasks=1000
```

Increase limits if you expect high throughput from multiple compute engines (e.g., Spark, Dremio, Snowflake). Decrease them to constrain resource usage on small or shared infrastructure.

Monitor queue depth and task latency via metrics to help determine optimal values.

Rate limiting with token buckets

To further protect Polaris from overload or abuse (intentional or accidental), you can enable rate limiting via a token bucket algorithm. This approach allows short bursts of traffic but limits the average request rate over time.

Enable token bucket rate limiting:

```
polaris.rate-limiter.filter.type=token-bucket
```

Then define the rate-limiting behavior:

```
polaris.rate-limiter.token-bucket.requests-per-second=1000
polaris.rate-limiter.token-bucket.window=PT10S
```

This configuration allows a maximum of 10,000 requests every 10 seconds (on average). You can fine-tune these settings based on expected usage and load testing. To disable rate limiting entirely (*not* recommended for production), set:

```
polaris.rate-limiter.filter.type=no-op
```

Scaling considerations

Polaris can scale horizontally behind a load balancer, especially when used with a shared metastore like PostgreSQL. If you're deploying Polaris in a containerized environment (e.g., Kubernetes), consider:

- Running multiple replicas with a shared external metastore
- Using externalized configuration (via ConfigMaps or mounted volumes)
- Scaling based on CPU or request latency metrics
- Monitoring thread pool and connection pool sizes, especially under heavy metadata workloads

Polaris is stateless from a service perspective, so scaling is largely a matter of infrastructure sizing and backend capacity.

By tuning concurrency limits, enforcing rate policies, and scaling your deployment appropriately, you can ensure that Polaris remains responsive and stable under real-world production conditions, even as workloads grow and new teams onboard.

Finalizing and Verifying Your Production Setup

At this point, you've laid the groundwork for a secure, durable, and scalable Polaris deployment. But before onboarding users or integrating compute engines, it's critical to validate that all the key components are functioning as expected. A properly configured deployment should not only serve metadata requests but also enforce access policies, persist state across restarts, and expose visibility through logs, metrics, and traces.

Here's a checklist you can use to verify your production setup:

- ☐ Issue an OAuth2 token using your realm's `client_id` and `client_secret` via the `/oauth/tokens` endpoint.
- ☐ Create a catalog and confirm metadata is durably stored in your configured metastore (e.g., PostgreSQL).
- ☐ Bootstrap a realm and use the CLI to create and assign roles, then test access with scoped credentials.
- ☐ Check the `/q/metrics` endpoint to ensure Prometheus-compatible metrics are exposed and tagged correctly.
- ☐ Validate that OpenTelemetry traces are reaching your configured collector and include realm and request IDs.
- ☐ Inspect logs to confirm they are structured, contain MDC fields, and rotate as expected.

☐ Confirm test defaults (like file-based storage and default catalog initialization) are disabled.

If all of the above checks pass, you've successfully transitioned Polaris from a development tool into a production-ready metadata platform. You now have a secure foundation for cross-team collaboration, multi-tenant data governance, and scalable catalog management.

Conclusion

Polaris is more than just a catalog; it's a foundation for building reliable, governed, and multi-tenant data platforms on Apache Iceberg. While earlier chapters introduced its architectural concepts and hands-on usage, this chapter focused on what it takes to run Polaris in the real world.

We explored how to secure a Polaris deployment with robust authentication, how to persist metadata durably using production-grade metastores, and how to harden system behavior through configurable feature flags. We also covered how to monitor and debug Polaris using a rich observability stack—metrics, traces, and logs—all designed to help operators understand what's happening and why.

Beyond its internal configuration, Polaris also provides a powerful command-line interface for managing catalogs, principals, roles, and privileges. This makes it easy to automate administration, integrate with CI/CD workflows, or maintain consistent governance across environments.

With these capabilities in hand, you're equipped to deploy Polaris with confidence—securely, at scale, and with the observability required to support production-grade data operations. Whether you're building for internal teams, external customers, or both, Polaris offers the flexibility and control to serve as the metadata backbone of your lakehouse architecture.

Looking to the Future of Apache Polaris

As Apache Polaris continues to evolve as a key part of the Iceberg ecosystem, its trajectory reflects both the maturity of open table formats and the growing demand for flexible, interoperable data catalogs.

This chapter looks ahead to what's next for Polaris. We begin by examining the broader Polaris ecosystem, including how Polaris is offered as a managed service by vendors such as Dremio and Snowflake. We then examine how Polaris integrates into the landscape of REST-compatible catalogs, facilitating seamless collaboration across engines and vendors. Finally, we delve into the Apache Polaris project roadmap, highlighting key features under development and the direction of community-led innovation. Understanding where Polaris is headed is essential for practitioners planning for the future of their Iceberg-based infrastructure.

Apache Polaris is a community-driven, open source project. The features and functionalities mentioned in this chapter are not part of Apache Polaris at the time of writing. There is no guarantee on whether, when, how, and to what extent these features and functionalities will be implemented. Only features and functionalities that are part of an official, binary release and not marked as experimental or the like are considered stable.

Managed Polaris

The Polaris ecosystem is rapidly expanding, supported by a vibrant community and significant contributions from Dremio and Snowflake. Apache Polaris's implementation of the Iceberg REST Catalog specification makes it an ideal foundation for managed catalog offerings that prioritize openness, governance, and interoperability. Both Dremio and Snowflake offer managed catalog services—Dremio Catalog and

Snowflake Open Catalog—that simplify the process of adopting Polaris in production environments.

As we introduced in Chapter 9, Dremio Catalog, powered by Apache Polaris, is an enterprise-grade solution that eliminates much of the operational overhead traditionally associated with managing Iceberg catalogs. Dremio Catalog supports on-premise and hybrid cloud deployments, an essential capability for organizations with diverse infrastructure needs. It also incorporates built-in automation for table optimization, including compaction and vacuuming, which helps users avoid performance pitfalls caused by small files or outdated metadata.

Additionally, tDremio has introduced features such as autonomous performance management and automatic clustering for Iceberg tables, making Polaris-backed catalogs easier to manage and more responsive to workload patterns.

Snowflake Open Catalog, which we introduced in Chapter 8, is also based on Apache Polaris. It provides centralized access to Iceberg tables for Snowflake customers while maintaining compatibility with a range of Iceberg-aware engines through the REST interface. Snowflake's implementation is integrated within its platform—including role-based access control (RBAC) and storage credential management—in order to maintain strong data governance without sacrificing openness.

Managed Polaris implementations lower the barrier to entry for organizations exploring Polaris, allowing them to adopt a production-ready REST catalog with minimal setup. By reducing the operational complexity and providing enterprise-grade enhancements, these solutions ensure that Polaris is open, interoperable, highly accessible, and reliable for modern data architectures.

The REST Catalog Ecosystem

The Apache Iceberg REST Catalog Specification is a standardized interface that enables decoupled, cross-platform interaction with Iceberg tables.

As we have noted throughout the book, the significance of the REST Catalog specification cannot be overstated. It eliminates the need for tight coupling between processing engines and specific metastore implementations, enabling users to build open and flexible lakehouse solutions that scale across teams, tools, and infrastructures. Polaris's full support for the REST API makes it a plug-and-play, highly interoperable catalog for any engine or service that supports the REST Catalog API. A growing number of tools natively support this standard, allowing you to use your preferred tools with zero friction.

Data Processing Engines

Data processing engines are at the heart of the analytics and data engineering work-flows that interact with Apache Polaris. These systems are responsible for ingesting, transforming, querying, and serving data at various scales—from real-time event pipelines to large-scale batch processing and interactive business intelligence (BI) workloads. Because Apache Polaris implements the Iceberg REST Catalog specification, all of these engines and more can interact with it directly by using a standard, vendor-neutral API.

Apache Spark

Apache Spark is one of the most widely adopted engines for both batch and micro-batch processing. Its support for the Iceberg REST Catalog spec enables seamless interaction with Polaris-managed tables. Spark is frequently used for ETL pipelines, feature engineering, and training machine learning models, all of which benefit from Iceberg's versioned, schema-evolving table format. Polaris brings Spark users a robust, REST-accessible metastore that eliminates the complexity of traditional Hive-based catalogs.

Apache Flink

Flink is the go-to engine for real-time, low-latency stream processing. It integrates with Polaris through the REST Catalog interface, allowing Flink jobs to write directly into Iceberg tables for use cases such as change data capture (CDC), real-time ETL, and streaming analytics. Polaris ensures that even rapidly changing data can be captured and governed using a consistent catalog, enabling Flink to participate in a unified lakehouse architecture.

Dremio

Dremio is a SQL engine designed for self-service analytics and data lake acceleration. It is deeply integrated with Apache Polaris in multiple ways. First, it can connect to any REST-compatible catalog, including Polaris, enabling federation across multiple Iceberg catalogs, as well as federation with databases, data warehouses, and data lakes. Second, Dremio offers a built-in, fully managed Polaris catalog, eliminating the need for users to provision or operate an external metastore. This integrated Polaris catalog works out of the box and is deployable in cloud, hybrid, or on-prem environments.

Dremio also introduces autonomous performance management features for Iceberg tables, including automatic clustering, automated maintenance tasks (such as compaction and vacuuming), and query acceleration. These capabilities ensure that data remains optimized without requiring manual intervention, delivering consistent performance for BI tools, dashboards, and data products.

Trino

Trino is a distributed SQL engine known for its ability to federate queries across heterogeneous data sources. Through support for the Iceberg REST Catalog spec, Trino can connect to Polaris and execute high-performance analytical queries on Iceberg tables, while simultaneously accessing other sources such as object stores, JDBC-compatible databases, and more. Polaris provides a consistent and versioned metadata layer that enhances Trino's reliability and governance.

Presto

Like Trino, Presto offers distributed query capabilities for large-scale data analysis. It connects to Polaris using the REST Catalog interface, enabling read access to Iceberg tables for interactive and batch SQL workloads. Presto's integration with Polaris enables it to efficiently leverage Iceberg's schema evolution, time travel, and partition pruning features.

StarRocks

StarRocks is a massively parallel processing (MPP) analytical engine designed for real-time and multi-dimensional analytics. With native support for Iceberg via the REST Catalog interface, StarRocks can query Polaris-managed tables with high throughput and low latency. Its focus on sub-second analytics makes it ideal for operational dashboards and complex OLAP workloads.

Streaming and Ingestion Platforms

In modern data architectures, real-time data ingestion is a crucial capability, enabling use cases ranging from operational analytics to anomaly detection and personalized experiences. Apache Polaris, with its support for the Apache Iceberg REST Catalog specification, can serve as the destination for streaming data ingested through various event-driven platforms. These platforms enable the writing of change data capture (CDC) events and real-time updates into Iceberg tables governed by Polaris, providing a unified, consistent, and up-to-date lakehouse.

Kafka Connect

Kafka Connect is a widely used framework for integrating Apache Kafka with external systems. It provides a declarative and scalable way to capture and push streaming data into data lakes, warehouses, and other storage systems. Through Iceberg sink connectors that support the REST Catalog spec, Kafka Connect can write streaming records directly into Polaris-managed Iceberg tables. This is ideal for use cases such as log ingestion, CDC pipelines, and IoT data collection, where event data needs to be captured and queried with strong consistency and schema control.

Confluent

Confluent—the commercial distribution of Apache Kafka—builds on Kafka Connect and adds robust enterprise capabilities including governance, schema registry, security, and monitoring. With support for Iceberg and REST-compatible catalogs, Confluent pipelines can ingest streaming data into Polaris with minimal configuration. Organizations using Confluent gain operational reliability and visibility while leveraging Polaris's table versioning, time travel, and access controls for downstream analytics and compliance.

Redpanda

Redpanda is a Kafka-compatible, high-performance event streaming platform built from the ground up in C++. Known for its low latency, durability, and operational simplicity, Redpanda can integrate with Polaris via REST-compliant Iceberg sinks. This allows Redpanda to serve as a drop-in Kafka alternative for real-time data delivery into the Polaris catalog. Use cases such as financial tick data, observability streams, and high-frequency logging benefit from Redpanda's performance characteristics when paired with Polaris for governed table storage.

Estuary

Estuary is a real-time data integration and pipeline platform that specializes in CDC and streaming ETL. It provides an intuitive interface and rich connectors for syncing data across operational databases, SaaS tools, and data lakes. With native Iceberg support through the REST Catalog interface, Estuary enables users to ingest fresh data into Polaris-managed tables in near-real time. This is particularly useful for powering up-to-date analytics, machine learning features, and dashboarding with strong data consistency and minimal lag.

Other Data-Stack Tools

Beyond processing engines and streaming platforms, Apache Polaris is supported by a broad and evolving set of tools that enhance metadata management, analytics, governance, and developer productivity. These tools leverage the Iceberg REST Catalog specification to integrate seamlessly with Polaris, enabling a rich, interconnected ecosystem. This section highlights additional notable tools that work with Polaris, expanding its utility across the modern data stack.

DuckDB

DuckDB is an in-process OLAP database designed for local analytics and prototyping. With support for reading Iceberg tables via REST-compatible catalogs, DuckDB can be used to explore Polaris-managed datasets directly from a developer's laptop or notebook environment. It's particularly valuable for data scientists and analysts performing rapid experimentation, ad hoc queries, or local validation of production datasets.

Polars

    Polars is a DataFrame library implemented in Rust with bindings for Python. It offers powerful data manipulation capabilities and is well-suited for use in data science and machine learning pipelines. Through its support for Iceberg and REST Catalogs, Polars can access Polaris-registered tables efficiently, bringing structured and versioned data into advanced analytical workflows with minimal friction.

DataHub

    DataHub is an open source metadata platform that provides centralized search, lineage tracking, and governance. It integrates with Polaris via the Iceberg REST Catalog specification, allowing teams to visualize and manage metadata for Iceberg tables in a unified user interface. DataHub helps organizations answer key questions about data provenance, schema evolution, and usage patterns, thereby strengthening governance and enabling trusted analytics.

The Apache Polaris Roadmap

Apache Polaris is evolving rapidly, with an ambitious and community-driven roadmap that reflects the priorities of a broad set of contributors, including users, vendors, and engine developers. The roadmap aims to solidify Polaris as a foundational catalog in the open data ecosystem, while continuously expanding its capabilities across governance, performance, security, and interoperability.

The roadmap is not a rigid release schedule but rather a transparent articulation of the project's long-term vision and current focus areas. Features are grouped into categories, including core catalog functionality, security and governance, catalog federation, observability, and AI/ML support. Many enhancements are already generally available (GA), while others are in active development or planned for future milestones.

In this section, we examine the most significant roadmap items that will shape the future of Apache Polaris. Each subsection highlights what the feature is, why it matters, and how it fits into the broader data platform strategy.

Generic Table Support

One of the most impactful and forward-looking additions to the Apache Polaris roadmap is support for Generic Tables (Initial Feature release in 1.0). This foundational capability expands Polaris beyond its current scope, which is currently limited to Iceberg. Until now, Polaris has operated solely as a catalog for Apache Iceberg tables via the Iceberg REST Catalog API. However, many organizations rely on multiple table formats across their data ecosystems, notably Delta Lake and Apache Hudi, and require a unified governance and cataloging layer that is not tied to a single format.

Generic Table Support addresses this need by allowing Polaris to register non-Iceberg tables, such as Delta, Hudi, or raw file-based tables, alongside Iceberg tables within a shared namespace and governance model. This creates new opportunities for inter-operability across engines, without requiring all workloads to conform to Iceberg.

The primary motivation for introducing Generic Tables is interoperability. Engines like Apache Spark, Trino, and Snowflake often interact with a mix of table formats. By enabling Polaris to manage these diverse formats, users gain a centralized, consistent, and format-agnostic catalog, which reduces operational overhead and promotes data governance best practices.

Key goals of the initial implementation include:

- Support for registering and managing non-Iceberg tables as first-class entities in Polaris
- A REST API for basic operations: create, load, drop, and list Generic Tables
- A dedicated Spark Catalog plugin to allow Spark 3.5+ to interact with Polaris-managed Generic Tables
- Clear separation of REST endpoints between Iceberg and Generic Table operations to maintain API integrity

API and architecture overview

Generic Tables in Polaris are managed through a new set of REST endpoints (/generic-tables) that exist in parallel to the Iceberg REST endpoints. These APIs support basic operations:

CreateGenericTable
: Registers a table with a given name, format (e.g., "delta"), and metadata properties like location

LoadGenericTable
: Retrieves metadata for a Generic Table

DropGenericTable
: Removes a registered Generic Table

ListGenericTables
: Lists all Generic Tables in a namespace

The design avoids overloading the Iceberg APIs to preserve the semantic clarity of each specification. For example, a loadTable call must explicitly target either the Iceberg or Generic Table endpoint, ensuring engines and users receive predictable behavior.

Spark integration

A notable component of the Generic Table initiative is the Polaris Spark Catalog Plugin. This plugin allows Spark to interact with both Iceberg and Generic Tables in Polaris through a unified interface. It can:

- Route create, drop, and load operations to the appropriate REST endpoint.
- Construct Spark table objects using returned metadata.
- Defer schema inference and transformation logic to the client (e.g., Spark).

Initial support focuses on Spark 3.5, with a runtime package (`polaris-spark-runtime-3.5_2.12`) and configuration options for easy deployment.

Governance and identity model

Generic Tables integrate with Polaris's existing governance model. They support standard table-level privileges (e.g., `TABLE_CREATE`, `TABLE_DROP`) and are organized within namespaces alongside Iceberg tables and views. Name uniqueness is enforced within a namespace, ensuring no conflicts across different entity types.

Looking ahead

While the MVP focuses on basic lifecycle management, the roadmap includes plans to extend Generic Table support with:

- Metadata converters to dynamically generate Iceberg-compatible metadata from Delta or file-based tables
- Enhanced read capabilities via the Iceberg REST API (e.g., reading Delta tables after conversion)
- Expanded engine integrations beyond Spark

This feature lays the groundwork for proper multi-format governance within Polaris, unlocking robust hybrid lakehouse architectures where Iceberg, Delta, and other formats coexist under unified control.

In essence, Generic Table support transforms Polaris from an Iceberg-only catalog into a format-flexible metadata platform, reflecting the diverse realities of production data environments and Polaris's commitment to openness and extensibility.

Policy Store

As organizations scale their use of lakehouse architectures, governance becomes a critical pillar, not just for security and compliance but also for operational efficiency. In line with this need, the Apache Polaris roadmap introduces a powerful *Policy Store*, which positions Polaris as more than just a metadata catalog. It becomes a centralized, versioned repository for declarative policy definitions governing access control, data lifecycle, and operational behavior across the lakehouse.

The vision behind the Polaris Policy Store is to enable centralized policy definition and lifecycle management while delegating enforcement to the execution engines (e.g., Spark, Snowflake, Dremio). This clear separation of concerns ensures that Polaris remains lightweight and scalable, while engines efficiently apply policies at query or processing time.

This design caters to a wide range of governance use cases, such as:

- Snapshot retention enforcement for compliance
- Automated compaction policies for optimizing performance
- Row-level access policies for secure data access control

Each policy is tied to tangible data assets—such as catalogs, namespaces, tables, and views—and can be inherited across entity hierarchies to simplify administration and promote consistency.

Architecture and key capabilities

Policies are first-class entities within Polaris, grouped under namespaces and governed by fine-grained privileges. Core capabilities of the Policy Store include:

Flexible policy types and custom schemas
> Polaris supports predefined policy types such as `system.compaction`, `system.snapshot_retention`, and `system.row_access_policy`, each with its own schema and versioning. It also allows custom policy types (e.g., `custom.myorg.data_masking`) to address domain-specific requirements.

Policy inheritance
> Policies can be defined at the catalog, namespace, or table level. Inheritance rules ensure that global governance can be enforced broadly, while still allowing for granular overrides. For example, a namespace-wide retention policy can apply to all tables unless superseded by a more specific policy at the table level.

CRUD and versioning APIs
> Polaris introduces REST APIs to create, retrieve, update, and delete policies, attach them to resources, and manage policy versions. Versioning enables rollback to prior policy states, allowing for safe experimentation and change control.

Secure, privilege-based access control
> Management of policies is governed by a detailed privilege model. Polaris distinguishes between privileges to read, write, delete, attach, and detach policies,

ensuring that responsibilities can be clearly distributed across teams (e.g., governance vs. platform ops).

Engine integration and policy evaluation
Policies are stored and versioned in Polaris, but enforcement occurs in trusted engines. For example, Snowflake can evaluate a row-level access policy defined in Polaris at query runtime. The roadmap includes mechanisms for *synchronous policy-table loading* to prevent discrepancies in policy enforcement during reads.

Validation and pluggability
Polaris includes schema validation to prevent invalid policies from being created or attached. It also supports a pluggable validator framework, allowing organizations to enforce custom rules for specific policy types.

Looking ahead

The Policy Store roadmap sets the foundation for enterprise-grade governance within Polaris. Future expansions may include:

- Tag-based policy assignments (e.g., apply retention to all tables tagged "PII")
- Deeper integrations with external policy systems like Apache Ranger
- Support for policy languages such as Rego or Cedar for advanced logic expression

By embedding policy definitions directly into the catalog layer, Apache Polaris provides a single source of truth for both data and governance, streamlining security, compliance, and operational consistency in Iceberg-based lakehouses. As organizations seek to unify policy management across multiple engines and environments, this feature positions Polaris as a cornerstone of open data governance.

Table Maintenance Framework

As Iceberg adoption grows, so does the need for automated, scalable table maintenance. Apache Polaris is evolving to meet this challenge with the introduction of a *Table Maintenance Framework*, a major roadmap item designed to streamline the configuration, inheritance, and enforcement of operational policies across large-scale data environments.

This framework does not aim to run maintenance jobs itself; instead, it establishes Polaris as a metadata coordination layer for maintenance tasks executed by external Table Maintenance Systems (TMS), such as those running in Spark or Flink. This architecture ensures that Polaris remains lightweight while still playing a critical role in policy management, configuration, and governance visibility.

The Table Maintenance Framework provides:

- A centralized place to define and manage table maintenance policies (e.g., compaction, snapshot retention)
- Granular control over which tables are subject to maintenance and under what conditions
- A communication model between Polaris and external TMSs that supports loose coupling, scalability, and asynchronous coordination
- Support for inherited policies across catalog, namespace, and table levels, ensuring consistent operational behavior

Metadata-driven maintenance coordination

Polaris enables TMS integration by exposing essential metadata and configuration values. This includes:

- Table schemas, partition specs, and Iceberg-native statistics (e.g., snapshot summaries, partition stats)
- Maintenance policies (e.g., compaction thresholds, retention windows)
- Enablement flags that indicate whether maintenance is active on a specific table

TMS systems then read this information and autonomously decide when and how to perform maintenance jobs. This separation of concerns ensures that the computationally intensive logic of optimization remains outside Polaris, while policy governance remains within the catalog.

Flexible policy definition

The maintenance framework supports defining policies at various levels:

Catalog level
    For universal policies such as snapshot expiration or default compaction behavior

Namespace level
    To scope operational policies across logical groupings of tables (e.g., all analytics datasets)

Table level
    For precise performance tuning or lifecycle configurations

Plans include support for tag-based grouping, allowing users to apply a policy to all tables tagged with a given label (e.g., env=prod or data_type=log).

Policy configuration is expressed in JSON format and uses standardized keys such as:

- `polaris.maintenance.data-rewrite.policy`
- `polaris.maintenance.snapshot-retention.policy`
- `polaris.maintenance.metadata-rewrite.policy`

These configurations can be embedded in entity properties or defined as first-class policy objects with clear privilege boundaries and versioning.

Inheritance and governance

Polaris implements policy inheritance and override logic, ensuring that table-level settings always take precedence over namespace or catalog-level defaults. This model enables administrators to define general rules globally, while allowing teams to fine-tune policies for specific datasets.

To support governance and operational safety, Polaris introduces dedicated privileges for managing maintenance policies. This allows site reliability engineering (SRE) teams or platform operators to manage these settings without requiring full write access to table content, reducing risk and promoting best practices.

Integration model with TMS

Polaris and TMS interact through an *asynchronous event-driven model*. Polaris emits events on entity changes (e.g., table created or updated), which are consumed by one or more TMS systems to trigger maintenance workflows. Required API touchpoints include:

`loadTable` *and* `listTable`
> To fetch metadata and understand current policies

`GetApplicablePolicies`
> To retrieve inherited or assigned maintenance rules

`GetTablesPerPolicy`
> To enable batch coordination of tables grouped by a shared policy

This architecture ensures high scalability and flexibility, supporting multiple TMS implementations and catalogs concurrently without tight coupling.

Looking ahead

The Table Maintenance Framework lays the foundation for intelligent, automated data optimization within the Polaris ecosystem. Looking ahead, we expect to see:

- Richer policy evolution features, such as time- or metric-based switching

- Multiple policies per entity with prioritization logic
- Tighter integration with governance features, including audit trails and enforcement controls
- Unified policy language and APIs shared across access control, retention, and optimization settings

By enabling Polaris to act as the authoritative source for operational policy metadata, this roadmap item makes Polaris indispensable for maintaining performant, cost-effective, and compliant Iceberg-based data lakes at scale.

SQL and NoSQL Persistence

One of the core strengths of Apache Polaris is its ability to manage metadata for large-scale, distributed data lakehouses. To meet the demands of diverse deployment environments—from ephemeral testing clusters to enterprise-grade, multi-region systems—the Polaris roadmap includes a major architectural enhancement: support for SQL and NoSQL persistence backends.

This initiative decouples the core business logic of Polaris from its underlying storage engine, allowing deployments to choose the most suitable metastore, whether it's a relational database like PostgreSQL or a NoSQL system like DynamoDB.

The default Polaris implementation currently uses an in-memory store (based on `PolarisTreeMapMetaStoreSessionImpl`) for fast development and testing. However, production-grade environments require durable, scalable, and transactional storage systems. The new persistence architecture aims to:

- Support relational stores (via JDBC) for structured, ACID-compliant deployments
- Enable NoSQL backends like MongoDB for flexible, cloud-native persistence
- Improve modularity by separating business logic from data access layers

This evolution is critical for making Polaris truly adaptable to any enterprise environment—whether deployed in the cloud, on-premises, or in hybrid configurations.

Deployment flexibility

With this enhancement, users will be able to choose the most appropriate storage backend based on their operational requirements:

PostgreSQL and H2
    Ideal for environments requiring ACID transactions, strong consistency, and well-established tooling

MongoDB, more NoSQL DBs possible
> Suited for cloud-native, high-availability architectures that prioritize scalability and fault tolerance over strict transactionality

This opens the door for Polaris to be used in high-availability, distributed deployments and better aligns it with modern platform-as-a-service and multi-tenant requirements.

Looking ahead

This decoupling effort sets the stage for additional innovations:

- Pluggable store backends via community-contributed implementations
- Easier scaling and HA, as metadata can now live in battle-tested distributed datastores
- Seamless upgrades and migrations, with a clean abstraction layer between the catalog and storage

By unifying the catalog's persistence interface across storage paradigms, Polaris is taking a significant step toward becoming a truly backend-agnostic, cloud-ready catalog service, adaptable to a broad spectrum of organizational needs and environments.

S3-Compatible Storage Support

One of the most practical and highly anticipated roadmap features for Apache Polaris is its support for S3-compatible object stores. While Polaris already integrates with Amazon S3, enterprises increasingly operate in on-premises or hybrid environments using S3-compatible solutions such as MinIO, Ceph, Backblaze B2, NetApp Storage-GRID, and Dell ECS. This enhancement makes Polaris significantly more versatile by enabling deployment in private clouds or air-gapped environments without sacrificing Iceberg compatibility or open architecture.

Many organizations require the flexibility to manage data across diverse environments that don't involve AWS infrastructure. Polaris's initial tight coupling with AWS-specific services and assumptions, particularly around Identity and Access Management (IAM) and Security Token Service (STS), posed limitations for these use cases. By extending its storage layer to support generic S3-compatible endpoints, Polaris breaks those constraints and opens the door to broader adoption.

This capability is crucial for:

- On-prem deployments that rely on MinIO, Ceph, or other S3-compatible appliances
- Regulated industries where data residency or sovereignty prohibits public cloud usage

- Multi-cloud strategies where different regions or teams may operate under different infrastructure stacks

Implementation overview

Polaris will introduce a new storage type to access on-prem S3 setups like MinIO and S3 appliances. Users can configure catalogs to use this storage type with a custom set of parameters.

Polaris respects the same dynamic credential scoping and vending behavior as AWS integration but introduces a flag (`skipCredentialSubscopingIndirection`) for environments that do not support STS or IAM. This ensures minimal disruption and maximum interoperability with simpler authentication models.

Deployment simplicity

Catalogs can be created using standard REST APIs, with the `S3_COMPATIBLE` type and associated fields configured during provisioning. This makes it easy for users to register internal catalogs that point to MinIO, Ceph, or other supported backends, while leveraging Polaris's cataloging and governance capabilities on top.

```
{
  "name": "my-s3compatible-catalog",
  "type": "INTERNAL",
  "storageConfigInfo": {
    "storageType": "S3_COMPATIBLE",
    "region": "eu-central-1",
    "s3.endpoint": "https://localhost:9000",
    "s3.stsEndpoint": "https://localhost:9000",
    "s3.pathStyleAccess": true
  }
}
```

This enhancement will be tested and validated with multiple S3-compatible systems, confirming its effectiveness across varied enterprise setups.

This feature enables:

- Full Polaris functionality on self-managed object stores
- Credential vending and policy enforcement for private clouds
- Deployment in disconnected or security-sensitive environments
- Support for open lakehouse architectures across cloud and on-prem

Although the initial PR proposing this feature encountered prolonged review cycles and was eventually closed, the design has garnered broad community support. Future iterations may incorporate:

- Expanded test coverage and Helm integrations
- Enhanced secrets management for catalog-level credentials
- Streamlined fallback behavior when IAM features are not available

By supporting S3-compatible backends, Polaris reaffirms its role as an open and adaptable metadata platform that can thrive in any infrastructure setting. This milestone greatly enhances its appeal to enterprises seeking to modernize their data architectures without being bound to a specific cloud provider.

Catalog UI

To ensure that Apache Polaris can be adopted by a broader range of users—including data analysts, governance teams, and platform administrators—the project roadmap includes a dedicated web-based Catalog UI. While Polaris already exposes comprehensive REST APIs and Swagger documentation for developers, a graphical interface will dramatically enhance usability and accessibility across the organization.

The Catalog UI is envisioned as a central control plane for metadata operations and governance within Polaris. It provides an intuitive, browser-accessible interface that lowers the barrier to entry for users who may not be comfortable interacting directly with APIs or command-line interface (CLI) tools.

Goals for the UI include:

- Visual browsing of catalog entities such as namespaces, tables, and views
- Creation and deletion of metadata entities through interactive forms
- Inspection of catalog configurations, including both internal and federated catalogs
- Visibility into policy management, such as applied maintenance or governance policies

This feature aligns closely with Polaris's ambitions to support not just platform engineers but also data stewards, compliance officers, and operational SRE teams.

The Catalog UI is more than a convenience; it's a key enabler of governance at scale. By giving non-engineering teams a self-service interface to Polaris, organizations can distribute responsibility for metadata hygiene, compliance tracking, and policy auditing across multiple roles.

Furthermore, in environments with multiple catalogs and namespaces—especially in federated or multi-tenant deployments—the UI provides critical transparency and discoverability for complex metadata topologies.

Feature scope

The first iteration of the Catalog UI is expected to support:

Entity browsing
  Navigate through catalog, namespace, and table hierarchies.

Entity management
  Create or delete catalogs, namespaces, and tables directly from the interface.

Policy visibility
  Display TMS and access control policies applied at various levels.

Catalog federation support
  View and manage external catalogs federated into Polaris.

Over time, the UI may evolve to include:

- RBAC role and permission visualization and management
- Integration with OpenLineage or other metadata visualization tools
- Search, filtering, and tagging support for large-scale catalog navigation

Looking ahead

While the initial work on this feature is still in its early stages, it has strong backing from the Polaris community. As Apache Polaris matures into a full-fledged, enterprise-grade metadata platform, a rich, interactive UI will be essential for driving adoption and accelerating productivity among both technical and non-technical users.

By unifying metadata management, governance visibility, and policy introspection under one interface, the Catalog UI brings Polaris closer to becoming the single pane of glass for the modern lakehouse.

Federated Catalogs

As enterprise data platforms increasingly span multiple regions, storage systems, and organizational domains, federation of metadata catalogs becomes critical. Apache Polaris is introducing Catalog Federation to unify disparate Iceberg REST catalogs under a single control plane while retaining robust governance, RBAC, and metadata management. This capability not only simplifies multi-catalog integration but also positions Polaris as a foundational layer for cross-catalog governance and migration strategies.

The Catalog Federation roadmap in Polaris aims to:

- Enable read-through and passthrough access to remote Iceberg REST Catalogs
- Introduce just-in-time (JIT) facade creation of entities such as namespaces, tables, and views
- Support Polaris-native RBAC and policy evaluation even when metadata resides in external systems
- Provide a smooth pathway for catalog consolidation and migration through intermediate federated states

Federation modes and facade types

Polaris classifies federated entities into three conceptual types:

Implicit entities
    No local metadata is available; entities are resolved on the fly.

Static facades
    A read-only snapshot of the remote entity is retained in Polaris.

Passthrough facades
    Fully dynamic proxies for remote entities, supporting both reads and writes, and JIT-creation when accessed.

By default, Polaris federation will begin with catalog-level facades, with deeper levels (namespaces, tables, and views) introduced via JIT creation and optional JIT refresh.

Milestone 1 scope

The first implementation milestone includes:

- Static catalog facades pointing to remote Iceberg REST Catalogs.
- No Polaris persistence for subordinate entities (namespaces, tables).
- RBAC is controlled at the catalog level.
- Remote reads and writes are passed through the Polaris server transparently.

This design ensures Polaris remains the gatekeeper for access control, while deferring execution to the source-of-truth catalog.

Milestone 2: JIT-creation of entity facades

A significant enhancement following the MVP is the envisioned support for *the JIT creation* of namespaces, tables, and views during access. This unlocks:

- RBAC granularity beyond the catalog level

- Entity-specific policy attachment within Polaris
- Seamless integration of federated metadata into Polaris UIs and governance tooling

Entities can be promoted from JIT-in-memory to persisted objects as needed (e.g., during a grant operation or as part of a migration).

Use cases

Use cases for catalog federation include:

Hybrid cloud governance
Manage on-prem and cloud-based catalogs centrally with Polaris.

Enterprise catalog migration
Use federated access as a transitional step before fully onboarding legacy catalogs into Polaris.

Looking ahead

The federation framework is designed for extensibility:

Non-Iceberg catalogs
While the MVP targets Iceberg REST, future support may include other possible connection targets.

Policy federation
Integration with external policy engines (e.g., Apache Ranger) is a natural evolution of the current access-control design.

Catalog Federation summary

Catalog Federation in Polaris brings together data unification, governance, and scalability. With support for dynamic facades, JIT metadata creation, and secure credential management, Polaris is evolving into a federated governance layer that can sit atop any number of Iceberg-compatible catalogs. This not only simplifies architecture for organizations operating in complex environments but also opens the door to centralized policy enforcement and catalog observability at scale.

Federated Role Support

Large-scale organizations often manage tens of thousands of users and rely on centralized services, such as Okta, LDAP, Entra ID, or Google, to control authentication and role-based access. With dynamic group membership and immediate privilege revocation needs, Federated User and Role Support is an essential capability for Polaris to provide scalable, secure, and enterprise-ready governance.

The goals for federated role support are:

Centralized identity management
Enterprises require a single point of control for users and roles, ensuring that changes in IdP group membership are reflected instantly across all dependent systems.

Dynamic provisioning
Automatically populate role entities in Polaris as users authenticate, aligning with System for Cross-Domain Identity Management (SCIM) and Single Sign-on (SSO) best practices.

The key design principles for the project are:

Pluggable identity providers
Polaris supports multiple identity providers (e.g., Okta, Google, LDAP [via OAuth/OIDC]), using a flexible authenticator framework and token broker model.

Federated entities
Roles provisioned via an IdP will be marked as `federated=true`, preventing unauthorized local modifications or credential assignments.

Architecture overview

Federated support in Polaris will follow these core mechanics:

Authentication
Tokens presented to Polaris will be validated using pluggable token brokers per identity realm.

Provisioning
Polaris dynamically creates PrincipalRole entities based on claims.

No entity is persisted unless it is needed for grants (PrincipalRoles must be persisted for CatalogRole assignments).

Grant restrictions
Grants *cannot* be assigned to or from federated entities via the Polaris API.

Federated PrincipalRoles are exclusively controlled by the external IdP.

Token scopes dictate access—roles not present in the token are not effective, even if they were previously granted.

Security enforcement
APIs such as `/oauth/tokens` and `/rotateSecrets` are *disabled* for federated users.

Federated Principals cannot assume or be granted non-federated roles, and vice versa.

SCIM and future synchronization

While the MVP centers around just-in-time (JIT) provisioning, Polaris is designed to support SCIM for push-based synchronization of users and groups. This enables:

- Pre-population of users and roles
- Easier visibility into role membership
- Support for compliance audits and entitlement tracking

Though SCIM is not part of the initial release, persistence of federated principals lays the foundation for future support.

Practical implications

Here are some of the results of this architecture when it comes to governance.

Token-driven access
A token issued by the IdP serves as the sole source of truth for current roles, with no local grant overrides.

Immutable role membership
Ensures firm security boundaries, where only the IdP governs access.

Safe delegation
Prevents scenarios where leaked credentials or misconfigured grants could give unintended access to sensitive data.

Federated User and Role Support in Polaris establishes a secure, scalable identity integration framework that aligns with enterprise SSO and governance needs. By enforcing strict boundaries between Polaris-managed and IdP-managed identities, the platform ensures both real-time access control and strong compliance guarantees while laying the groundwork for future features like SCIM synchronization and fine-grained multi-IdP federation.

Polaris Event Listeners

As Polaris matures into a platform supporting varied use cases across large-scale deployments, extensibility becomes a key requirement. While configuration flags and dependency injection can handle a subset of customizations, these approaches quickly become unmanageable for dynamic, runtime-specific needs or for fine-grained internal process visibility. To address this, Polaris is planning to introduce a first-class event listener framework to support safe, pluggable hooks at key lifecycle stages.

The goal of Polaris Event Listeners is to expose well-defined "event hooks" at critical execution points within the platform, allowing users to:

- Observe or react to internal state transitions
- Augment behavior in a modular, non-intrusive way
- Avoid forking Polaris or performing brittle dependency injections

These event listeners will support observability, analytics, auditing, and custom policy enforcement while maintaining core stability.

Event hooks will only be introduced where:

- The behavior cannot be achieved with existing configuration or dependency injection.
- There's a tangible use case that benefits users or downstream systems.
- The event is distinct enough not to be addressed by existing listeners.

This approach encourages deliberate and thoughtful extensibility, rather than blanket instrumentation.

Initial event set

The initial implementation proposes the event hooks shown in Table 11-1.

Table 11-1. Polaris event listeners

Event Name	Trigger	Use Case
OnBeforeRequestRate Limited	Prior to applying request rate limiting	Observability, dynamic throttling adjustments
OnBeforeCommitTable	Before committing table metadata	Anomaly detection, pre-commit validation
OnAfterCommitTable	After successful table commit	Audit logging, metrics capture
OnBeforeCommitView	Before committing view metadata	Anomaly detection, pre-commit validation
OnAfterCommitView	After successful view commit	Audit logging, metrics capture

Event Name	Trigger	Use Case
OnBeforeRefreshTable	Before internal table metadata refresh	Monitor refresh patterns or cache invalidation logic
OnAfterRefreshTable	After table metadata refresh	Metadata validation, metrics capture
OnBeforeRefreshView	Before view metadata refresh	Monitor refresh patterns or cache invalidation logic
OnAfterRefreshView	After view metadata refresh	Metadata validation, metrics capture
OnBeforeAttemptTask	Before Polaris launches an asynchronous task	Workflow tracking, task filtering
OnAfterAttemptTask	After an async task finishes	Audit trails, error analysis

These form the foundation for a future in which all major Polaris lifecycle steps are optionally observable or interceptable.

Implementation options

Two implementation strategies are under consideration:

Jakarta events
  These use the Jakarta EE standard event system. They are simple and familiar but lack support for modifying event payloads (e.g., altering metadata before commit).

Custom listener interface
  This provides richer functionality, including bi-directional hooks that allow the event handler to modify the object being processed (e.g., intercept and change table metadata before commit).

While Jakarta offers immediate integration benefits, the custom interface provides greater flexibility and power, significant in the Polaris context where metadata mutation and validation are essential.

Looking ahead

As Polaris evolves, the event system will likely expand to include:

- Security-sensitive actions (e.g., before/after authorization checks)
- Integration events for external systems (e.g., lineage tracking, observability platforms)
- Extension points for data governance workflows

A registry of active listeners, error-handling strategies, and performance isolation mechanisms will also be part of future discussions.

The addition of Event Listeners represents a strategic enhancement to Polaris's extensibility. It aligns Polaris with other mature platforms that offer runtime hooks for advanced users while preserving the OSS project's maintainability and stability. This feature will empower platform engineers, observability teams, and governance administrators to customize Polaris with confidence and precision.

Unstructured Data in Polaris

As the data landscape evolves with the surge of AI/ML and multimedia applications, managing unstructured data (such as logs, images, and videos) has become a core need for modern data platforms. Polaris is extending its architecture to accommodate this by introducing first-class support for unstructured data within the same governance and access control fabric as structured Iceberg tables.

Traditional catalogs, such as Polaris, have excelled at managing structured tabular data via Iceberg but have had limited capabilities in organizing and governing unstructured data. Users typically interact with object stores directly for files, limiting governance, access control, and query capabilities. The proposed *Volume* abstraction in Polaris addresses this by introducing a new table-like entity designed explicitly for unstructured file metadata.

A Volume in Polaris is a logical container within a namespace that represents a group of unstructured data files. It enables:

- Logical grouping of related unstructured files
- Access control enforcement and credential vending using Polaris' privilege model
- Queryable metadata for files (e.g., size, timestamps, checksums)
- Asynchronous metadata sync via a backing directory table

Volumes allow file management (add/update/delete) using standard object store operations, such as `aws s3 cp` or `gsutil`, without the need for Polaris-specific upload APIs.

Architectural overview

Each volume can optionally be backed by a directory table, implemented as a read-only Iceberg table maintained by Polaris. This table provides query capabilities across volume file metadata, such as:

```
CREATE TABLE dir_table (
  relative_path STRING,
  size BIGINT,
  last_modified TIMESTAMP,
  md5 STRING,
  file_url STRING
)
```

Directory tables are automatically refreshed in the background, either:

- By delegation to a remote engine
- A Polaris-integrated TMS job (similar to compaction or snapshot expiration workflows)

These directory tables reside in a reserved path under the catalog's location and enable users to run SQL analytics or scans over file metadata.

Volume properties and behavior

Here are some details regarding the possible properties and behavior and properties that exist in this proposed feature:

- Belongs to a Polaris namespace
- Inherits the catalog's storage type (S3, GCS, Azure Blob, or local filesystem)
- Can include optional metadata like file format
- Supports metadata refresh intervals

Users do not need to register files manually; Polaris automatically detects and reflects changes during its scheduled refresh cycles.

API design

To support this new functionality, Polaris may introduce a dedicated set of REST APIs:

Create Volume
```
POST /v1/{prefix}/namespaces/{namespace}/volume/
```

Drop Volume (with optional purge)
```
DELETE /v1/{prefix}/namespaces/{namespace}/volume/{volume}
```

List/Filter Files in a Volume
```
GET/POST /v1/{prefix}/namespaces/{namespace}/volume/{volume}
```

These APIs enable seamless creation and management of volumes while providing visibility into the files they contain.

Limitations and looking ahead

Here are some of the limitations of this early proposed version of this feature:

- This initial feature does not provide transactional guarantees—no versioning, branching, or rollback of files.

- Sharding or partitioning within a volume is not supported. Files are managed as flat lists.

- Cross-catalog syncing of volumes is not a design goal, unlike Iceberg table federation.

- Open questions include whether to unify directory tables with standard Iceberg table listings and how to separate or denote them in the UI visually.

With the introduction of Volumes and directory tables, Polaris is extending its reach into unstructured data management, bridging the gap between traditional data lakes and modern, multimodal AI/ML data ecosystems. This architecture provides a scalable, secure, and queryable interface over files, natively integrated into Polaris' governance model, positioning Polaris as a complete data catalog solution for all data modalities.

Conclusion

The future of Apache Polaris is incredibly promising. As organizations increasingly adopt open, interoperable lakehouse architectures, Polaris is emerging as a corner-stone for secure, scalable, and multi-engine data cataloging. With the rise of managed Polaris services, such as Dremio Enterprise Catalog and Snowflake's Open Catalog, enterprises no longer need to choose between flexibility and operational simplicity. The expanding ecosystem of tools supporting the Iceberg REST Catalog specification ensures that Polaris can serve as a neutral foundation for a wide variety of engines, including Spark, Flink, Dremio, Trino, DuckDB, and beyond.

The Polaris roadmap reflects a forward-thinking and community-driven vision. Innovations such as generic table support, federated catalogs, policy-based governance, metadata-driven table maintenance, and unstructured data management all point toward a robust, extensible platform ready to meet the evolving demands of the data lakehouse landscape.

We hope this book has helped deepen your understanding of Polaris and the broader lakehouse ecosystem. Together, we explored:

- The foundational concepts behind data lakehouses
- What makes Apache Iceberg a modern table format
- The role and architecture of a lakehouse catalog
- The purpose and design of the Iceberg REST Catalog specification
- How Apache Polaris brings modern governance and interoperability to Iceberg
- Polaris's built-in access control and fine-grained privilege model
- The ability to onboard existing data via external catalogs

- How to work locally with Polaris and Spark
- How to integrate Polaris OSS with Snowflake Open Catalog
- How Dremio's integration with Polaris provides unified experience via the Enterprise Catalog
- A look at the future roadmap of Polaris, where the project is headed, and how it is positioned to shape the future of open data architectures

Thank you for joining us on this journey. Whether you're a platform engineer, data architect, or open data enthusiast, we hope Polaris empowers you to build a more open, interoperable, and governed data platform.

Index

About the Authors

Alex Merced is head of DevRel at Dremio with experience as a developer and instructor. His professional journey includes roles at GenEd Systems, Crossfield Digital, CampusGuard, and General Assembly. He co-authored *Apache Iceberg: The Definitive Guide* published by O'Reilly and has spoken at notable events such as Data Day Texas and Data Council. Alex is passionate about technology, sharing his expertise through blogs, videos, podcasts like Datanation and Web Dev 101, and contributions to the JavaScript and Python communities with libraries like SencilloDB and CoquitoJS.

Andrew Madson is an experienced data leader with 17 years of experience leading technical teams. Currently the head of evangelism and education at Tobiko—the creators of SQLMesh and SQLGlot—Andrew has held senior leadership positions at institutions such as JP Morgan, LPL Financial, MassMutual, and Arizona State University. In addition to leading data teams, Andrew is a professor of data science and analytics at several universities, where he teaches graduate courses in machine learning, statistics, SQL, R, Python, Tableau, and Power BI.

Tomer Shiran is the founder and chief product officer of Dremio, an open data lakehouse platform that enables companies to run analytics in the cloud without the cost, complexity, and lock-in of data warehouses. As the company's founding CEO, Tomer built a world-class organization that has raised over $400M and now serves hundreds of the world's largest enterprises, including three of the Fortune 5. Prior to Dremio, Tomer was the fourth employee and VP product of MapR, a big data analytics pioneer. He also held numerous product management and engineering roles at Microsoft and IBM Research, founded several websites that have served millions of users and hundreds of thousands of paying customers, and is a successful author and presenter on a wide range of industry topics. He holds an MS in computer engineering from Carnegie Mellon University and a BS in computer science from Technion — Israel Institute of Technology.

Colophon

The animal on the cover of *Apache Polaris: The Definitive Guide* is a walrus (*Odobenus rosmarus*). This remarkable, fin-footed mammal is a relative to seals and sea lions and can be found in the Arctic and subarctic regions in the Northern Hemisphere, specifically in the Atlantic and Pacific oceans.

Walruses are known for their incredible size. Their body lengths typically range from 7 feet to 11 feet 10 inches. While most males weigh between 1,800 and 3,700 pounds, those found in the Pacific can weigh as much as 4,400 pounds. Females weigh about two-thirds as much, with Atlantic females averaging between 880 and 1,230 pounds; females found in the Pacific weigh around 1,800. Blubber (a thick, fatty tissue) is the main cause of this high body weight, but it serves an important purpose: it keeps walruses warm and serves as a source of energy for the mammals.

Walruses are also famous for their incredible tusks, a feature that is present in both males and females. Males primarily use their tusks for fighting and establishing dominance within social groups. Since walruses spend about two-thirds of their lives in the water, their tusks serve as useful tools for keeping breathing holes in the ice open and are also used to haul their heavy bodies onto ice floes, which they sometimes ride during migration.

A walrus's diet usually consists of soft-bodied invertebrates from the seafloor, such as sea cucumbers, snails, mollusks, and clams. Adult walruses eat about 3% to 6% of their total body weight per day, with some eating as much as 6,000 clams in a single feeding session. Walruses might also consume seals, though this is very rare.

Due to their formidable size, walruses do not have many predators, aside from orcas and polar bears. Despite this, walruses are unfortunately listed as a vulnerable species by the International Union for Conservation of Nature due to loss of sea ice from climate change and warming oceans. Commercial fishing and bottom trawling also threaten these wonderful mammals, since these activities break up sea ice and destroy their feeding grounds.

Many of the animals on O'Reilly covers are endangered; all of them are important to the world.

The cover illustration is by José Marzan Jr., based on an antique line engraving from *Brehms Thierleben*. The series design is by Edie Freedman, Ellie Volckhausen, and Karen Montgomery. The cover fonts are Gilroy Semibold and Guardian Sans. The text font is Adobe Minion Pro; the heading font is Adobe Myriad Condensed; and the code font is Dalton Maag's Ubuntu Mono.

O'REILLY®

Learn from experts.
Become one yourself.

60,000+ titles | Live events with experts | Role-based courses
Interactive learning | Certification preparation

**Try the O'Reilly learning platform
free for 10 days.**

www.ingramcontent.com/pod-product-compliance
Lightning Source LLC
Chambersburg PA
CBHW082110220326
41598CB00066BA/6056